NO REFUGE

NO REFUGE

Ethics and the Global Refugee Crisis

Serena Parekh

OXFORD
UNIVERSITY PRESS

Oxford University Press is a department of the University of Oxford. It furthers the University's objective of excellence in research, scholarship, and education by publishing worldwide. Oxford is a registered trade mark of Oxford University Press in the UK and certain other countries.

Published in the United States of America by Oxford University Press
198 Madison Avenue, New York, NY 10016, United States of America.

Library of Congress Cataloging-in-Publication Data
Names: Parekh, Serena, 1974– author.
Title: No refuge : ethics and the global refugee crisis / Serena Parekh.
Description: New York, NY : Oxford University Press, [2020] |
Includes bibliographic references.
Identifiers: LCCN 2020003047 (print) | LCCN 2020003048 (ebook) |
ISBN 9780197507995 (hardback) | ISBN 9780197508015 (epub) |
ISBN 9780197508022
Subjects: LCSH: Refugees—Europe—Social conditions. |
Humanitarian assistance—Moral and ethical aspects. |
Refugees—Public opinion. | Refugees—Government policy—Europe. |
Europe—Emigration and immigration—Government policy.
Classification: LCC HV640 .P366 2020 (print) | LCC HV640 (ebook) |
DDC 174/.936287—dc23
LC record available at https://lccn.loc.gov/2020003047
LC ebook record available at https://lccn.loc.gov/2020003048

1 3 5 7 9 8 6 4 2

Printed by Sheridan Books, Inc., United States of America

For my father and in loving memory of my mother

If you look at the statistics, you get depressed, but if you look at the people, you find hope.

—Filmmaker working in the Democratic Republic of the Congo,
quoted in Milliband, *Rescue*, p. 67

CONTENTS

Preface: Turbulence and Fear *ix*

Introduction: A Tale of Two Refugee Crises 1

PART I
THE FIRST CRISIS: THE CRISIS FOR WESTERN COUNTRIES

1. Who Is a Refugee? 27
2. Moral Obligations, or Why We Should Help People Even If We Don't Like Them 50
3. Reasons for and against Accepting Refugees: A Philosophical Overview 76

PART II
THE SECOND CRISIS: THE CRISIS FOR REFUGEES

4. Refugee Camps and Urban Settlements: The Problem We Have Created 101

5. The Price We Demand for Asylum 121

6. Structural Injustice 151

Conclusion: What Should We Do? What Should I Do? 177

Acknowledgments *201*
Notes *205*
Bibliography *219*
Index *239*

PREFACE: TURBULENCE AND FEAR

I used to have a terrible fear of flying. It all went back to an episode of turbulence so awful that I couldn't put it out of my mind. The plane dipped and dived seemingly out of control, leaving me nauseous, dizzy, and scared. After that, I avoided flying as much as I could, and if I had to get on a plane, I spent the entire flight terrified.

Because it's almost impossible to avoid flying these days, I eventually had to find some way of coping. My local adult education center advertised a "fear of flying" course taught by a pilot, and I signed myself up. The instructor calmly explained the mechanics of flying, how difficult it was, in fact, for a plane to crash, and all the various safety measures airlines put in place. But he never actually addressed the thing that had brought me in: turbulence. When he came to the end of his lecture, I raised my hand and asked him about this, the thing that was so crucial to my fear of flying.

According to the instructor, turbulence was such a nonissue that he tended to forget to mention it. A plane in turbulence was just going with the flow, so to speak, following the natural air current. The pilot could easily correct for this and it posed no threat to the safety of the plane. There was nothing to be afraid of at all.

How could it be that the source of my fear of flying, the thing that had cast a shadow over every travel experience and caused me so much anxiety, was objectively not dangerous? Yet the pilot was unequivocal: there was nothing to fear from turbulence.

It took a while for my body to catch up to my brain. Getting on a plane, my anxieties still made themselves known, and I had to calm them by reminding myself of what I had learned. But eventually I stopped being afraid of flying.

When I speak about the treatment of refugees I feel as though it is my turn to play the role of the pilot defusing baseless fears. In the winter of 2017, the refugee travel ban had just been put in place in the United States, and my book *Refugees and the Ethics of Forced Displacement* had just come out. I gave lectures about why we should accept refugees for resettlement in the United States and why, in my opinion, we should be doing more to help refugees around the world. Once my talk was over, an audience member would invariably ask: but aren't refugees dangerous? In other words, it may be that we should help people, but given that at least some refugees enter our countries with the intention to hurt or kill us, shouldn't we protect ourselves? It was perfectly obvious to me that refugees in the United States had absolutely no connection to terrorism. The data are very clear that there is no correlation in the United States between refugees who are resettled and terrorism. Though the issue of security is the question that may have brought people to my talk, I never mentioned it. I was just like the pilot who had forgotten to discuss turbulence.

By 2017, fear of refugees was widespread. It had colored many people's views of the roles we should play in helping refugees. Not only did I need to address this fear, but I couldn't talk about anything else regarding refugees until I addressed it.

People's views of refugees around the world have shifted since 2017. Though refugees are still feared by some, the nature of the fear has changed. Refugees are depicted less frequently as terrorists, and more as criminals and sexual predators. Others now also worry about the economic cost of dealing with large numbers of asylum seekers who have sought refuge in the West in recent years. So before I go on to talk about how we should understand our moral obligations to refugees, let me first get turbulence out of the way by addressing some of the big worries people have about refugees.

ARE REFUGEES TERRORISTS?

One of the biggest concerns with refugees, especially in the United States, is that they are terrorists in disguise. The most common claim is that a would-be terrorist might be able to use the refugee resettlement program to sneak into the United States to commit terrorism. Several Republican presidential candidates put forward this idea during debates ahead of the 2016 election. While every Republican candidate promised to close the border to refugees, some went further. So dangerous are refugees, claimed New Jersey governor Chris Christie, that we shouldn't even let in orphans under five years of age.[1] Politicians across Europe have adopted a similar position. Hungarian Prime Minister Viktor Orbán claimed that refugees were "the Trojan Horse of terrorism."

This reaction was due in part to the terrorist attack in Paris in November 2015. One of the terrorists involved in this attack reportedly carried a Syrian passport, sparking fears that terrorists had come to Europe posing as refugees along with the hundreds of thousands of other refugees who arrived in Italy and Greece that year. Lax border control and overly generous refugee policies received the lion's share of the blame for the attack. News reports eventually emerged to reveal that the passport itself was forged and that the majority of the attackers were French or Belgian nationals, but it was too late. The connection between refugees and terrorism was already cemented in many people's mind.[2]

Yet this link between refugees and terrorism is not borne out by the evidence. Between 1975 and 2015, the United States resettled more than 3.2 million refugees. Of these, only 20 refugees out of 3.2 million attempted or carried out a terrorist attack (six Iranians, six Sudanese, two Somalis, two Iraqis, and one Yemeni have been convicted of attempting or executing terrorist attacks on US soil during that time period).[3] In the 1970s, three US citizens were killed by refugees—Cuban exiles.[4] However, since the United States implemented its rigorous screening process for refugees in 1980, not a single refugee has been involved in a terrorist attack.[5] That means an American citizen has a 1 in 3.6 billion chance of being killed by a refugee in a given year.[6]

Yet in the United States, many remain skeptical. The belief that terrorist attacks are committed by refugees is a hard one to shake—but the evidence simply does not support it. Take the attacks in San Bernardino in December 2015: though the attackers were Muslim, they were not refugees. The main attacker, Syed Farook was an American citizen, born in Chicago. His wife, Tashfeen Malik, was born in Pakistan but came to the United States on a fiancée visa and was a permanent resident. Excluding refugees would not have prevented the Boston Marathon bombings of 2013 either. The Tsarnaev brothers, who carried out the attacks, came to the United States as children. Their parents were granted asylum once they were in the United States because they were fleeing persecution in war-torn Chechnya. Similarly, the Orlando nightclub shooter was a US citizen, though his parents were immigrants (not refugees) from Afghanistan.

For anyone who has gone through the resettlement process in the United States, the fact that no refugees have turned out to be terrorists is not surprising. The hardest way to gain access to the United States is through gaining refugee status. No one simply applies to be a refugee in the United States; the United Nations chooses whom to recommend for resettlement and passes their case files on to the United States. The United States will only consider refugees who are of "special humanitarian concern," that is, only those refugees whose life, health, or dignity cannot be protected in the refugee camps where they are living, such as torture survivors, women, and children. The United States then begins a two- to five-year vetting process for refugees that includes screening by eight federal government agencies (Immigration and Customs Enforcement, FBI, etc.) using six different security databases; five separate background checks; four biometric security checks; and as many as nine in-person interviews that can range from one to six hours each. This long, intensive screening process interrogates every detail of the refugee's story. Take the in-person interviews. Questions that refugees have been asked include these: "Can you remember how many stars were on the jacket of the military officer that raped you?" "What kind of a knife was the man that killed your father holding?" "How many hours were you on the boat that night the smugglers shot your brother and threw him overboard?" There is no group of people in the United States that have been more thoroughly vetted than refugees.[7]

The EU and Australia are much the same. In Europe, according to counterterrorism experts, the main terrorist threat comes from "home-grown extremists," not newly arrived refugees or asylum seekers.[8] According to the head of Australia's intelligence agency, they have "found no evidence to suggest that there is a connection between refugees and terrorism."[9] The people who understand public security and counterterrorism simply do not consider refugees to be a serious threat. By all accounts, if you are worried about people committing terrorism in your country, refugees are not the group with which you should be most concerned.

Some might object that if there is *any* risk from refugees, we should not allow any in. This is the wrong way to think about things.

If security is the most important good in a society, there are far greater threats to individual security. Rather than devoting resources in the United States to keeping refugees out, time and money would be better spent addressing gun violence, pollution linked to disease, or domestic extremism. Further, if the United States were to close its doors to refugees, it would require giving up its image of itself as a nation that welcomes people from all backgrounds and walks of life, a view that has been part of the national self-image for most of the country's history. The security of individuals in a state is an extremely important good that governments must work to achieve; but excluding refugees and asylum seekers, besides being ineffective, would require us to give up on the values that have defined most Western countries. In my view, this isn't a trade-off worth making.

ARE REFUGEES SEXUAL PREDATORS AND CRIMINALS?

A persistent claim about refugees, especially in Europe, is that they are likely to be criminals and sexual predators. Some have argued that crime increased after the 2015 rise in asylum seekers in formerly peaceful European cities. Others have suggested that rates of sexual violence against women also increased substantially, making it unsafe for women to walk by themselves in cities with large refugee populations. Let me look at each of these in turn.

Depictions of refugees as sexual predators circulated widely in Europe after 2015 and even made their way into the speeches of political figures. Nigel Farage, the British politician, insisted that after taking in large numbers of single, male refugees, the Swedish city of Malmö became the "rape capital" of Europe, maybe even the world.[10] He warned that this is what would happen to all of Europe if more refugees were let in. This seemed to be supported by several highly visible incidents of sexual violence by refugees across Europe, culminating in the 2015–2016 New Year's Eve attacks in Cologne and other cities across Europe.

Despite these highly publicized cases, statistics show that Farage's claim that refugees are responsible for the upswing in rape and sexual violence is wrong. There has been a general upward trend in *reports* of sexual violence against women in Sweden since 2005, but not an actual increase in sexual violence. The increased reports of sexual violence actually result from a change in how rape and sexual violence are understood in Swedish law. In 2005, a new Swedish law expanded acts that would be counted as rape, which would have been previously counted as "sexual exploitation" and included acts that the victim did not resist (in Germany, by contrast, until 2016, rape could not be prosecuted unless the victim could demonstrate that she had been forced and resisted).[11] In other words, Sweden broadened its understanding of what is included as "rape," and this understanding is much wider than how rape is conceived in other European countries and the United States. Rates of sexual assault seem to have gone up since 2005 because more acts now fall within the legal definition of sexual assault. In other words, rates of sexual violence were lower prior to 2005 not because fewer sexual crimes were being committed, but because they were not classified and counted as rape.[12]

Second, not only does Sweden define rape more broadly than other countries, it also *counts* incidents of rape differently. In Sweden, each act of sexual violence is counted distinctly. For example, if a woman said that her husband raped her every night for a year, Sweden would count that as 365 acts of rape, while most other countries would count it as one violation.[13] Finally, there is more support for women in Sweden who report sexual violence. Unlike in other countries, Swedish women do not worry that they will be shamed or retaliated against and, as a result, are more likely to report sexual violence than in other countries such as the United States.[14]

What about crime more generally? In Germany, for example, there is a broad concern that the influx of refugees has created a problem of crime that did not exist before. Again, though there have been some highly visible crimes committed by refugees in Germany, as a whole, crime is at its lowest level in thirty years.[15] In Italy, another country with a large number of asylum seekers, crime fell by 25 percent between 2007 and 2016.[16] In Sweden, though crime is frequently blamed on immigrants and refugees, it's actually being committed by European criminal gangs, not asylum seekers.[17] In the United States, contrary to claims made by the Trump administration, not only are immigrants, including refugees, considerably less likely to commit crime than native-born citizens, those jurisdictions with larger immigrant populations actually tend to have less crime.[18] There is simply no evidence for the claim that refugees and asylum seekers lead to more crime.

Why, then, do so many people continue to believe that refugees are a threat to society? One explanation is that the presence of those perceived to be racially, ethnically, or religiously different can create a sense of fear and uncertainty, feelings that lead people to believe that they are losing control over their countries. Especially in recent years, politicians have found this fear to be a useful tool. Regarding Syrian refugees, some US presidential candidates in 2016 found it very useful to increase fear so that they could be seen as keeping the country safe from potentially dangerous people. We know now that Russia participated in spreading fake stories about refugees, including exaggerating the attacks in Cologne on New Year's Eve 2014 for propaganda purposes.[19] When claims are repeated frequently enough—that Malmö, Sweden, is the rape capital of Europe, for example—people start to believe it. Fear is a very powerful emotion, not easily assuaged by knowledge and facts.

I don't mean to downplay the genuine challenges each country that takes in refugees will face around resettlement and integration.

It's true that some refugees will not be familiar with norms of gender equality that many take for granted in the West, for example (for this reason, Norway has started programs that teach refugees these norms).[20] The transition from being a refugee—likely traumatized, separated from one's community, with few material possessions and little savings—to being a productive citizen is a hard one. It's hard for all societies, even ones that are full of immigrants like the United States and Germany, to adapt to changing populations. Though the challenges of integrating refugees are real, it's not helpful to exaggerate them by falsely claiming that refugees are terrorists, criminals or sexual predators.

AREN'T REFUGEES TOO EXPENSIVE?

Refugees are often described as a financial burden on societies that take them in. There is an intuitive logic to this claim. After all, a country has to pay for them to travel to their country, cover the initial costs while they get on their feet, and shoulder the financial burden of security and health screenings as well. Though figuring out the exact cost of certain policies is a complicated matter, the data actually show pretty consistently that refugees and asylum seekers are an economic benefit to Western countries. Though they pose more challenges for countries in the Global South, even there they find ways to cope economically.

In countries like the United States that have historically resettled refugees, refugees are decisively a net economic gain. This point was made dramatically in 2017, when a report about the cost of refugees to the US economy was leaked. The report had been commissioned by the Trump administration in the hopes of finding evidence to support their refugee ban. In fact, it showed the opposite. The report, by the Department of Health and Human Services, showed that over a ten-year period, refugees contributed a net $63 billion dollars to the US economy.[21] It takes about six to eight years for refugees to integrate and start contributing to the economy, but once they do, their contributions are substantial.[22] Though the United States had to fund the short-term costs of background checks and initial resettlement, this proved to be a smart long-term economic strategy.[23]

What about European countries that have faced such large numbers of asylum seekers in recent years? Headlines often spoke of how much it was costing Germany to host refugees. In 2016, Germany spent almost twenty billion euros, much more than originally estimated, on refugees.[24] Though this was a lot of money to be sure, the International Monetary Fund is optimistic about the potential benefits. In the IMF's view, the large influx of asylum seekers and migrants that began in 2015 will raise economic growth in the long term by contributing young, energetic workers to the European workforce.[25] Even in the short term, the European Commission found that countries that allowed refugees to settle (Germany and Sweden in particular) showed positive economic effects on growth and employment rates. They too foresee high economic growth in the long term if refugees continue to come in high numbers.[26]

Less affluent countries in the Global South that host the majority of the world's refugees do face financial challenges.[27] The economic strain of taking in refugees can exacerbate existing economic problems. The situation isn't wholly dire though: in 2015, with 2.2 million refugees, Turkey's economy expanded by 3 percent; Lebanon, which took in 1.1 million refugees, saw economic growth of 2–3 percent; and Jordan, which hosts over 600,000 refugees, also had 3 percent economic growth that year.[28] Political, economic, and social challenges nevertheless remain. For example, in Turkey in areas where Syrian refugees live and work illegally, rents overall have increased, causing strain for local Turks searching for affordable housing.[29]

Yet despite this, for reasons that remain almost unfathomable to people in the West, countries in the Global South continue to take in refugees, often with great public support. For example, in July 2018, the government of Jordan decided that it had done enough for Syrian refugees and would cease taking them in. At that time, there were already 650,000 registered refugees in Jordan, about 7 percent of the Jordanian population. This is an extraordinary number. If the United States had taken in as many refugees as Jordan had in the past four years, relative to the US population, the United States would have had to take in sixty-three million refugees;[30] compared to that, the four million refugees the United States has accepted in the past twenty-eight years seems relatively small. Some government officials blamed Syrian refugees for Jordan's economic woes, like increasing public debt, rising poverty, and unemployment. Despite the financial burden of hosting refugees, Jordanian citizens reacted not with relief at the border closing, but with anger. Citizens called the action shameful and began organizing private relief operations for Syrian refugees stuck at the border. The Twitter campaign #OpenTheBorders became one of the top hashtags.[31] This is not to say that all Jordanians agreed. Many Jordanians are frustrated with what they perceive as competition for jobs, overuse of water resources, and rising housing prices. But by and large, even though they are poorer than Western countries and host much larger numbers of refugees relative to their populations, countries like Jordan continue to allow refugees in and share a commitment to helping them, despite the economic cost.

OPEN BORDERS

Regardless of what I've explained—that, like turbulence, we have little to fear from refugees—some may continue to insist that openness to refugees will threaten their country in another way. The fear is that anyone who advocates for more humane treatment of refugees and better asylum policies will be committed to a policy of open borders. "Open borders" refers to the view that states do not have a legitimate right to control their borders or control immigration, and we should allow anyone who wants to enter a country to enter. The worry, of course, is that wealthy, democratic countries would be overwhelmed by the global poor and have no basis to defend themselves or protect their cultures and institutions.

The position that I defend in this book is consistent with the right of states to control their borders and doesn't require that we adopt a policy of open borders. In fact, my starting assumption is that states have a legitimate right to control who is allowed in and who can become a member of the state. However, I reject the all-or-nothing view that this sometimes entails.

Some people believe that if states have a moral right to control their borders, then any kind of refugee or immigration policy is justifiable and states can treat outsiders however they think best. Australia, for example, uses border security as a reason to put all asylum seekers who arrive by boat in detention facilities outside of Australia that have been described as hell on earth—places where adults have set themselves on fire, children have been sexually abused, and healthcare is routinely denied with terrible consequences.[32] People who are reluctant to criticize Australia worry that if they are not allowed to treat asylum seekers in this way, they will not be allowed to control immigration at all.

This all-or-nothing approach is simply wrong. I believe that states should balance their right to control their borders with a basic ethical consideration for the individual human beings who bear the consequences of these policies. For example, states have a right to reject people who do not fit the criteria they have established for asylum. But it doesn't follow that this gives them the right to treat people they reject for asylum without concern for their dignity or rights. I'll argue later in the book that it should be seen as morally unacceptable to detain would-be asylum seekers and put them in conditions like the ones described in Australia.

States ought to consider the ways that their policies on immigration and border control are actively harming some of the most vulnerable human beings on the planet. They ought to exercise their right to control immigration in ways that are consistent with the human rights of these vulnerable people. There is no inherent conflict between an ethical refugee policy and a state controlling its borders.

CONCLUSION

There is no reason to believe that refugees are more likely to be terrorists, criminals, or sexual predators than any other group, and if these are categories of people from whom we want to be protected, it would be far more effective to concentrate on native-born populations. Long-term trends suggest that when coupled with effective integration policies, refugees are a sound economic investment. There are of course still challenges associated with resettling and integrating refugees that ought to be treated seriously. But these problems shouldn't be exaggerated in ways that add to antirefugee rhetoric and contribute to declining support for refugees. In many ways, excessive fear undermines our ability to make rational policy decisions about refugees and asylum seekers in ways that can benefit Western countries, help refugees, and strengthen our ties with countries in the Global South. Of course, for many the point is to generate fear, but data simply do not support these pernicious depictions of refugees.

When I was recovering from my fear of flying, it wasn't enough just to learn that flying was safe and turbulence was not dangerous. Though important, facts and data alone are rarely convincing.[33] The same is true about fear of refugees. For many, suggesting that we have stronger moral obligations to help refugees, as I do in this book, makes people feel that their country is out of control—it induces a kind of turbulence—and simply telling them that they are safe, objectively speaking, will do little to calm fears. Because facts alone are not enough, I've included stories in this book, accounts of the experiences of refugees around the world, that may resonate with readers and help generate a personal connection to refugees. I hope that the facts and data in this preface, along with stories of refugees throughout the book, will allow readers to put aside their fears and take seriously the main claim of this book: that we have ignored the ethical dimensions of our treatment of refugees for too long and that this ethical perspective is absolutely crucial when we think about the place refugees ought to have in our global community. I now really enjoy flying, and this has made many parts of my life much better, such as visiting family and traveling for work or fun. Once we get past our fears, welcoming refugees may also have a similar benefit for our political communities.

Introduction

A Tale of Two Refugee Crises

In 2015, Sina Habte's limp, pregnant body floated off the coast of Greece.[*,1] Already past her due date when she boarded a flimsy boat to cross the Mediterranean Sea, Sina wanted nothing more than to deliver her baby somewhere safe. A chemical engineer and citizen of the small African country of Eritrea, she'd spent six months fleeing almost certain lifelong imprisonment, if not torture or death, for violating one of Eritrea's draconian rules. In her case, she wanted to live with her husband, Dani, instead of where the government assigned her. Eritrea is a country so repressive that it is considered the North Korea of Africa. After escaping Eritrea, sneaking across borders and living in the shadows of several different countries, she had nowhere else to go. If she returned home, she would be imprisoned, tortured, or killed, and if she stayed in a refugee camp in Africa, it was likely that she would be found by Eritrean agents and returned home to the same punishment. So Sina, like tens of thousands of others like her, paid the last of her money to smugglers and boarded a small, overcrowded boat bound for Europe in the hope of claiming asylum.

* All the stories in this and the following chapters are based on published accounts written by journalists and scholars who have traveled around the world and spent time with refugees and asylum seekers. This book owes a debt of gratitude to them for their work, and to the refugees themselves for sharing their stories.

When her boat capsized, as so many boats did that summer, she became one of those refugees that people saw on the news. And for many, images of bodies like hers, drowned at sea or still alive in an overcrowded lifeboat, struck a nerve. Shock turned to horror when the images were of the bodies of young children who had drowned at sea. People could no longer ignore the plight of asylum seekers and began to demand a response to this crisis.

The summer of 2015 marked the beginning of the so-called European refugee crisis. While people had been entering Europe as asylum seekers for a long time, the rate intensified dramatically in 2015, when more than 1.3 million asylum seekers arrived asking for refugee status, tens of thousands more than previous years.[2] The arrival of over a million refugees in a relatively short period of time was seen by many observers as a crisis. Such an unprecedented increase raised questions for European citizens. Many people wanted to know: Do we have obligations to help all these refugees? Is it enough to give them food and send them home, or must we let them stay? Do we really have the capacity to help everyone?

Italy and Greece, easiest to reach by boat, were quickly overwhelmed. With more asylum claims to process and longer wait times, it wasn't long before living conditions deteriorated for refugees in these countries. We began to see pictures of fetid refugee camps in Greece, and of refugees desperate to leave, in the news. Unable to get help in Greece and Italy, asylum seekers began walking in large numbers across the pastoral European countryside, children and belongings in tow, camping out at European train stations, in the hopes of reaching Germany, Sweden, or the United Kingdom—countries perceived to be more welcoming, more efficient at responding to asylum claims, and more willing to allow family reunification.

Soon, a core principle of the European Union became a casualty of the crisis: open borders. Border guards in countries across Europe began forcefully pushing back refugees. Borders began to close and fences were erected to keep refugees out. Antirefugee sentiments spread across Europe, contributing to the rise of right-wing, anti-immigrant parties in many countries in Europe. Refugees, Hungary's prime minister said, are not fleeing for their lives but are "Muslim invaders" from which his country required protection.[3] Sixty-seven percent of British citizens approved of using the army to keep migrants and asylum seekers from entering the United Kingdom from France.[4] Significantly, antirefugee sentiment contributed to the Brexit referendum, where the United Kingdom voted to leave the EU altogether. Sympathy turned into fear, and refugees became people that Europe needed to be protected from, rather than vulnerable and sympathetic people, like Sina, who needed our help.

For most people, *this* was the refugee crisis—the arrival of large numbers of asylum seekers, the struggle that ensued in Europe, and the political changes that resulted from governments' handling of it. But this is only part of the story. While the 2015 crisis in Europe shocked many around the world, it was actually the background to another, less visible crisis.

What lay behind the European refugee crisis was a second crisis, the crisis for refugees themselves. The crisis is that refugees around the world are largely unable to get refuge, that is, they are unable to access the minimum conditions of human dignity while they wait for a more permanent solution (either to go home or to be resettled permanently elsewhere). The majority of refugees, about 85 percent, will remain in the Global South, either in inadequate refugee camps or without international aid in urban centers. Many others will leave and seek asylum directly in a Western country, a choice that entails paying smugglers their life savings, putting themselves at risk of violence, and, all too often, losing their lives.[5] Only 2 percent of refugees will be able to find a new home either by being resettled or by being able to return home;[6] the remaining refugees will persist in this period of limbo and without access to the basic conditions of human dignity, for years and often decades.

Because this second crisis has been largely invisible for most people in the West, few have raised the kinds of moral questions that became pressing when bodies of refugees began washing onto the shores of Italy and Greece or were found decomposing in trucks in Austria. Few have asked: Why are these the only options for refugees? Whose responsibility is it to help them while they are in this limbo state? How did this dire situation come about? These are questions that urgently need to be addressed, as the two crises—the European refugee crisis and the crisis for refugees unable to get refuge—are interconnected. This book will show that the European refugee crisis cannot be understood or adequately responded to without understanding the role Western states have played in shaping this second crisis.

A STORY IN NUMBERS

I will explain this second crisis in much more detail in the second part of this book, but as an overview, let me explain three key numbers that make the crisis what it is.

First, the total number of people forcibly displaced from their home as of 2019 is 70.8 million. While most are displaced within their own countries and never leave—41.3 million are *internally displaced* and not technically considered refugees—about 25 million are considered refugees, half of whom are children.[7] Another 3.5 million are asylum seekers. In other words, there are *a lot* of people who do not have a place in the world where their human rights are secure. It's important to remember, though, that while 25 million is a lot of refugees, it's a number that many consider manageable. In the view of some, in a world of over 7 billion people, it would be possible to find a place for all refugees if there were only the political will to do so.[8]

The second number is 1 percent. This is the approximate percentage of refugees who are resettled in a new country each year.[9] Resettlement refers to the process whereby countries work with the United Nations to bring over refugees who are living in refugee camps. About 1.4 million of the 25 million refugees are considered by the UN to be too vulnerable to be protected in refugee camps in the Global South and are in need of resettlement.[10] Because so few are resettled, the vast majority of refugees, including those in the most vulnerable group, remain in the poorest countries in the world, where they first seek refuge. About half live in camps run by the UN and the other half live in urban centers, though this proportion can vary greatly from country to country. Those who live outside of refugee camps often have little access to international assistance. For example, less than 10 percent of the Syrian refugees living outside of camps in Turkey, Lebanon, and Jordan receive support from the UN or its partner organizations.[11] This is in part because for every $135 of public funds spent on asylum seekers in Europe, only $1 is spent on refugees in the Global South.[12] This is true even though roughly 85 percent of forcibly displaced people live in developing countries, with Turkey, Uganda, Pakistan, Lebanon, Jordan, and Iran hosting the highest number of refugees. These countries, though agreeing to *host* refugees, do not allow them to integrate, work, or settle permanently (with the exception of Uganda and Ethiopia, which allow refugees the right to work). Because many refugees believe that it is not likely that they will be able to return home in the near future and know that the odds of being chosen for resettlement are extremely low, they choose to bypass this system and seek asylum directly in Europe and other Western countries.[13]

The final number is seventeen. This is the average number of years that a person is likely to remain a refugee once becoming one.[14] If you are a refugee escaping war, the average length of time as a refugee is even longer: twenty-five years.[15] About half of all refugees are in "protracted" situations, and the average length of their exile is twenty-six years.[16] In other words, millions of refugees are spending their lives in "a permanent state of temporary living."[17] This is both because the conflicts that generate refugees are more complex and entrenched than in previous periods (denying refugees the ability to return to their homes) and because resettlement countries are taking in relatively few refugees. Far from a short or temporary status, being a refugee is how most refugees will spend their lives, and many refugee children will remain refugees well into adulthood.

All three of the factors highlighted by these numbers contributed to the refugee crisis of 2015 in Europe. Many refugees from Syria were aware of their options—squalid refugee camps or urban poverty for years on end—and chose instead to pay smugglers to help them come to Europe, where they could claim asylum. They made informed, calculated decisions about the best course of action based not only on their need to leave their home country but also on an understanding of how badly refugees are treated around the world. Keeping these two crises in mind can help us to understand the decisions of more than a million people who, in 2015, chose to risk flimsy boats on the Mediterranean rather than put up with the status quo life as a refugee.

There is another connection between the two crises that is important. The way that Europe and other countries chose to respond to the first crisis, the European refugee crisis, only worsened circumstances for refugees by making it harder to find refuge. In 2018, fed up by the challenges European countries faced, the EU made agreements with Libya and Turkey[18] to ensure that these countries, in exchange for various economic benefits, would prevent asylum seekers from departing for Europe from their coasts. These agreements made it even more difficult for refugees to claim asylum and access the minimum conditions of human dignity. These deals essentially ended the European refugee crisis—from January to June 2018 only thirteen thousand refugees had made it to Europe, a far cry from the hundreds of thousands who had arrived previously. Train stations in Italy, Hungary, and Germany that had formerly been filled with exhausted refugees trying to get across Europe returned to their pristine appearance.[19]

For refugees, of course, these deals only deepened their inability to access asylum in the West and worsened the second crisis. Take the situation in Libya. The EU funded the Libyan coast guard to return refugees who tried to leave Libya by boat for Europe, essentially preventing asylum seekers from seeking asylum. Libya, far from offering the minimum conditions of human dignity for refugees, is known for abusing refugees and migrants, sometimes in horrifying ways.[20] Many are put in overcrowded, unsanitary detention centers. Torture, forced labor, and other forms of cruel treatment are common in these places, and some refugees are even sold into slavery.[21] Most Europeans, of course, don't see where refugees have ended up and what life is like for them in places like Libya. Though the crisis has effectively ended as far as Europeans are concerned, the crisis for refugees has only been pushed further out of sight.

ETHICS AND THE GLOBAL REFUGEE CRISIS

This book is an attempt to make visible this second crisis. It seeks to reveal the conditions in the twenty-first century for refugees who are virtually unable to get refuge, and to consider our moral obligations to them in light of this reality. I will suggest throughout that the discussion of how states and their citizens should respond to refugees has been impoverished because it has not taken seriously our moral responsibilities to all refugees, both those who seek asylum and those who languish in camps and urban spaces. When morality has entered into such discussions, it has not done so in a way that takes seriously our obligations to *all* refugees, not just the ones on our shores.

At the core, we cannot understand our moral obligations to refugees without understanding the second crisis. I'll argue that our primary moral duty is to address the political structures that unjustly prevent refugees from accessing the minimum conditions of human dignity while they are refugees. We may not be able to stop ongoing conflicts around the world or prevent new ones from starting, but we must ensure that the international community responds to refugees in ways that protect the minimum conditions of human dignity.

MAKING SENSE OF THE CRISES

Life for refugees in the twenty-first century as I've just described it stands in stark contrast both to what most people imagine happens to refugees and to what the international community envisioned for refugee protection after World War II. Many people want to believe that once refugees flee their countries, they reach refugee camps where they stay for a short time, receiving food, shelter, and healthcare, before starting their new lives in another country. They imagine that conditions for refugees are at least decent, if not good, and that time spent as a refugee is fairly short. There is a tacit assumption that if one country chooses not to resettle refugees, another will or they will return to their home country.[22] Given these assumptions, many people cannot understand why so many refugees are willing to risk their lives on flimsy boats or on foot through the brutal desert heat to come to Europe, the United States, or Australia.

This situation would also be surprising to the politicians who first sought to find an international solution for refugees at the end of World War II. When developing the Refugee Convention in 1951, the drafters imagined one of three solutions—voluntary return to the home country, integration into the country hosting the refugee, or resettlement in another country—would be accessible to all refugees within a short amount of time. Article 17 of the Convention guarantees the right to access employment. It makes clear that if restrictions are placed on this right to protect the domestic labor market, they need to be removed after three years in the unlikely event that a refugee should find herself in a camp longer than that. It was hard for the drafters of the Refugee Convention in the 1950s to imagine that refugees would remain dependent on international aid for more than a few years.[23] This was the case, by and large, in the 1960s and 1970s, when most refugees were integrated among local host populations in the Global South.[24]

It is hard to make sense of how far the situation has declined since then. There are some historical reasons: during the Cold War both communist and capitalist societies could claim a political victory if people from one kind of country claimed asylum in the other;[25] but when the Cold War ended, so did the appeal of using asylum to score points on another superpower. Political factors have also played a part: wars stretch on much longer, and states have grown more unstable, among other reasons.[26]

From another perspective, the situation results from two important moral principles clashing with one another. On the one hand, there is the widely accepted principle of national sovereignty. States have a right to control their internal affairs, including who they allow into their countries. The principle of national sovereignty holds that states should not be told by other countries what laws they can enact or how they should structure their democracy. In order to be self-governing democracies, states must have the self-determination embodied in the principle of national sovereignty.

On the other hand, states also have an obligation to protect human rights.[27] Human rights, the rights that all people have just in virtue of their humanity, are recognized in some way by every state. Most states have signed human rights *treaties* and have agreed to uphold human rights. The 1951 Refugee Convention[28] is the piece of international law that lays out how states should treat refugees and what they can and cannot do to them. Most states want to be seen as protecting and defending human rights, and many go to great lengths to do so.

Two morally legitimate principles—national sovereignty and human rights—come into conflict in the refugee crises. States try to balance their sovereign right to control immigration with the protection of human rights of refugees and asylum seekers that they have formally agreed to. In practice, it can be hard to do both at once. States try not to violate refugees' human rights, for example, by sending asylum seekers back to their home country if they have a genuine fear of persecution (this is known as the principle of non-refoulement). But most states consider it a legitimate exercise of their national sovereignty to implement deterrence policies that make it difficult, and dangerous, for refugees to claim asylum in the first place.

This is why asylum has come to resemble a cat-and-mouse game—refugees seek their human rights, while Western states try to prevent them from doing so on Western territory. Further, it is why millions of refugees are confined to camps and hidden away in urban spaces—they are not forced to go back home (which would violate their rights), but states are unwilling to grant them citizenship, legal residence or, in most cases, even the right to work (which most countries believe they have the sovereign right to do in order to protect their national goals).

Though significant, this conflict of rights doesn't have to prove as harmful for refugees as it does and can be moderated to some extent by *morality*. I'll suggest in this book that though we may have a *right* to exclude refugees or make their entrance to our countries difficult on principles of national sovereignty, we ought not to. There are many reasons people have given for why we have moral obligations to refugees. One reason is that we may be the cause of their becoming refugees in the first place; perhaps our state contributed to a conflict that destabilized their country and resulted in their displacement. Another reason is simply humanitarian: perhaps their need is great and we are in a position to help. A third reason leading many to believe that we have obligations to refugees is that our commitment to human rights requires that we help refugees who have no one else to help them. In Chapter 6, I'll suggest another reason for thinking about our moral responsibility for refugees. The reason is that we participate in various global institutional structures that have contributed to the second crisis. This is not to say that we intended to harm refugees in the ways I've described in this chapter, but rather, we contribute to and benefit from a global system that has the effect of preventing refugees from gaining refuge. This is why we must take the second crisis, the crisis for refugees and their inability to secure the minimum conditions of human dignity, more seriously than we do.

MINIMUM CONDITIONS OF HUMAN DIGNITY

Throughout this book, I will use the phrase *minimum conditions of human dignity*. Here I refer to a common-sense understanding of what any human being needs in order to live a life with dignity. I stress that I am considering a *minimum* level. There may be many things that are needed for a good life—advanced education or sophisticated medical procedures, for example—but I'm concerned with what is absolutely necessary by virtually any measure of human dignity. There is an important debate on what refugees and asylum seekers should be entitled to in Western countries that can provide more elaborate resources, beyond the minimum. But virtually no one openly denies that refugees and asylum seekers are entitled to the basic, minimum conditions of human dignity wherever they find themselves; their inability to obtain these conditions in most places is precisely what I hope to draw the reader's attention to.

What exactly are these minimum conditions that refugees should have access to? We can begin to understand what they are by looking at what life is like when they are absent. Throughout this book, we will see what the lives of refugees are like in camps, urban settings, and the deserts and oceans they cross to seek asylum. The father who worries that his children will be bitten by rats at night in the refugee camp, the refugee mother who has to send her small children to work in the city to survive, and the family that hires smugglers to take them on an inflatable raft to cross the sea to claim asylum are all denied the minimum conditions of human dignity. When a German diplomat described the conditions where asylum seekers are held in Libya as being like a "concentration camp," where execution, torture, and rape are the norm,[29] the minimum conditions for human dignity have not been met.

For a definition with more precise content, we can turn to the Universal Declaration of Human Rights or to the conventions (legally binding commitments) that followed from it, such as the International Convention on Civil and Political Rights and the International Convention on Social, Economic and Cultural Rights. The Universal Declaration of Human Rights is so widely accepted as the basic standard of humane treatment that it is considered to be *customary* international law, binding on states whether or not they have signed and ratified any piece of human rights law. According to Article 25, all human beings have the right to a standard of living that is adequate for their health and well-being. This includes an *adequate* level of food, clothing, housing, and medical care. Children in particular are entitled to special care and assistance in achieving this adequate standard of living, and for them, the right to an education (Article 26) is part of this minimum standard. All human rights documents stress the importance of the right to security of one's person (Article 3).

Of course, what counts as an "adequate" level of food, housing, or medical care is the subject of some debate. Regarding food, a minimum threshold is food that is sufficient in quantity, nutritionally adequate, culturally appropriate, and accessible. A minimum threshold for adequate housing is that it is safe and habitable, including access to basic sanitation, not just a roof and walls. A right to a basic level of medical care includes access to medical services that are necessary for sustaining life and protecting health and should include access to hospitals, clinics, and health professionals. Some advocates for rights include basic access to mental health care on this list. In terms of education, everyone has the right to free, elementary education that promotes literacy and other basic skills. What precise form these provisions take will depend on the country, culture, and economic state of the place in question. What I want to stress here is that there is a widely accepted minimum level considered necessary for people to be able to live lives of dignity. Though many people around the world who are not refugees do not have access to this minimum standard, it's still important to use it to evaluate the help we give to refugees.

However you define the minimum conditions of human dignity—whether, for example, it's food amounting to 1,000 calories a day or 1,500—millions of refugees are not able to access these conditions. As we will see throughout this book, refugee camps often lack sufficient food and security; urban settings often make it hard for refugees to find adequate housing or education; and, increasingly, refugees seeking asylum in Western countries find themselves in circumstances where they too lack these minimum conditions of human dignity. It's clear from the stories that refugees tell about their experiences that many do not live lives that would be considered secure. Virtually everyone agrees that most refugees do not have access to sufficient material conditions, education, or security.

WHO ARE "WE"?

I wrote this book with a specific audience in mind: people who want to understand the global refugee crisis from an ethical perspective and who may not be aware of the second crisis, the crisis for refugees, I have described. I drew from conversations that I have had with students in my classes, people in my community who came to my public talks, academics at conferences in North America and Europe, and friends and colleagues who asked me about my work and challenged me to think more deeply about my answers. Though my argument is addressed to this broad group of students, scholars, policymakers and curious citizens, I recognize the extraordinary amount of diversity among readers. But by and large, I hope most readers will recognize themselves in the "we" who are trying to understand the challenges and benefits of refugees.

But there is another sense in which I use the term "we." The main question that I ask in the book is what moral responsibilities *we* have to refugees around the world. Here I am referring primarily to relatively wealthy, liberal democratic states and their members, states that have historically played a powerful role in shaping the global system of refugee protection. I will refer to this group of states as "Western" throughout this book not because it's the most accurate term, but because it's the mostly widely agreed upon. This is not to suggest that other countries don't have obligations to refugees. I think they do. But Western countries have a special obligation to help—their greater capacity to help, their stated commitment to liberal democracy, and their role in shaping the second crisis ground their responsibility.[30]

Western states are in a position to help because they have the capacity to do so. The relative wealth of Western states is important, especially in a world of extreme global inequality. Relatively wealthy Western states are in a position to take in refugees, either through asylum or resettlement. Their population density, especially countries like Canada, the United States, and Australia, tends to be lower than in other places. Most are multicultural societies, and they have a tradition of including immigrants. In other words, most Western states are able to take in refugees and absorb them into their communities at relatively low cost to themselves. As David Miller has pointed out, responsibility for refugees should be shared by all states that "are able to help the refugee by admitting her."[31] Further, the financial power of Western states means that, at least relative to other countries, there are resources to invest in refugees and the global refugee protection system. As I discussed in the preface, refugees tend to be a net economic gain, though the upfront cost of helping refugees can be steep. In this sense, the economic capacity of a country matters. The philosopher Henry Shue argued that affluent states have a duty to aid poor ones because they are the ones controlling resources globally.[32] The same idea applies to helping refugees.

Second, the fact that Western countries consider themselves to be liberal democracies is significant. Western states claim that they are guided by principles of justice, fairness, and human rights. As the philosopher John Rawls put it, democratic countries "recognize principles of justice as governing their own domestic conduct."[33] The moral obligations of Western states to refugees, in some cases, will simply entail applying their own principles of justice to this group of people.

Finally, I think the history of Western states in shaping the norms and practices around the treatment of refugees, norms that have benefited Western countries at the expense of refugees, is also significant. Western states, as I'll argue in the book, have played a powerful role in shaping the second crisis. While some countries have taken in refugees and granted asylum, almost all Western states have been working to make the second refugee crisis invisible by keeping refugees far from Western states. Further, they have supported refugee camps as the primary way of responding to refugees. This is in part because Western states believe it is in their interest to keep potential asylum seekers far from their shores and ultimately, in the words of one scholar, "to keep Third World refugee problems from inconveniencing the developed states."[34] They have in this way contributed to the crisis refugees face, and their responsibility to them is grounded in this history. Relative wealth, commitment to principles of justice and human rights, and historical connection are the key reasons Western states have a particular moral responsibility to refugees.

In my view, both states themselves (their leaders, policymakers, and institutions) and individuals share obligations to help refugees. On the one hand, states have the capacity to change laws and policies affecting the treatment of refugees. States are in charge of budgets that fund refugee programs, both domestically and abroad. The number of refugees accepted in the United States each year is set by the president. The province of Quebec in Canada provides assistance for refugees once they are in Quebec. The individuals who are in positions of power in these institutions set the rules.

However, these rules are influenced by the citizens of these countries. Heads of state often, though not always, take cues on the treatment of refugees from their constituents. In democracies, whether or not people support policies matters. How refugees are treated while they are in a country is determined both by individuals and by institutions in that country. Individuals can help shape the terms of the debate, such as how refugees are depicted in the media, talked about in policy debates, and considered in funding strategies. In many countries, individuals have played large roles in supporting refugees by allowing them to live in their home, protesting harmful policies, and making films and art that teach others about refugees and increase understanding of them. Individuals and institutions are important, and we need think about the moral responsibility of both groups. In the conclusion of this book, I'll come back to this idea and suggest actions that both individuals and institutions can take to support the moral obligations we have to refugees.

Though Western states and their citizens are the focus of this book, other countries also have an obligation to refugees, though the ground of this obligation may be different. I use the term "host states" to talk about the countries in the Global South, which are by and large much poorer than Western countries but house the vast majority of displaced people in the world. Over 85 percent of refugees are in countries like Uganda, Pakistan, Jordan, Lebanon, Turkey, Bangladesh, and Kenya. While these countries are generous in allowing refugees residence, they too have an obligation to respect, protect, and fulfill the human rights of all residents on their territory, including refugees. Often this is not the case—freedom of movement and the right to work are routinely denied—and these states should be held to a rights-based standard. There are, of course, many other countries that are neither Western states nor host states—the Gulf States, China, and Russia, for example—which can and should be doing much more for refugees. The relative wealth of some of these countries—the Gulf States and South Korea, for example—can ground an obligation to contribute financially, if not in other ways. This is the approach Japan has taken: it resettles very few refugees but is one of the top donor states to the UNHCR. But this book is not addressed to wealthy non-Western states, though my hope is that a larger, more global approach might one day be possible.

MOVING BEYOND RESCUE

It's not entirely true that morality is absent in the debate over how states should respond to refugees. Philosophers have been engaged in a robust debate over this topic for years, but because they have not taken seriously the second crisis of how refugees are treated while they are refugees, they have not, in my view, been able to adequately explain what we owe to refugees. This is in part because Western states are too often seen only as *rescuers* and not as in part responsible for the inability of refugees to find refuge.

In the view of some philosophers, Western states are like someone who comes across an injured person at the side of a road and steps in to help.[35] In this view, the refugee producing states (Syria, Myanmar, etc.) are the parties who have done something wrong by harming their citizens and creating refugees who need to be rescued by other countries. They are the ones responsible for the situation of refugees. Refugees, those in need of being rescued, are the (mostly) innocent victims of the situation. Western states, then, are positioned as the rescuers who come to the aid of those in need and who are unconnected to the situation. Because this is a *positive* duty of rescue—a duty to provide aid, not the fulfillment of a *negative* duty, a duty to refrain from harming, which is generally considered stronger and more demanding —the rescuers cannot be asked to sacrifice too much.[36] When framed in this way, the moral question becomes how to best help refugees while balancing the interests of the rescuing state, which has a right to control its borders, limit immigration, and determine the amount it is willing to spend on refugees. This way of thinking introduces another consideration: separating out those who are genuine refugees from those merely taking advantage of generosity. This task becomes paramount in order to ensure that the generosity of rescuing states is not taken advantage of.

What underlies the rescue frame is that Westerns states, the rescuers, have not done anything wrong. They have not caused the refugees to come into harm's way but are merely stepping in to help. In other words, this is not a duty of justice, a duty that might come into play if a state had done something wrong. If a country that was able to help refugees failed to do so, we would perhaps think it ungenerous or unkind, but would not consider it unjust. Because it's sometimes unclear who should be helping which refugees, especially in contexts where there are many countries that could be providing aid, it is hard to blame any one country when refugees go unaided. We may praise states that step up and help refugees, but we rarely criticize other states for doing too little.

The real story is more complicated than this. While it's true that refugee-producing states harm refugees by failing to protect their human rights and that many Western states do a lot to help refugees, there are some important facts of the global refugee crisis that are left out of this way of framing the story. What needs to be included is the harm experienced by refugees *as they seek refuge* and the role that Western states have played in this outcome.

If we broaden our frame in this way, we can see two distinct sets of harms. The first is the one already mentioned that receives the most focus: the circumstances that drive refugees to leave their homes in the first place. The risk of torture by the police, the barrel bombs that killed relatives, the fear of kidnapping by a militant group. Yet escaping this dangerous environment is not all that refugees need to fear.

The second set of harms that refugees must overcome occur once they seek refuge outside of their home country. We have created a situation in which the vast majority of refugees are unable to get refuge in any meaningful sense; they are not able to access the minimum conditions of human dignity. Refugees must choose from among the options of impoverished camps, urban poverty and insecurity, or risking life and limb to seek asylum.[37] As I'll detail throughout the book, each choice comes with its own kind of harm. Refugee camps produce a loss of autonomy and hope for the future; urban settlements mean greater freedom, but even less security, access to food, and education for children; and asylum often means risking everything, including life itself. Each choice exposes refugees to a different kind of deprivation.

This second set of harms must be understood as something that Western states and the international community have played a role in creating and sustaining, and this is why I refer to it as *the problem we have created*. Because of our policies with respect to immigration and border security—which I will assume that states have a moral right to establish as they see fit—states have more or less ensured that the vast majority of refugees will not be able to access the conditions that would allow them to lead a minimally decent life, one that includes autonomy, dignity, and basic material goods, in other words, the kind of life they aim at when they flee their countries. We must consider this outcome one of the harms refugees need to be rescued from. Not only have the international community and powerful Western states failed to genuinely rescue refugees, but the options we have given them often undermine their human rights.

When the problem we have created is brought into the frame, it becomes clear that we must ask a broader set of moral questions: What do we owe to people living in refugee camps and urban centers for years or decades? Is it morally justifiable to make seeking asylum so difficult as to require risking bodily integrity and even life? What do we owe to refugees who will never make it to our shores? My answer, in short, is that we have a moral obligation to ensure that refugees can access the minimum conditions of human dignity while they are waiting for a solution to their situation (either returning home or finding a new one). This will require us to rethink our relationship with refugees and how we respond to them.

OVERVIEW OF THE BOOK

How can we ensure that refugees can access the minimum conditions of human dignity? For many people in Europe, North America, and Australia, refugee policy is a matter of national security, economics, or perhaps foreign policy. Yet if we are going to take seriously the dignity of refugees, it's crucial that we consider the demands of morality. To that end, I want to give readers the resources to think about the moral issues raised by the existence of refugees in the twenty-first century and the tools to think critically about not just the current refugee crisis, but future challenges as well.

Because this book was written for a wide audience of curious citizens, students, policymakers, and scholars from different disciplines, Part I offers an overview of both the refugee crisis and the philosophical debate over what states owe refugees from the point of view of morality. Chapter 1 will introduce the key terms and definitions that are used when talking about refugees. It answers such questions as who counts as a refugee, how they are different from asylum seekers, what obligations states have to them, and the needs of climate refugees and economic migrants. The question—who is a refugee?—turns out to be one that is answered differently by different countries in ways that make it seem that the definition is applied in a morally arbitrary way. This chapter gives readers the necessary background to understand both the crisis for Western states and the crisis that refugees themselves face in their inability to find refuge. Chapter 2 provides a general introduction to ethics and explains what it means to say that we have moral obligations. Some people think that we should keep political or economic concerns at the top of our mind when thinking about how to respond to refugees. This chapter shows why morality is equally important and how morality can apply *globally* and not just to those close to us, such as family, friends, or fellow citizens. This is particularly important since I argue throughout the book that we have a moral obligation to provide refugees with the minimum conditions of human dignity. Both Chapter 1 and Chapter 2 are important background information for the following chapters. Chapter 3 gives a more specific introduction to the ways that philosophers have discussed our moral obligations to refugees. As I have already suggested, I don't fully agree with the conclusions reached because I think philosophers have framed the problem too narrowly. But nonetheless, the question of whether or not we have moral obligations to resettle or grant asylum to refugees, even if it goes against our national interest, is an important one to consider.

In the second part of the book, I present my own views on our treatment of refugees and argue that we must expand the way we frame the refugee crisis to include the crisis for refugees who are unable to get refuge. I explain this crisis in detail in Chapters 4 and 5. Chapter 4 is a detailed discussion of what it means to be a refugee living in a refugee camp or in a city without help from the international community. Well over 85 percent of refugees, half of whom are children,[38] live in one of these two circumstances, though most people in the West are scarcely aware of this. Nor are people aware of the ways that Western states have supported this outcome.

Chapter 5 describes the price we ask refugees to pay to claim asylum. During the 2015 refugee crisis, almost every single person who made it to Europe used a smuggler at some point in the journey.[39] This was because states have made it so difficult to enter in order to claim asylum that spending your life savings to pay a smuggler is virtually the only option. Refugees must overcome deterrence policies designed to make claiming asylum as difficult as possible so as to discourage asylum seekers. Detention, destitute refugee camps, and policies of separating children from parents are now normal approaches for handling asylum seekers. In my view, we have not grappled with asylum policies that harm refugees sufficiently. This chapter shows the ways in which our immigration policies intertwine with the options refugees have and their inability to get refuge without sacrificing their safety, health, and dignity.

In Chapter 6, I present my own approach to our moral obligations to refugees in light of the realities described in the previous two chapters. I draw on the philosopher Iris Young to suggest that we ought to frame the crisis for refugees as a kind of *structural injustice*—an injustice that wasn't intentionally caused by any particular state but that nonetheless we must take responsibility for. I explain why Western states are *politically* responsible. In the conclusion to the book I suggest practical ways to think about how individuals and states can address the structural injustice that refugees around the world experience.

CONCLUSION

Sina Habte, the pregnant Eritrean asylum seeker whose story this chapter began with, had a happy ending. Because her boat capsized close to the shore, an off-duty Greek army sergeant saw the wreck, jumped into the water, and swam out to rescue whomever he could. One of the people he rescued was Sina. She was taken to the hospital and delivered a healthy baby whom she named Andonis, after the person who saved her life. She was really fortunate. That summer thousands of asylum seekers had no one to rescue them and died crossing the Mediterranean Sea.

When we consider what Western states owe to people like Sina, people who risk their lives and the lives of their children to gain entry to the countries we live in, it's important to consider why she believed this was her only option. Why would anyone risk her life and the life of her unborn child as she did? Part of what we owe people like Sina is consideration of the larger context that forced her to risk her life before we would even think about helping her and that made risking her life her only viable option. This larger context is what I've referred to as the second refugee crisis, the crisis for refugees who are unable to get refuge. What we owe Sina and the millions of others like her is the ability to access a minimum amount of human dignity while they are seeking refuge. Providing this dignity will require that we reconsider how we respond to refugees around the world. My hope is that this book will provide some guidance in this crucial task.

PART I

THE FIRST CRISIS

The Crisis for Western Countries

Chapter 1

Who Is a Refugee?

Normally, when one citizen threatens another, the authorities can be called in. If your neighbor sends you a death threat, you can call the police, file a complaint, and ask for protection. That's not how things work in El Salvador.

Before things went awry, Alberto was raising five thriving children with his wife.[1] He had a business breeding livestock and dogs, his wife ran a food stand, and they had many friends in town. But gangs disrupted everything.

A local gang tried to get one of Alberto's sons to be a drug mule. His son was beaten for resisting. Another gang leader made it known that he wanted Alberto's ten-year-old daughter to become his "girlfriend." When Alberto refused to give her up, he began receiving death threats. As Alberto was fully aware, gangs in El Salvador do not make idle threats.

Living in a country where the police were bribed by gangs and the government was powerless to intervene, Alberto had a choice. He could stay in his home and try to enjoy his life, but risk having his daughter raped and his son killed. His other option? He could leave his home and the life he had created and try to find safety elsewhere.

He chose the latter, heading north with his family, taking only what they could carry. At first Alberto moved his wife and children to a more northern part of El Salvador. He rebuilt his business and his children went back to school. But when one of the gangs caught up to him, he had no choice but to move again. He relocated twice within the country, but the gang found him wherever he went. He soon made his way to Mexico. He had never heard of "asylum" until he arrived at the US border and only learned about this possibility from other migrants.

Should we consider Alberto to be a refugee? The question of who "counts" as a refugee is one of the most contentious in the current debate about refugees. What's at stake in the answer is who gets the legal rights guaranteed to refugees by law, the social and economic benefits states extend to refugees but no other immigrants, and the sympathy that people are willing to express only for those migrants who qualify as refugees. Many in the West are concerned that economic migrants, people immigrating because they want better economic opportunities, are posing as refugees and should not qualify for the benefits of this status. For Alberto, this is a question of life (if he is seen as a legitimate refugee and allowed to stay in the United States) or death (if he is seen as an economic migrant and deported back to El Salvador, where the gangs he was fleeing from will be waiting).

It turns out that, globally speaking, there is little consensus on who is a refugee. "Refugee" is a term that is used in many different and sometimes inconsistent ways. The UN Refugee Convention of 1951 contains the official legal definition of a refugee. Yet this definition is not applied consistently by different countries. To be a refugee under the UN Convention you must be *persecuted* on one of several grounds. But what precisely counts as persecution, who has to do the persecution for it to count, and how bad the persecution has to be are all questions that different countries answer differently at different times in history. To complicate matters, the UN considers people to be refugees in a much broader set of circumstances than most countries. In short, while there is an official legal definition, it is interpreted so widely that it might be clearer to say that there are several different definitions. What this means in practice is that who gets refugee status is almost arbitrary. It is for this reason that philosophers have taken up the more abstract question of who *should* be considered a refugee. What precisely must people have gone through before they are entitled to the protection of the international community and potentially even a new home in a desirable Western country? What makes a refugee morally distinct from other kinds of immigrants? Many philosophers believe that it is the severity of the harm and the need for international protection, rather than the source of the harm, that should ground our definition of a refugee.

I think this is the right approach. I suggest that we adopt a fairly broad understanding of who counts as a refugee and hence who should be included in our moral consideration. We should think of refugees as people who have had their human rights severely violated, regardless of the source of the violation, and have been forced to flee their home country and seek international protection. This is an understanding of refugees that is broader than the strict legal definition, though it stops short of including most economic migrants.

The point of this chapter, however, is not to engage in an argument over who should or should not count as a refugee. My goal is to show that because there is no universally agreed-on definition of a refugee, one that is consistent with law, our moral intuitions, and on-the-ground practice, we cannot be confident that we are categorizing the right people as refugees, and others as not deserving of help. Sheer luck plays too big of a role in determining who counts as a refugee. Some years people fleeing domestic violence will receive asylum in the United States, and in other years they won't; some countries will recognize Eritreans as refugees nearly 100 percent of the time, while other countries will refuse them entirely; a mother and daughter fleeing the same circumstances at the same time may end up with one of them getting refugee status and one being denied it simply because different judges saw their situation differently.[2] The seemingly arbitrary way that refugee status is given in some cases is a feature of the global refugee regime that contributes to the second crisis I discussed in the introduction. If you are a person fleeing your home state for whatever reason, it's hard to know exactly where to seek refuge.

Determining who is a refugee in a way that does not lead to these morally arbitrary outcomes is a real challenge. The line between refugees and other kinds of forced migrants is blurry at best, and a rigid distinction is perhaps impossible. As a result, we need to be cautious—even humble—about who we exclude and decide is not worthy of sympathy and help. We should be wary of denying refugee status to whole groups of people without taking seriously their circumstances. Given the reality of forced displacement in the twenty-first century, it's important to consider what we owe to all people who find themselves seeking international protection of their rights, however we define them.

DEFINITIONS: REFUGEE AND ASYLUM SEEKER

The primary legal definition of a refugee comes from the 1951 Refugee Convention. According to this document, the term "refugee" applies to any person who, "owing to a well-founded fear of being persecuted for reasons of race, religion, nationality, membership of a particular social group or political opinion, is outside of the country of his nationality and is unable or, owing to such fear, is unwilling to avail himself of the protection of that country."[3] In other words, refugees are those who are *forced* to flee their country and are unable or unwilling to return due to a *well-founded fear* of persecution.

This definition emerged in the aftermath of the horrors of World War II. The war had demonstrated that it was almost impossible to protect the human rights of people who had lost their citizenship, such as Jews in Germany after 1939—human rights were useless unless you had a government to which you could appeal to uphold them. A moral consensus emerged: states have a responsibility to come to the aid of those who do not have the protection of their own state or who are, in fact, being persecuted by their state. The Refugee Convention was an attempt to put that sense of moral responsibility into practice through international law, ensuring that refugees could access their basic human rights. At the same moment, an international body, the United Nations High Commissioner for Refugees (or UNHCR for short), was created to oversee the implementation of the Refugee Convention and to take charge of refugee protection around the world.

The term "refugee" is the broadest term that is used for those who are forced to flee their country of nationality because of persecution, war, or violence. But the Refugee Convention's definition is very specific. An individual must meet all parts of the definition in order to legally be considered a refugee: one's location (outside one's home country) and the reason one was persecuted (one of the five grounds) must align exactly with the terms of the 1951 Refugee Convention, and on some interpretations, the persecution must be done by the state.

First, refugees must be outside of their home countries, that is, they must enter another country before they can claim to be refugees. Generally speaking, refugees go to a *host country*, usually proximate to the country they are fleeing, register with the UNHCR, and wait there until the UN is able to find a country willing to grant them refugee status (the United States, Canada, Australia, and the European Union are the most likely ones and are sometimes referred to as *resettlement states*). We call people internally displaced persons, or IDPs, if they have lost the protection of their state but have not left their country of nationality (40 million out of the 70.8 million forcibly displaced people around the world are in this situation). Such people are in many ways even more vulnerable than refugees because they are not entitled to the same legal protections, and humanitarian agencies have a harder time accessing them to provide aid.

Second, to be classified as a refugee, a person must be persecuted on one of the five grounds listed in the Convention. These include race, religion, nationality, political opinion, and membership in a particular social group. War, violence, and poverty are not enough—people fleeing from these circumstances will have a harder time making a claim for refugee status. Moreover, if the persecution stems from something other than one of the five grounds, for instance, sexual orientation, a person may not count as a refugee under the Convention. Countries—and even different courts within the same country—may differ on what counts as the *persecution* that entitles a person to refugee status. For example, should people who are persecuted because they are gay, lesbian, bisexual, or transgendered be considered "members of a social group" and entitled to asylum? Countries disagree. Canada, for example, considers this a ground for asylum, while other countries, such as the United Kingdom, often do not.[4] The bar for resettlement is even higher, and in some circumstances persecution itself is not enough. The United States, for example, won't consider refugees for resettlement unless they are also of "special humanitarian concern."[5] This means that the refugee is so vulnerable and the circumstances are so dire that the person can be helped only through resettlement.

Finally, individuals must be fleeing from persecution at the hands of their state, that is, by public and not private actors. Jews massacred by the Nazis, Christians escaping communist regimes, and Tutsis killed at the command of Hutu leaders are all clear examples of state persecution. However, in the twenty-first century, many people are fleeing *failed states,* states that are not trying to harm them but are unable to protect them from threats to their dignity. Many Central Americans, for example, seeking asylum in the United States are fleeing gang violence or domestic violence, not persecution by the state. Their states are either *unable* to protect individuals from these harms (some gangs in Central America are more powerful than the state) or *unwilling* (some states don't consider domestic violence against women a crime worthy of enforcement). Many countries do grant refugee status to people fleeing violence by private actors, but it's up to the discretion of individual state, and states can and do change their policies. The United States, for example, used to consider women fleeing domestic violence from certain countries refugees but reversed that policy under the Trump administration.[6]

While most refugees go through the UN to apply for refugee status, others go directly to the country they hope will grant them refugee status. Such people are referred to as *asylum seekers.* If they meet the definition of a refugee as interpreted by the particular country they are in, they are *granted asylum*—that is, given refugee status—and allowed to stay indefinitely. Asylum seekers are not considered refugees until they gain this legal recognition. People who are denied asylum (sometimes referred to as "failed asylum seekers" or even "rejected asylum seekers") can be deported to their countries of origin.

Asylum seekers, people who come directly to countries like Greece, the United States, and Australia and make their claims in person, have one of the strongest rights in the international system—anyone who claims asylum has the right to have one's claims heard and cannot be sent back to the country of origin unless it can be determined that the person does not have a well-founded fear of persecution. This is the right of *non-refoulement,* and its strength in international law can be seen in the lengths countries will go to avoid having to uphold it, primarily by preventing people from coming onto their territory to claim asylum.

Though asylum seekers are sometimes criticized for being "illegal migrants," since they often enter Western countries without official documentation or not through official borders, this is not, strictly speaking, accurate. All human beings have a *human right* to seek asylum. This right comes from the Universal Declaration of Human Rights, signed in 1948, which articulates the most widely accepted list of human rights. Not everyone has a right to *receive* asylum, since countries don't have an obligation to give asylum to everyone who asks for it, but everyone has a right to seek it. Article 31 of the Refugee Convention says explicitly that *irregular entry*—people who cross borders without permission, that is, *illegally*—should not negatively affect whether or not a state considers them refugees. In other words, the hundreds of thousands of people traveling around the planet trying to find a secure place to live are not doing anything illegal; seeking asylum is not a crime, even when it requires that individuals illegally cross borders. This makes sense: we would hardly accuse the Von Trapp family—the family featured in *The Sound of Music*—of being criminals for crossing "illegally" into Switzerland from Austria to seek refuge from the Nazi persecution.

Though the criteria for who should count as a refugee appear to be clear, this coveted status is often granted in an arbitrary fashion. In fact, "refugees in identical circumstances will be granted asylum in the courts of some nations but refused it in others; even within the same country, they will be granted asylum in some years but not others."[7] For example, in 2014, Iraqis were recognized as refugees in Greece 14 percent of the time but 94 percent of the time in France. In the same year, Eritreans were considered refugees in France 26 percent of the time but 100 percent of the time in Sweden.[8] The arbitrary nature of asylum can be seen in the US context as well. In 2019, a mother and daughter from Honduras sought asylum in the United States on the grounds that they were persecuted in their country because they were both HIV-positive. Though they had identical circumstances (same country of origin, same reason for persecution), their outcomes were different: the mother was believed by the asylum officer and allowed into the United States, but her daughter was not and was sent back to Honduras by herself.[9]

The inconsistency and increasing strictness of the process has created a new category: the "rejected." This is an informal category that refers to people who remain in a country after they have been denied asylum. Having traveled thousands of miles to get to Europe from the Middle East or Africa, refugees are understandably unwilling to return voluntarily to the conditions that forced them to leave in the first place, and so choose instead to remain in the country illegally and without state recognition or protection.[10]

To complicate things further, the UN itself uses a broader definition of a refugee than the one found in the Convention. The UNHCR, the UN body tasked with overseeing the protection of refugees, goes beyond the Refugee Convention definition to include all people it considers to be "persons in refugee-like situations," including people fleeing war, violence, and extreme poverty. These are people who face the same risks as refugees but who are unable to gain refugee status "for practical or other reasons."[11] The UNHCR sometimes uses the term *forcibly displaced person* to refer to *all* people who are forced to flee their home, regardless of how they come to be classified under international or domestic law. Forcibly displaced persons include refugees, asylum seekers, IDPs, and stateless people (people who have had their citizenship revoked or were never granted citizenship; they are not considered citizens of any country, even though they have never left the country they were born in). The term *forcibly displaced person* also includes people fleeing war and other violent conflicts who, though not persecuted for one of the five grounds in the Refugee Convention, are in need of international protection. The UNHCR considers people in all of these categories de facto refugees, even if they do not precisely align with how the Convention or individual states define the term.

To give you a sense of how complex it can be to define a person's legal status and how many different ways the same person can be categorized, take the example of a Liberian displaced by civil war.[12] This person would become a refugee once she crossed a border and entered a UN refugee camp in Guinea. If she leaves the refugee camp to work in a different part of the country, she then becomes an *illegal alien.* Should she choose to pay a smuggler to travel to Europe and end up in France, she becomes an *asylum seeker* (with a 90 percent chance of being rejected). France may decide not to grant her asylum but will acknowledge that the circumstances she fled from are too dangerous to send her home. In this case, she will be considered a *non-expellable irregular* (the United States will give people in these circumstances *temporary protected status*). These legal statuses can be changed at any time. If the temporary protected status is revoked and the person refuses to leave, she ends up classified as an *illegal immigrant.* The Liberian in this example can go from being a refugee to illegal alien, depending on where she happens to be, whom she is asking for help, and what the political climate of the day is. Did she become less deserving of aid or moral consideration once she left the refugee camp? Because she was from a country that France considered less dangerous than others—regardless of the conditions she was fleeing—does she deserve less protection? Morally speaking, it doesn't seem that this should be the case, but this is how the international system has developed.

WHO IS NOT A REFUGEE?

Perhaps the most controversial distinction is between refugees and *economic migrants.* On its face, the difference may seem straightforward. If you're fleeing persecution, you're a refugee. If you're fleeing poverty or just looking to improve your overall quality of life, you're an economic migrant. The former person is entitled to all of the rights and protections in international law—and perhaps a good deal of sympathy as well. The latter person is not entitled to anything, certainly not the right to immigrate to a country of one's choice. Countries generally believe they have no obligations to economic migrants over and above not violating their human rights.

Yet this distinction is controversial. In practice, calling refugees "economic migrants" has become an easy way to dismiss any legitimate claim they may have on a state for protection and benefits. It was common in 2015 for European leaders to dismiss refugees as economic migrants, coming to leech off the EU, when in fact, according to the UN, 84 percent of people arriving in Europe by boat in 2015 came from the world's top ten refugee-producing countries.[13] If they are indeed economic migrants, and have no "well-founded fear of persecution," they are considered by the UN to be persons "not in need of international protection"[14] and can be deported without violating international law. However, if they are refugees, states have an obligation to allow them to stay and provide shelter and other benefits while they work toward integration and citizenship.

Because of the complexities of the world in the twenty-first century, it is often impossible to make this distinction clearly and consistently. Many people who flee their homes come from *failed states,* states unable to protect the human rights of their citizens or provide a minimum level of security in which people can access what they need to live with dignity. Citizens from countries as different as Nigeria, Sudan, Honduras, and Libya are fleeing their states because their government cannot protect them from the violence caused by *nongovernmental actors,* for example, Islamic organizations like Boko Haram and al-Shabaab, in the cases of Nigeria and Sudan, and violent gangs in the case of Honduras and Libya. But these are also very poor countries, and citizens' insecurity is compounded by their poverty.

At the very least, it's hard to disentangle which specific factor *caused* them to leave their home and seek protection in another country. In the United States, many asylum seekers are fleeing gang violence in Central America, but because many economic migrants come from these same countries, skeptics are reluctant to receive them as genuine asylum seekers. They prefer to treat them as economic migrants whom the state can deport at will.

Categorizing someone as a "refugee" or an "economic migrant" can tap into existing sympathies and prejudices. In the United States, economic migrants are accused of taking jobs away from American citizens. In Europe, they're accused of coming to take advantage of generous social benefits. In both cases, they are seen as a threat, something the government must protect its citizens from, both for the sake of the economy and for basic security.

Though the distinction between refugees and economic migrants is important, it is one we should be wary of. Relying too heavily on this distinction runs the risk of complicity in an artificial separation of those supposedly deserving of our help from those who are undeserving. The philosopher Kieran Oberman illustrates this absurdity in the following way.

> Imagine a health system working upon similar lines. Instead of treating the sick and injured, it treats only those who are sick or injured for particular reasons. Victims of assault are seen to; those suffering from disease or malnutrition are ignored. Doctors attend to a superficial knife wound, but walk past a man having a stroke. Now imagine, under this healthcare system, that some patients pretended to be the victims of assault in order to obtain treatment. Would we condemn them as "bogus treatment-seekers" for "abusing the system"? I do not think so. More likely, we would regard their behavior as a reasonable reaction to arbitrary discrimination.[15]

Many have seen the distinction between genuine refugee and economic migrant, founded on the narrative of the "good" versus "bad" migrant, as a way to justify policies aimed at excluding non-Westerners. In practice, it's a distinction that allows a kind of racial division between refugees, where in Europe people from the Middle East are seen as genuine refugees, while people from Africa are not. This does not correspond to the experiences of people fleeing these places. The journalist Charlotte McDonald-Gibson writes: "Twenty-six percent of the world's refugees are in sub-Saharan Africa. The largest number of migrants to arrive in Italy so far this year [2016] are Eritreans, who are fleeing a dictatorship that the UN has accused of crimes against humanity. The second biggest group is Nigerians. The International Organization for Migration has told me that at least 80 percent of Nigerian women and girls [who flee Nigeria] are trafficked for sexual exploitation. And many of the people trying to reach Europe this year are not fleeing conflict in their own lands, but in Libya, where they have suffered kidnapping, torture and imprisonment."[16] It's important to keep in mind that the distinction between economic migrants and refugees can be used to exclude people from certain countries from the benefits of asylum when they may in fact have a genuine claim. It's clear that categorizing people for the sake of determining our moral obligations is no easy task, as circumstances make it difficult for us to put people into neat boxes.

CLIMATE REFUGEES

The concept of *climate refugees*, though increasingly necessary, can make categorization even more complex. Broadly speaking, this term is used to refer to people who become refugees—that is, people who are forced to leave their countries of origin and seek help elsewhere—as a result of climate change, rather than persecution.

Because the international system still sees refugee status as largely tied to the political rather than environmental circumstances of a country, climate migrants are generally not recognized as *refugees*.

We have good reason to believe that human-caused changes to the environment will result in sea levels rising and dramatic weather events, such as droughts and hurricanes. There are two scenarios describing the effects these changes may have on refugees—one acute and one more gradual. Because the coming changes will have the most dramatic impact on the poorest and most unstable countries, since they are the ones least able to mitigate these changes, there is the possibility of an acute rise in climate refugees. According to this acute scenario, climate change *directly* causes displacement and will make millions of people climate refugees in the coming years. By some estimates, there could be between fifty million and two hundred million climate-induced refugees by 2060.[17]

Alternatively, a more gradual scenario would take into account the way that climate change exacerbates already difficult situations. According to this perspective, climate would be one of many factors causing people to move. Climate change will certainly affect people's ability to grow food, how close to water they are able to live, and the frequency of hurricanes and other extreme weather events wiping out homes and livelihoods. But these changes are likely to be slow and incremental—and because these changes are likely to be subtle, it's possible they will be ignored until they finally contribute to people being forced to migrate.

There is at least some reason to believe that the acute scenario of a sudden increase in climate refugees is less likely than the gradual scenario. Jane McAdam has argued that though climate change will produce rising sea levels and other dramatic climate events, these are likely to cause *internal* movement as people seek shelter with others whom they know and in places that they are familiar with, rather than go abroad.[18] This is not to say that no one will seek refuge abroad, but only that the numbers are likely to be smaller than the acute view would have us believe. Climate change will contribute to refugee movements in the more subtle ways already described—making land and other resources scarcer, increasing the severity of weather events, making it harder for countries to develop, and generally contributing to socioeconomic decline and instability. But these changes, in most cases, will not directly cause people to leave their home country.

Yet regardless of how the coming years play out, the fact remains that current international law does not include climate migrants as refugees or grant them any kind of protected status. Given how reluctant states are to grant refugee status, it will be a hard sell to convince states to include in the category of refugees people fleeing because of the sometimes subtle effects of climate change. It may turn out that we will have a moral obligation to resettle climate refugees because of the large role developed economies, and the United States in particular, have played in climate change through emitting greenhouse gases. But regardless of their legal classification, *climate refugees* is a term we are likely to hear a lot in the future.

IS A MORAL DISTINCTION EVEN POSSIBLE?

Between the inconsistencies in definitions, the arbitrary way refugee status is given, and the looming concerns about climate refugees not qualifying as refugees, one may wonder whether the term *refugee* has any *intrinsic* meaning, meaning not connected to the political circumstances, at this point in history. Perhaps there is no getting around this ambiguity given how much is at stake in deciding who gets the status of refugee. We've created an all-or-nothing system, where those we call refugees get all the benefits and those who are not quite refugees are entitled to virtually nothing, though they may be equally vulnerable and in need of help.

While many observers focus on the benefits that come with refugee status—the right to residence within a country and the associated benefits, including the right to be reunified with your family—there is less focus on what happens to individuals who are given instead the status of "rejected," "false asylum seeker," or "illegal." The assumption, of course, is that if they are not genuine refugees, they can go back home—though they may have already endured grueling trips for thousands of miles through desserts and oceans, and may have been raped, brutalized, and tortured along the way.[19] Failed asylum seekers and people who have been denied refugee status are in a unique state of vulnerability given that no state is willing to recognize them as a member and protect their human rights, including their own state. Most migrants themselves do not believe returning home is a realistic course of action. Those realities point to the fact that the legal categories into which we sort people are not just administrative but contain real power, the power in some cases to offer a life with dignity versus a life in misery.

Is it possible *in principle* to distinguish between refugees and other kinds of forced migrants, to draw a hard line between those migrants deserving of sympathy, resources, and perhaps even a place in our society, and those we can detain, jail, and send back to face poverty and insecurity at home? To answer this question, it's helpful to look at the answers given by a few different philosophers to the question of what makes an individual a refugee.

Philosophers rarely agree on much, but there is consensus about one thing: states have stronger obligations to refugees than they do to immigrants in general. The explanation given for this is that refugees have been persecuted by their own governments and forced to leave their home country, and consequently, have no choice but to ask the international community for help. Immigrants, by contrast, are not forced to leave but choose to leave in order to seek a better life. As the philosopher Michael Walzer said, being a refugee is a condition of "infinite danger." Unlike other immigrants, such individuals can claim, "If you don't take me in . . . I shall be killed, persecuted, [or] brutally oppressed."[20]

Another point of agreement by a number of philosophers is that persecution by one's government should not be the only ground for refugee status. Instead, we should take seriously the *harm* from which individuals are fleeing. For the philosopher Joseph Carens, "What is most important is the severity of the threat to basic human rights and the degree of risk rather than the source or character of the threat."[21] In other words, we shouldn't be asking whether an individual was persecuted by a government, but rather how serious the threat was to life, even if the government was not the cause of the threat. Similarly, Luara Ferracioli has argued that we should include in the *legal* definition of a refugee all those who we think have a *moral* right to asylum, that is, people who are fleeing serious harms and threats to human dignity.[22] David Miller also thinks the definition should be expanded to include those whose human rights cannot be protected for any reason and cannot be helped except by crossing a border.[23]

In short, there is a growing recognition that we must take seriously the harm individuals are fleeing from, rather than the source of the harm, and broaden our definition of a refugee accordingly. I am inclined to agree that the best way to think of refugees is as people whose human rights are so severely under threat that they have been forced to flee their homes and seek international protection. This way of thinking is broader than the legal, Convention definition but stops short of including people who move only to improve their economic situation.

Regardless of what definition you hold, it's important to acknowledge that the line between refugees and other forced migrants is one that is, at best, blurry. I think it's impossible to maintain a rigid distinction between refugees and other kinds of forced migrants and we ought to recognize that people are separated not categorically but in terms of degrees. This perhaps complicates the application of law and policies, but it has the virtue of more fairly assessing those who are demanding our moral attention.

WHAT OBLIGATIONS DO STATES HAVE TO REFUGEES AND ASYLUM SEEKERS?

Even if the international community could agree on who precisely should count as a refugee, it would not settle the question of how states should treat them. As much as the international community has struggled to agree on the definition of a refugee, it has struggled even more to agree on what obligations states have to refugees. This lack of agreement in terms of both who should be considered a refugee and what is owed to them is partly responsible for the current global refugee crisis and the inability of refugees to gain refuge.

When, in the wake of World War II, the Refugee Convention solidified the view that refugees were entitled to aid from the international community, the international community imagined three "durable solutions" for refugees. These were voluntary return (repatriation) to a refugee's original country of residence, integration into the country that the refugee first sought refuge in (local integration), and residence in a new country that allowed the refugee to move there (resettlement). Each durable solution was a way for a refugee to once again be a member of a political community, with legal standing and civil rights. It was only extreme or "hardcore" cases that the UN imagined would need long-term assistance from the UN.[24]

As it turns out, the hardcore cases would become the norm. In fact, today fewer than 2 percent of refugees globally are able to access one of the three original durable solutions. About 40 percent of refugees spend the duration of their exile in camps, completely dependent on international aid and not permitted to work. Those who remain in the Global South and refuse to go to refugee camps live almost without international protection or legal rights in urban spaces (I'll discuss life for such refugees in much more detail in following chapters). One might wonder how we got to the point where the reality of refugee protection is so far from the ideal envisioned in the Refugee Convention. One answer to this question has to do with the way obligations to refugees were envisioned in it.

What obligations were agreed in the Refugee Convention? The Convention contains two sets of normative obligations for states: one set relates to what states are required to do when asylum seekers arrive on their territory, while the other set has to do with state obligations toward refugees who have fled their own country and are living in refugee camps or informal settlements. European countries, for example, have different normative obligations to Syrian asylum seekers who arrive in Italy and Greece than they do to the millions of other Syrian refugees who remain in Turkey, Lebanon, and Jordan.

The strongest moral and legal norm relates to people seeking asylum. The principle of *non-refoulement* holds that a state cannot return a person to her home country if she has a "well-founded fear of persecution." In other words, if an individual can demonstrate persuasively that she will be raped, killed, tortured, or put in jail indefinitely if she were to return home, countries are not allowed to send her back. In practice this has meant that people who arrive in a country and claim asylum must be given a hearing before they can be deported; if it is determined that their fear is justified, they must be allowed to stay and be granted refugee status. In most countries, this status means that refugees are entitled to certain social benefits, language and job training, and ultimately the ability to gain membership in the society. Over time, a strong normative and legal framework has developed to support this norm, and most states acknowledge its legitimacy, at least in principle. It is for this reason that Greece, Italy, and the United States, among others, could not just deport the large numbers of asylum seekers who found their way to these countries in the past few years.

By contrast, according to the Refugee Convention, states have minimal obligations to refugees in refugee camps or other informal spaces not on their territory. It is especially important to note that there is no legal obligation to resettle refugees. Many countries consider it a *moral* obligation to resettle refugees who have no chance of returning home, but this not a *legal* obligation in the Convention. Because there is no consensus on this obligation and no formal mechanism for dividing up this responsibility, relatively few refugees are resettled. Until recently, the main resettlement state was the United States.[25] In 2015, about 107,000 refugees were resettled in total around the world, and 66,500 of these were resettled in the United States.[26] Since the election of Donald Trump, who ran on an antirefugee platform and claimed that refugees were security threats, that number has dropped precipitously. In 2018, the United States resettled only 23,000 refugees.[27] Globally, fewer than 1 percent of refugees are resettled annually.[28]

The Refugee Convention is also silent about funding for refugees. Any aid states give to refugees abroad, either through financial contributions or by agreeing to resettle them, is considered a matter of generosity and goodwill, rather than the fulfillment of a legal norm.[29] States consider aid to refugees and the UNHCR to be more or less discretionary. This is in part why the UNHCR has almost always been underfunded.[30] For example, in 2018, the UNHCR estimated that it needed 8.2 billion dollars, and received 45 percent of the requested funding.[31] This in part explains why refugee camps are largely underfunded and why it's so difficult to provide more robust forms of aid, such as better primary education or help for urban refugees. The funding simply isn't available because states are willing to donate only so much to refugee protection.

While the Refugee Convention does contain obligations that relate to states that host refugees—such as allowing freedom of movement (Article 26), access to courts (Article 16), treatment at the same level as or better than other aliens (Article 7), access to employment (Article 17), access to elementary education (Article 22)—these obligations are routinely violated with no repercussions. The UNHCR and other NGOs may encourage the state to behave differently, but there is no legal penalty. There is a reluctance to even criticize host states for failing to provide these rights to refugees since they are doing something that other countries are unwilling to do, namely allowing refugees to live in their countries.

What is clear is that there is an asymmetry between these two sets of obligations: the former set (obligations toward asylum seekers) is much stronger and more widely recognized than the latter (obligations toward refugees who remain in host states). This asymmetry has a number of implications.

One outcome of this asymmetry is the discrepancy in "burden sharing." This refers to the fact that countries in the Global South play a much larger role in hosting refugees than the Western democracies. Over 85 percent of refugees live in the Global South, and less than 1 percent of the displaced are resettled in Western states.[32] We can see this clearly in the case of refugees from Syria fleeing the civil war. Of the 5.5 million Syrian refugees that have left Syria since 2011, the vast majority remain in the five countries that surround Syria, with Turkey alone hosting more than 3 million refugees.[33] By contrast, the United States, despite its large economy, has resettled just over 18,000 refugees since the war broke out in 2011.[34] There is rarely a discussion in Western countries about whether or not it is morally acceptable for some of the poorest states in the world to bear the brunt of hosting the majority of refugees.

The crisis for refugees—that refugees, however they are defined, are not able to access the minimum conditions of human dignity—is in part the outcome of this asymmetry in obligations. Western states have few obligations or incentives to help refugees not on their territory, but because of the strength of the principle of non-refoulement they have strong incentives to prevent refugees from arriving on their territory and keep refugee populations contained in the Global South.

The result is that Western states have favored policies that contain refugee flows outside their own regions. It is at least in part why long-term encampment and urban destitution have essentially become the de facto durable solutions to the global refugee crisis. As noted in the introduction, refugees in the twenty-first century are likely to remain in exile for long periods of time, either in camps where they are forbidden to work and remain entirely dependent on international aid for survival, or in urban centers where they live precariously with little or no help from the international community. This becomes less surprising when we realize that there are few incentives for states to treat refugees otherwise.

CONCLUSION

Any reader who was hoping for a simple answer to the question of who counts as a refugee will be disappointed by the current state of the global refugee regime. There are no easy answers and yet so much at stake for the refugees themselves and for states that worry about the burden imposed on them. The UN considers over seventy million people to be forcibly displaced from their homes, and of this number, roughly twenty-five million are considered refugees who are in need of international protection and ultimately, a new home.[35] When a person finds herself displaced from her home country—whether due to war, political persecution, gang violence, environmental destruction, or another reason—she will remain displaced for years, possibly decades, with only a 2 percent chance of accessing a genuine solution like resettlement or voluntary return.[36] This situation is complicated by the lack of agreement of who among the forcibly displaced is a refugee and what, precisely, such a person is entitled to. Appreciating the complexity of this situation will, I hope, lead us to be more cautious about whom we exclude from our moral consideration and deem unworthy of aid.

What this chapter shows is that it is imperative that we move away from thinking of our obligations solely in terms of helping only those who have met the criteria of a narrow, limited definition of a refugee or asylum seeker. Politically, it is often useful to dismiss the claims of some by calling them economic migrants or not genuine refugees because their persecution was not by the state. The complexity of the refugee system also leads many to neglect all those refugees who remain in the Global South simply because Western states have few legal obligations to them. I hope this chapter shows why we should be wary of this way of thinking about our moral obligations. In my view, we must consider our obligations to all people whose human rights are so severely under threat that they have been forced to flee their home and seek international protection, whether they are fleeing state persecution of their religious practices, violence by private actors the state won't protect them from, or climate change-induced drought. We owe all refugees the ability to access a minimum amount of human dignity while they are seeking refuge. Or so I will argue in the remainder of this book.

Chapter 2

Moral Obligations, or Why We Should Help People Even If We Don't Like Them

Muna's mother and father escaped Somalia when she was six months old.[1] The three of them were among the first Somalis to arrive in the Dadaab refugee camp in Kenya. There were still animals everywhere—gazelle, zebra, and giraffes—and the refugees hunted them for food. In time, the animals would disappear, but Dadaab would grow to be one of the biggest and most populous refugee camps in the world.

Muna was part of the first generation to be raised entirely in the camp and would go on to raise her own family there as well. At fourteen she married. When she became pregnant, her husband returned to Somalia to visit his sick father but died of cholera before he could return. Now widowed with a newborn, Muna was expected to marry her husband's elder brother. Though she disliked him and tried to refuse, she was forced to marry him anyway. She became pregnant again and returned home to live with her mother even though her uncles threatened to kill her. After months of dispute, Muna had to give her youngest child to the husband, who continued to threaten her. Muna then left her oldest child with her mother and went to live on the UN compound in Dadaab, hoping for a job that would allow her to sleep inside the razor wire that surrounded the compound so that her husband could not kill her. There she met and fell in love with a Sudanese Christian man named Monday. Muna became pregnant once again. Because of the scandal of a Muslim woman having the baby of a Christian, many advised her to have an abortion. She refused. People called her fetus a "mutant," and Muna's own brother threatened to kill her for ruining their family name. She went to live in the Sudanese part of the refugee camp with Monday, who tried to keep her safe. It would not be easy: there were rumors that Somali nurses at the hospital would assassinate their baby with a lethal injection the moment she gave birth.

Muna managed to give birth to a baby girl they named Christine. Muna and Monday settled into life in the camp, trying to keep their new baby safe while waiting, like hundreds of thousands of others, for resettlement.

Helping the millions of refugees like Muna worldwide is a big task. Even providing basic goods, like adequate levels of security, food, and water, in refugee camps like Dadaab is a significant challenge. Muna is likely to be among the 8 percent of refugees that the UN considers too vulnerable to remain in a refugee camp—fellow refugees were, after all, trying to kill her baby—and in desperate need of resettlement. Yet she is still unlikely to be among the 1 percent of refugees who are actually resettled each year. It is more likely that she will spend years, perhaps decades, struggling in the conditions just described.

Some might think that being given a place to live in a refugee camp is sufficient. But is this really enough? Or do we owe something more to refugees, especially those who are likely to be unable to return to their homes? In my view, the international community has not done enough and has largely not succeeded in providing Muna with the minimum conditions of human dignity, including security.

In order to do this, many countries would have to contribute a lot and be willing to resettle many more refugees than they currently do.

This is a lot to ask. Despite that, the core of this book is an argument that Western liberal democracies have moral obligations to help refugees achieve the minimum conditions of human dignity. This will require states to rethink the way that refugees are treated during their displacement in order to ensure that refugees can access refuge and dignity in the long term. Given that a minimum threshold for dignity often cannot be met in refugee camps, states have moral obligations to resettle the most vulnerable refugees as well.

Yet many people do not believe that we have moral duties to refugees. For many, moral questions are almost by definition deeply personal—so much so that ascribing morality to a country or to a political problem can be uncomfortable in the extreme. On this view, morality is up to the individual: those thinking they have a moral obligation are free to act on it and are praiseworthy, but that obligation doesn't extend to anyone else. For others, policies need to be pragmatic and economically efficient, and morality simply has no place in the calculus of what is best for the country. Yet I'll argue in this chapter that morality is not merely personal but can and should be extended globally and that politics and economics are not the only aspects that we should consider.

Those who believe that morality is up to the individual may also believe that charity is the best way to address the needs of refugees. People are free to help refugees if they want but are also free to donate their money to other causes or save it for their vacation. This is how we respond to other global crises like tsunamis or earthquakes. People see victims whose lives have been devastated and, moved by compassion, they donate money to charity. Many people like the idea of charity because it is comfortable. We get to say how much we're going to give, when, and to whom. We remain in control of our giving. Further, it does not entail any recognition or acceptance of blame for the problem. We are not giving in order to make up for some harm that we've caused either directly or indirectly. Charity allows individuals to act according to their personal morality or not act at all if they so choose.

I think this view is mistaken. Though voluntary giving is important it is simply not sufficient to provide the help refugees need. It reflects a very good part of human nature—our compassion and the desire to help others in need. But in the case of refugees it is not enough to meet the vast needs of refugees around the world and is insufficient to meet our moral obligations. For example, the UN body that deals with refugees, the UNHCR, is chronically underfunded, often by millions of dollars.[2] It would be almost unimaginable for private donations to make up this difference. Hundreds of other charities and NGOs (nongovernmental organizations) are likewise in need of donations to do their work. As a practical matter, even the most generous people rapidly develop "donor fatigue" and simply stop paying attention after months of pleas for donations.

The argument in favor of moral obligations to refugees is crucial for more than just academic reasons. Recognizing that we have such duties is important to solving the problem. It is unlikely that countries or individuals would provide the kind of help that is needed if they acted out of self-interest alone. Individuals and governments often act when they feel they have a good reason to, and having a moral obligation is often taken to be a good reason to act. This is why showing that we have moral obligations plays an important role in actually addressing the core of the refugee crisis. If states and their citizens do not consider it an obligation to fund refugee protection and resettle refugees, there is little chance that they will be willing to provide the kind of help refugees need. My claim that we have a moral obligation to refugees to provide the minimum conditions of human dignity requires us to do a lot, perhaps an amount that might exceed what many think we should provide as a matter of charity or what we would be willing to do if we acted out of self-interest alone. This is why morality is so important and recognizing our moral obligations to refugees is so crucial.

This chapter is intended to address some of the concerns of those who disagree. Some may ask: do we really have moral obligations? This is the challenge of moral skepticism. Others may agree that we have moral obligations but think that they only apply to family and friends. How can moral obligations extend to refugees, people we don't know and may never have any contact with? The traditions of both religious and secular ethics I discuss in this chapter oppose this view. They hold that morality applies to all people, regardless of who they are or whether or not we have a personal connection to them. Many will still have a final concern: if we have obligations to refugees, what exactly are they? The answer to this is surprisingly simple and has a good deal of consensus: human rights. I argue that we owe refugees the minimum conditions of human dignity, an idea based on the view that all people are entitled to basic human rights. This is an idea that is widely accepted, enshrined in both international and national law, and has broad, overlapping consensus. Moral obligations to refugees, I'll conclude, have a strong foundation.

DO WE REALLY HAVE MORAL OBLIGATIONS?

Most people respond to moral demands all the time, though few outside of philosophy use the words "moral obligations" to describe things they feel they *should* do just because it's right. Still, the concept of moral obligations has a deep and rich history worth exploring.

To give a very broad definition: a moral obligation is something that you are required to do (for yourself, for other people, for your country, etc.) because it is morally the right thing to do. In everyday life, we have many sorts of obligations or, as they are sometimes alternately named, duties. We have legal obligations to pay our taxes, contractual obligations to go to work in order to receive our salary, and familial obligations to visit our grandparents on their birthdays. In other words, there are things we are required to do or have a very strong reason to do independently of whether we want to do them.

Obligations can take different forms. Legal obligations and contractual obligations are widely recognized to be legitimate kinds of obligations. The reason why we might fulfill legal or contractual obligations is easy to see: there are external mechanisms of enforcement. If I break the law, I may be fined or go to jail. If I break the terms of my employment contract, I may lose my job. But these forms of external enforcement aren't always essential to the obligation. There are other kinds of obligations that do not have these external forms of enforcement. Many people recognize that we have reasons to do things for our family, help our friends, and not to lie to people for fun. Even though there is no law that would punish me for lying to a friend, most people would agree that I owe it to my friend to be truthful. We take ourselves to have reasons not to do these things whether or not they benefit us or can be coercively enforced. When I say we have obligations to refugees, what I mean is that we have this kind of obligation: we have an obligation to help even absent an external enforcement mechanism and regardless of whether or not it benefits us.

Many readers will have doubts about morality as such. *Moral skepticism* has been around as long as people have been doing philosophy. Some readers may agree that we do indeed have some moral obligations, but still think that morality is so deeply personal that it's just up to us to decide what those obligations are and no one else can tell us what we should do or how we should treat people. For them, morality is *relative* or up to each individual or perhaps each culture. Stronger skeptics may hold the view that morality doesn't really exist. People may *seem* like they are acting in the name of moral principles, but they are really just following social custom, doing what they think will help them gain an advantage, or following the law. Morality is an illusion, followed only for the sake of personal gain or fear of the consequences. If a politician claims to be moved by the sight of a child refugee washed up on the shore of her country and insists we have moral obligations to help others like her, a skeptic would think this was just a way to gain sympathy from voters or appear more humane.

While some readers may be genuine moral skeptics, thinking there are no good reasons for moral obligations, most of us take ourselves to have at least some moral obligations. Most people act in their day-to-day lives with at least a minimum commitment to the idea of moral duties. Further, most people recognize that we should be consistent in our moral beliefs, treating similar cases alike. For those readers, making the moral case for refugees will mean articulating the sources of our obligations and arguing that they compel us to treat refugees in ways that are consistent with morality. It is my hope that in doing so, even moral skeptics may come to recognize that we have some moral obligations.

JUSTIFYING MORAL OBLIGATIONS

For skeptics or those wondering how we are going to justify obligations to refugees, we can start by looking at where people have found a foundation for moral obligations. There are several ways to *justify* or give reasons for morality that have proven durable and intuitive through the years, and I will focus on two. One source is the consequentialist view, which holds that obligations are based on the idea that we should aim to maximize overall well-being. This view is sometimes known as utilitarianism. Another is the view of Immanuel Kant, who roots morality in human reason. Though each view has its limitations, each highlights an approach to identifying the kinds of reasons we have for acting morally.

Perhaps the most intuitive basis for a moral obligation is that the action produces a good outcome. This is the basis of consequentialism, a view made popular by Jeremy Bentham and taken up in the nineteenth century by the great liberal thinker J. S. Mill. This view holds that the outcome or consequences of an action, typically understood in terms of the happiness or well-being of those affected, determine whether or not the action is morally correct. If you are a consequentialist, you think that we ought to do what produces the best consequences. Indeed, consequentialism *requires* choosing the course of action that produces the best outcome for the most people.

For many this way of thinking about morality makes sense. If I have to choose between two courses of action, it makes sense that I would choose the one with the better outcome, the one that produces the most good. If the finance minister of your country was choosing between two sets of policies, one that created more wealth for more people or one that created less wealth, most people would intuitively think that the right thing to do is to choose the first course of action. Moral action should aim at good outcomes, improving the world in terms of overall happiness or well-being, and not just in improving my own individual welfare. This seems to many people to clearly be the right course of action.

An important feature of this account is that everyone counts equally in determining the best outcome or how to maximize well-being or happiness. Everyone is equal—the happiness of a prince doesn't count for more than the happiness of a schoolteacher. Though this appeals to a sense of equality that many people share, its implications are very demanding. We are not allowed to aim for the best consequences for ourselves, nor for those we care more about (our children or best friend, for example) or those we have special relationships with (such as fellow citizens). This, for most people, is very hard to do in practice.

When used as a moral framework guiding political or economic policies, consequentalism is similarly demanding. It requires that we consider the effects of our policies not merely on our own citizens, but on all those the policy affects. For example, if a country is considering implementing a trade policy that would benefit its citizens by opening a market for a good produced in that country, a consequentalist would ask how this will affect the other countries involved.[3] If the result of this policy is that, globally speaking, more people will be made worse off, even though your own country might be made better off, the policy would not be morally permissible. What matters is the overall outcome, not which people benefit. This is one of the radical dimensions of consequentalism: a politician who adopted this standpoint and considered the impact on all those affected, not just her fellow citizens, would no doubt be considered radical.

One implication of consequentalism is that in principle, individuals may have to suffer bad consequences for the sake of maximizing the greater good. A trade policy that used consequentalism to maximize overall well-being might well require that a certain group of workers lose their livelihoods and their ability to provide food for their families. If we find ourselves in a situation where some need to be harmed or have their human rights neglected for the sake of increasing the overall well-being of the group, such actions may be permissible. What's missing from consequentalism is what the philosopher John Rawls called a sense of the separateness of persons and a requirement that we treat each individual as a singular entity, entitled to equal moral concern.[4] For Rawls and others who share this view, it is never morally acceptable to sacrifice the good of an individual for the sake of improving life for the group.

This is where the philosopher Immanuel Kant comes in. His view of morality requires that we treat others as individuals with their own needs, rights, and interests—as "ends in themselves," to use his phrase—and never merely as a means to my own ends, no matter how much happiness doing so would produce.

Kant will appeal to those who believe that doing what is right is not a matter of trying to get the best outcome. Some actions, we might think, are just right or wrong in themselves, regardless of the outcomes they produce. For example, many people consider friendship to be something that is just a good thing to have in one's life. Even though friends might bring certain benefits (season tickets to the Red Sox perhaps), most people want to have friends even without material benefits. Friendship, philosophers say, has an *intrinsic* value. Approached from the negative side, many think that killing an innocent person is just bad in itself. Maybe someone is annoying or standing in the way of your promotion, but we still don't think that it would be morally permissible to kill the person. While the list of actions that are good or bad in themselves (that is, independent of the outcomes they bring) might be debatable, most people easily recognize that there are some things that fall into these categories.

But what makes some actions right or wrong in themselves? Kant did not agree that what made actions right were the consequences they produced. But if he rejects this common-sense justification for moral obligations—that maximizing good outcomes grounds our reasons for acting—what is the alternative?

Kant's answer is rationality. It is through the use of our reason that we are able to figure out for ourselves what is right or wrong. We do this by applying what Kant rather cumbersomely calls "the categorical imperative." The categorical imperative asks us to consider whether or not the *principle* that we are acting on could be used by everyone; in his words, whether it could be applied *universally*. Perhaps I'm trying to decide whether or not I should lie to my boss to get out of going to work. Kant asks us to think about the principle or the core of what I'm doing. In this case, the principle would be that it's okay to lie if it gets you something you want. Now, what would happen if this were applied *universally*, that is, if all people acted on this principle? Imagine a world in which all your friends, colleagues, strangers simply lied whenever they wanted something. In such a world, we could hardly believe what anyone told us since we know that people are likely to lie to us. You certainly wouldn't be able to lie to your boss because she would not believe you—lies only work if people think we're telling the truth most of the time. In Kant's view, this leads to a *contradiction*: if we universalize the principle of lying for convenience, the practice of lying wouldn't make any sense: we actually wouldn't be able to engage in "lying" (or truth-telling) as we now understand that practice because no one would believe anything we said. The value of truth would have been eliminated. Lying, then, is morally wrong for everyone.

Yet not all moral decisions are quite so clear. Principles can be framed in different ways and may not lead clearly to a contradiction when they are universalized. If I am trying to decide if I should lie to help a friend out of a dangerous situation, is the principle in play "You should help friends in need" or is it "You should lie when it's helpful"? The latter principle, as we saw earlier, could not be universalized, while the former could.

Kantian and consequentialist ethics give us, I think, a good place to start to think about moral obligations to refugees. Their views point to nonarbitrary resources that most people will recognize as giving rise to reasons to act in certain ways that are independent of enforcement. Despite the challenges that come along with their positions, each view demonstrates that there are good reasons for acting morally. Whether it's for the sake of maximizing a value like happiness or general welfare or doing what reason shows us is the right thing to do, both views give us compelling reasons to take moral demands seriously whether enforced or not. They help us to think about what the *right* course of action is in a given situation, something that most people aim to do in their lives.

WE HAVE MORAL OBLIGATIONS, BUT DO THEY EXTEND TO REFUGEES?

Are these moral theories helpful in determining our moral obligations to refugees? To a certain extent, yes. They allow us to apply our moral compass to a global problem in a relatively straightforward way. If you're a consequentialist, you may ask what policy would increase the amount of happiness or well-being of both refugees and citizens of the country that would help them. For refugees who have lost their home, their place in society, their ability to earn a living and take care of their families, a policy that allowed them a place in a new country would increase their well-being astronomically. The good gained in being able to envision a future and know that your children will be safe, educated, and fed is incalculable.

What about citizens of the country refugees resettle in? They may experience a decline in well-being in the short term because they have to pay the cost of resettlement and must adjust socially and culturally to a new group of people. There may be other costs as well. Citizens may be more wary of their security or believe that they are losing their national heritage. Consequentalism would take seriously both the objective costs (the amount a country would have to spend on a resettlement program) and the subjective costs (how the policy changes people's feelings about themselves, their lives, and their country). It would also take into account the medium- to long-term benefits of having refugees. After all, refugees have proven to be both economically and culturally beneficial over the years. One need only think of all the Jewish refugees that were resettled after World War II—Albert Einstein, Sigmund Freud, Billy Wilder, Hannah Arendt, Marlene Dietrich, Vladimir Nabokov—to realize the important cultural contribution refugees can make. In resettlement countries like the United States, refugees have contributed billions of dollars to the economy.[5] On the whole, it seems that admitting refugees, at least to a certain level, would produce the most good, both for refugees and for the states that take them in and so would be the policy most consistent with consequentialist principles.

Kant's approach to our moral obligations to refugees would be different. He would ask us to think more about the principle that was underlying our treatment of refugees. Take a country's resettlement policy. In order to determine its morality, we would need to look at the principle underlying the policy and ask whether we could live in a world where this principle was universalized. The principle might be the following: you should help others in need when you are able to. Universalizing this principle would not entail any contradiction, and if I were in need of help, it would certainly be the kind of world that I would want to live in.

What about a policy based on the opposite principle: one should never help others who are in need? Such a principle, if morally permissible, could be used to reject the resettlement of refugees in a country. Kant says that even though the principle that we should not help others in times of need could be universalized—the human race would still be able to survive—we should still reject this principle. This is because it would lead to a different kind of contradiction.[6] By willing a world in which no one helped anyone, we would be denying ourselves the help of others when we needed help. But we are often in need of help, and "the love and sympathy" of others, in order to achieve our own goals.[7] Such a world, where nobody helped people in need, is not a world I could want to live in because I will inevitably need help at some point.

You might agree that consequentialism and Kantian ethics *can* be applied to refugees but *should not* be. This is the view that says that moral obligations only extend to people we have special connections to, like friends and family. On one understanding of patriotism, for example, we have stronger moral obligations to our fellow citizens than we do to noncitizens, either in our own country or abroad.

Are there compelling reasons for why our moral obligations should extend to people we may have no connection to, such as refugees and asylum seekers? I think compelling answers can be found in both secular global ethics and religious ethics.

FROM INDIVIDUAL TO GLOBAL ETHICS: SECULAR AND RELIGIOUS VIEWS

How can we extend the moral obligations I have discussed—rooted either in consequentialism or in Kantian ethics—to distant strangers we may be indifferent to or perhaps even dislike? Both philosophies are committed to *moral universalism*. The core idea behind this is that because all human beings are inherently equal—a strong commitment of many philosophical views and the basis of liberal democracies—all people should be given the same moral consideration. Consequentialist ethics treats everyone's pleasures and pains as counting equally. Kant similarly asks us to consider the world in which all people live, not just fellow nationals or friends. Both perspectives consider it immoral to restrict our obligations to only one subset of the population. Morality, on both views, is universal in its reach.

But the farther people are from an unfortunate situation or people suffering, the less connected they feel and the more likely they are to ignore it. It's one thing to donate money to a local family displaced by a fire; it's quite another to donate money to an aid agency working in a country I may not know anything about. One might ask: is this distance—both physical and intellectual—morally relevant in thinking about whom we ought to consider in our moral decisions?

One of the best-known responses to this question comes from the philosopher Peter Singer.[8] He asks us to consider the following scenario: imagine that you were walking past a shallow pond and saw a small child playing in it, unaccompanied by any grown-ups. You notice that the child is drowning. Singer asks, should you rescue the child, even if it means ruining your new shoes or being late for work? Almost everyone would agree, he thinks, that we have a moral duty to rescue the child, and that it would be wrong to let the child drown because we didn't want to sacrifice a pair of shoes.

Why is this? Just imagine what you might say to a friend who said that she didn't rescue the child because she hates having wet feet. Singer thinks that if you can prevent something very bad from happening, at a relatively low cost to yourself, you ought to do so. This principle gets to the heart of what makes morality universal. What should matter is the harm and your ability to address it, not who the person you are aiding is. The duty to help comes merely from the fact that the person in need of rescuing is a human being and we know how awful it is for any innocent child to drown, especially one who could easily have been saved.

Philosophers will sometimes call this the principle of humanity or the Good Samaritan principle. The story of the Good Samaritan, told by Jesus in the Gospel of Luke, is well known. A person has been robbed, beaten, and left by the side of the road. The first two people who come across him ignore him. The third person, a Samaritan, stops, and, as Luke says, "takes pity on him." He carefully bandages the man's wounds and brings him to an inn where they can take further care of him, offering to reimburse the inn for any expenses incurred (Luke 10:25–37). What it has come to mean to be a "Good Samaritan" is that you help strangers in need, when others fail to help, even if it means going out of your way. The principle of the Good Samaritan has become so much a part of our moral landscape that almost everyone recognizes the ideal behind it, even if we don't always live up to what it asks us to do.

Can this principle be applied more broadly? Many philosophers, including Peter Singer, think so. Singer has argued that we can apply this principle to global challenges such as poverty. The same intuition that tells us that we ought to rescue a child drowning in a shallow pond ought to compel us to donate the money we would spend on luxuries like eating out or bottled water to the extreme poor around the world since we could save many lives by doing so. The larger point that this thought experiment shows is that when someone is in extreme need and we are in a position to easily help, it should not matter who the person is, whether we have some kind of special connection to the person, or whether we share some important features, such as our nationality, our religion, or our political convictions. When a human being is in desperate need, we ought to help, especially when we can do so without much cost to ourselves.

Several philosophers appeal to this idea in order to justify our moral obligations to help refugees, as we'll see in the next chapter. Refugees, the argument goes, are like the child in the shallow pond—they risk suffering greatly or even dying if we do not intervene to help, and we can do so at relatively low cost to ourselves. It is not a duty that is based in any kind of special relationship—they don't need to share my religion or nationality—but simply in the fact that their need is great and we are in a position to help at relatively low cost to ourselves.

I'll return to this argument in more detail in the next chapter. For now it's worth pointing out that this principle has the benefit of providing clear and almost unassailable grounds for why we ought to help strangers in need, though it is limited in that it doesn't tell us much about what help we ought to provide or how much we are required to help. It also doesn't help us to understand our moral obligations when there are other people who are equally well suited to help. Imagine a pond scenario where there are three or four other people who notice the child drowning. Some are not rushing to work; maybe others are already wearing swim clothes and would be able to jump in without even the minimal consequences you would suffer. Does this change what morality says we ought to do? If other countries can equally help refugees but refuse to do so, does my country still have an obligation to help? Suffice it to say for now that the principle of humanity is an important starting point for thinking about what we owe to others, but the complexity of global problems requires that we go beyond it.

For many people of faith, religious ethics offer a way of complementing philosophical support for extending our moral obligations to distant strangers. Though religious traditions differ in many ways, there is a tremendous consensus over how we should treat strangers who are in need, and in many cases, religious texts discuss how we should treat people who have been forced to flee their homes, such as refugees.

In the three Abrahamic religious traditions—Judaism, Christianity, and Islam—the refugee is seen as a vulnerable individual who is deserving of special treatment: refugees should be welcomed, cared for, and treated with compassion. In these traditions, our obligations to refugees are rooted in an understanding of both sacred texts and the charitable traditions that have emerged from each religion that focus on supporting refugees. Many of the most active NGOs that support refugees explicitly claim a religious foundation: Catholic Charities, Jesuit Refugee Service, Hebrew Immigration Aid Society, Jewish World Relief, Muslim Aid, and Islamic Relief, among many other smaller organizations. Churches, mosques, and synagogues have themselves been sites of support for refugees and resistance against what they see as unjust treatment of refugees. A church in the Netherlands recently organized one thousand priests and pastors to hold a nonstop prayer vigil for three months, twenty-four hours a day, to protect a refugee family from deportation, since Dutch police are forbidden from interrupting a church service.[9]

The holy texts of these traditions offer support for these actions. In the Torah, obligations to refugees (or "aliens," as the Hebrew word is sometimes translated) are rooted in the fact that the Israelites were themselves refugees. Moses commands, "You shall not wrong or oppress a resident alien; for you were aliens in the land of Egypt" (Exodus 22:21). For the same reason, we find in Leviticus, "You shall love the alien as yourself, for you were aliens in the land of Egypt" (19:33–34). Loving aliens in this context means not only that you should not mistreat them, but that you must treat them as "native born" or "citizens" (depending on the translation). Perhaps most poetically, the Israelites are enjoined to "show hospitality to strangers, for by doing that some have entertained angels" (Hebrews 13:1–2). This has inspired the creation of the Hebrew Immigration Aid Society (HIAS), a group founded in the United States in 1881. While the original mission was to help Jewish refugees fleeing pogroms in Europe, it has changed to aiding refugees around the world. This work remains rooted in the organization's understanding of what it means to be Jewish: "Now we welcome refugees not because *they're* Jewish, but because *we're* Jewish."[10]

For Christians, the Gospels written by Matthew, Mark, Luke, and John are considered the word of God and contain specific injunctions of their own to help vulnerable people such as refugees. There is one particularly prominent place where this comes up. In the Gospel according to Matthew, when Jesus is telling his disciplines what they need to do to enter the Kingdom of God, he tells the story of separating the sheep and the goats on Judgment Day, where the sheep on the right are allowed into heaven and the goats on the left are not. The sheep represent people who fed the hungry, clothed the naked, visited the sick, and importantly for our purposes, welcomed the stranger (Matthew 25:31–46). Jesus tells his audience that whenever people did these things to the "least of my brothers," they did it to Jesus himself. Not only is "welcoming the stranger" a requirement for entering the Kingdom of God, or heaven, but welcoming the refugee is tantamount to welcoming Jesus himself. In the twenty-first century, the leader of the Catholic Church, Pope Francis, has been outspoken in his support of refugees: "You cannot be a Christian without doing what Jesus teaches us in Matthew 25. . . . It's hypocrisy to call yourself a Christian and chase away a refugee."[11]

The Islamic tradition contains similarly robust injunctions to help refugees.[12] In the Holy Qur'an, believers are told, "If anyone of the disbelievers seeks your protection, then grant him protection so that he may hear the word of Allah, and then escort him to where he will be secure (Surah 9:6).[13] The Koran speaks sympathetically of people fleeing oppression, and some verses even make seeking refuge from oppression an obligation if people are able (Surah 4:97–99). Given this, it is unsurprising that the 1990 Cairo Declaration on Human Rights in Islam grants a person the right, "within the framework of *sharia,* to free movement and to select his place of residence whether inside or outside his country and, if persecuted, [he] is entitled to seek asylum in another country. The country of refuge shall ensure his protection until he reaches safety" (Article 12).

WE HAVE MORAL OBLIGATIONS TO REFUGEES, BUT WHAT ARE THEY?

There is one final challenge to morality that I've alluded to throughout this chapter: even if we recognize the importance of morality, that we ought to act in ways consistent with moral principles, it's often not clear how exactly we should act. The *content* of morality remains unspecified. I want to suggest that one way of answering this question, especially regarding distant strangers, is by appealing to *human rights.*

Many who are familiar with and believe in human rights won't need to look to consequentialism or to Kant to understand that we have moral obligations. A basic definition is that human rights are rights that we have simply in virtue of our humanity (regardless of our nationality, race, religion, gender, etc.). Human rights are premised on the view that all human beings have an equal moral status and that this justifies us in making demands or claims for rights that are essential for our dignity.[14] For example, if I have a right to basic education, I can justifiably demand that my town build schools, train teachers, and purchase books and equipment. If it fails to do this, my rights have been denied. In building a school the town is not just being compassionate or doing something that might have positive economic benefits; it is upholding my rights. We may have rights because of all sorts of roles we have in society—I have certain rights as a resident of my town (to run for local office), as a citizen (to vote in elections), and as a renter of an apartment (to live with privacy). But human rights are the justifiable demands that we have just in virtue of being a human being.

Many human rights are also legal rights, as they have become part of international law and the law of the countries that have signed on to international treaties. But human rights are also important because they point to the way humans should be treated regardless of what the law says. For example, many countries, including the United States, put people into solidarity confinement for prolonged periods of time. This is widely considered to be a violation of an individual's human rights and a form of torture. When human beings are unable to have physical contact with other human beings, they lose something that is essential for their dignity. Solitary confinement thus is one of many things that governments do that may be legal but, in the view of many human rights supporters, is still immoral.

Equally important to the definition of human rights is the emphasis on dignity. In its simplest formulation, dignity implies that human beings have an equal and inherent value—that is, we have worth just in being human that does not derive from anything we do and cannot be taken away. The core idea here—that each human life is valuable—is not unique to human rights. It can be found in many, perhaps all, religious traditions. In the Catholic tradition, for example, human dignity results from the fact that we are all made in God's image, giving all people an inherent worth that cannot be violated. In this tradition, the basic fact of human dignity means that we ought to take the needs of the poor, the homeless, and other marginalized people as seriously as the needs of our family and friends. Shared among so many religious traditions, the concept of human dignity is familiar across cultures.

Because human rights apply to all human beings regardless of who they are, like the moral philosophies previously discussed, they are *universal*. While at one time it was radical to say that all human beings—including women, the poor, religious or ethnic minorities, criminals, immigrants, members of the LGBT community—were entitled to human rights, it may no longer strike us as terribly important. But consider it in other contexts: terrorists, authoritarian dictators, child molesters, and any other person who willfully ignores the rights and dignity of others—even these people have human rights that states cannot wantonly degrade or deny. This is among the most radical features of human rights.

Human rights are crucial to understanding our moral obligations to treat others in certain ways. Human rights tell us specifically how we, as individuals and members of states, ought to treat each other and people in other countries. In other words, they are both moral claims and widely agreed-upon political norms. They are a way of putting our moral commitments into political practice.

Perhaps the clearest expression of human rights comes from the Universal Declaration of Human Rights, signed by almost every country in existence in 1948. The very first article expresses the universal consensus that "all human beings are born free and equal in dignity and rights." This document includes two broad categories of human rights: civil and political rights (such as the right to freedom of speech, the right to equality before the law, and the right to freedom from slavery) and social and economic rights (such as the right to own property, the right to join trade unions, and the right to an adequate standard of living). Since 1948, human rights have been further entrenched in all kinds of legally binding human rights conventions, such as the Genocide Convention, the Convention on the Rights of the Child, and the Convention on Civil and Political Rights. The Universal Declaration of Human Rights remains the touchstone of human rights to this day.

I said earlier that there has been near universal consensus both that human beings have certain rights based on their humanity and, to some extent, what these rights consist of. This is not to say that there is no disagreement—there certainly is, even among politically and culturally similar countries like the United States and Europe. The EU, for example, considers the death penalty a human rights violation, while the United States does not. But, by and large, there is agreement on a wide range of basic human rights. Almost every country recognizes the human rights I refer to in this book as the rights needed for the minimum conditions of human dignity. It's certainly not the case that all countries are devoted to protecting human rights and never violate them—quite the contrary seems to be the case; the implementation of human rights has always been a problem. Yet despite these limitations, human rights are the common language of international policies and are the mark of legitimate and accountable states.

But what actually justifies these rights? Sure, they may be legally recognized and politically important, but why should I believe in them and act in ways that support them if doing so does not benefit me? Though there is widespread agreement that humans have *dignity* that must be protected, there is no singular answer to the question of *why* this is so.

In fact, there are many answers. The philosopher John Rawls called this phenomenon an *overlapping consensus*—we all come to believe the same thing (that people have human rights), though there are many different sets of reasons a person can give for this belief. Philosophers have argued that human rights can be grounded in our rationality, our agency, and our capacity for self-determination.[15] In addition to the secular, philosophical justifications, every major religion has some features of human dignity that can ground human rights. This is true for cultures more broadly. When the Universal Declaration of Human Rights was being drafted in the 1940s, the drafters sent a survey to scholars around the world asking how human dignity was understood in their cultures. It turned out that there was consensus on the fact that human beings had dignity, and this dignity required special care and treatment. The Declaration was a way of codifying the rights that were necessary to support the human dignity that all cultures could agree to.[16]

Human rights, then, give us a clear picture of the content of our moral obligations—we have to respect people's human rights, and if we come across people whose human rights are being violated, we have moral obligations to help them. This is particularly true for certain extreme forms of human rights violations such as genocide (the extermination of an entire people because of their particular identity), crimes against humanity (extreme and widespread human rights violations), and certain other egregious violations of human dignity.

In practice, each country is responsible for protecting the human rights of its own citizens and others who live in the country's territory. In normal circumstances, your government's job is to respect, protect, and fulfill your human rights.[17] A government respects your human rights by making sure it doesn't violate them; it protects them by making sure that others don't violate them; and it fulfills them by creating an environment where people feel secure claiming their rights. If we take sexual violence as an example, the government must make sure that sexual violence isn't being perpetrated by government representatives, police officers, for example, or in government institutions such as prisons. It must also pass and enforce laws that punish others for committing acts of sexual violence. Finally, creating an enabling environment means that the government must make clear that sexual violence won't be tolerated and promote grassroots and educational efforts to support this right. Of course, even if this is done to the fullest extent possible, sexual violence may still happen. But if a government has taken the steps just outlined, it can't plausibly be accused of violating human rights.

Needless to say, governments do not always live up to this standard. Imagine a country that decides to imprison and torture all of its political enemies or members or an ethnic minority. Whose job is it, then, to protect their human rights? The answer usually given is the internationally community. This means the UN would step in—perhaps the Security Council would pass a resolution condemning the action and put diplomatic and financial pressure on the rights-violating nation. If the violation is particularly egregious, military action may be warranted (though this happens infrequently—too infrequently in the view of some who think that human rights should be more robustly protected by the international community).[18] The fact that a state violates the human rights of its members makes it an illegitimate state in the eyes of the international community, which can become a justification for other states to engage in humanitarian intervention.

Human rights, then, explain how states are supposed to treat their own citizens and the obligations they have to noncitizens suffering rights violations. Thinking about the international human rights system in this way makes it easy to see how this concept can apply to refugee protection. Refugees are by and large people whose basic human rights are not protected by their state, and the only way they believe they can get protection is by seeking help internationally. Members of the international community—that is, all other countries—are expected to step in to protect their human rights. For refugees, the only way this can be done is through giving them a new place to live, either temporarily or permanently. Before any other human right can be upheld, people need a place to live with a basic sense of security. An obligation to take in and help refugees can be built on the obligation to protect human rights that emerges when other states systematically fail to uphold their citizens' human rights.

While a human rights perspective suggests that states have a general obligation to help refugees, states still have discretion in determining what this demands of them. Some countries take seriously the moral obligation to host refugees and welcome them as much as possible, the immediate costs notwithstanding.[19] Other states, even though they have more economic resources, have ignored the weight of this moral demand. It is both a virtue and a failing of human rights that they leave unanswered the question of how to provide aid for those who have suffered human rights violations. It is a virtue because it allow states to remain autonomous and decide for themselves how to interpret human rights norms, but this often results in human rights left unfulfilled.

The language of human rights makes clear how we *cannot* treat people. The term *negative rights* describes what we are obliged to refrain from doing. We cannot arbitrarily kill refugees, detain them, deny them freedom of movement, deprive them of housing, food, or education, any more than a state can do these things to their own citizens. As we'll see later in the book, many states violate these rights. Doing so has become politically expedient—indeed totally normal—and goes unchallenged by other states. The language of human rights may not always constrain these states' actions, but it affords us historically grounded, legally backed, and morally sound grounds for saying that this treatment is wrong.

CONCLUSION

I hope that it is now clear that there are good reasons to believe that we have moral obligations, that these obligations extend to refugees, and that these obligations consist in protecting basic human rights and dignity. This is in part why I think that Western liberal democracies have moral obligations to refugees that require we rethink our policies around their treatment during their displacement, both in the short and the long term. As I think will be clear after reading the stories of refugees in the rest of the book, our current treatment of refugees, on the whole, would not stand up to moral scrutiny on any considered view of morality. For the most part, we have not treated them with the basic moral consideration most people would agree is owed to other human beings.

Of course, many questions about morality and our treatment of refugees remain. But having established the importance of thinking morally about our treatment of refugees, we can move on to more specific questions about what we owe them. For example, given how long people remain refugees, do economically prosperous democracies have an obligation to resettle refugees? If not, how should they support refugees living in other countries, countries that are themselves quite poor? How should liberal democracies be permitted to treat refugees who arrive on their territory as asylum seekers? Answering these questions requires that we engage in moral thinking about how we can provide the minimum conditions of human dignity to refugees in a world that has largely ignored their human rights.

Chapter 3

Reasons for and against Accepting Refugees

A Philosophical Overview

On the evening of his son's birthday in 2012, Hashem al-Souki, a thirty-seven-year-old, middle-class Syrian, heard a knock at his door.[1] Men from the Assad regime were going house to house arresting all the men in his neighborhood in the suburbs of Damascus. Sometime before, supporters of President Assad had killed two boys, and though most people had been too afraid to say anything, some of the family and friends of the boys who were killed had protested by chanting in the street. The government's response was collective punishment.

All of the men in the neighborhood were now brought to an underground network of cells. Hashem was stuffed into a crammed room with hundreds of other men. Each day a few were taken out to be tortured. Hashem spent twelve hours hung from his wrists with the cords cutting into his skin; but his treatment was not as bad as others who hung there longer and had to have their hands amputated. After some months in the cell, so crammed that they had to take turns lying down, suffering regular beatings by the guards, Hashem was released. He learned that while he was in prison two of his brothers-in-law had been shot by the government. He moved his family further away from Damascus in an attempt to keep them safe. But when bombs dropped near his sons as they walked home from school, he realized that he could not keep them safe so long as they were still in Syria. He applied for a passport in the hopes of leaving but was arrested and again dragged to prison. When he was let out a second time, he was desperate to evade prison and torture again and to keep his family safe.

Rohima Kadu also had her life and safety threatened by her state, Myanmar.[2] In August 2017, Myanmar military forces began a "clearance" operation against those they called Islamic terrorists in a predominantly Muslim part of Myanmar. Though the military claimed to be fighting against terrorism, its indiscriminate violence attracted the attention of the international community, which likened its actions to "ethnic cleansing." Before the crackdown, Rohima Kadu had lived a relatively peaceful life with her six children. Her husband had passed away a few years earlier, but her sons were able to find work as laborers and thereby support her.

Though there had always been simmering hostility toward Muslims in Myanmar, this new wave of violence seemed for many to come from nowhere. When the military came to Rohima's village, she was at home taking care of her eldest daughter, who was suffering from malaria, and her grandchildren. As the military began to set fire to the village, Rohima didn't know what to do. Her daughter was too weak to leave the house, but if she didn't flee with her grandchildren, they would die too. So she made the decision to grab her grandchildren, running into the forest nearby. They survived. When she returned to her home, all that was left of her daughter was the black remains of her skull. Knowing that her village was no longer safe, she joined the hundreds of thousands of other Rohingya and began the journey to a refugee camp in Bangladesh with her young grandchildren.

The stories of Hashem and Rohima, painful as they are, make clear the reason that many refugees leave their home countries. Given their suffering and their need for a safe country to live in, how should we respond? Is there a moral obligation on the part of relatively wealthy countries to take in people like Hashem and to offer them membership in their political communities? Is there an obligation to resettle people like Rohima, who may end up raising her grandchildren in destitution and insecurity in a refugee camp?

Though most countries would recognize the extraordinary hardship that Rohima and Hashem have gone through and their desperate need for help, most countries remain unwilling to provide the profound help they need. For most states, helping Rohima and Hashem, either financially or through resettlement, has to be balanced with other domestic considerations, and this may entail limiting the help they can provide.

We can see that refugees pose a moral dilemma. Almost everyone recognizes that refugees are in need of help and that the help they require often amounts to permission to live in another country. Yet every state fiercely guards its sovereignty, which is to say, its ability to determine who can and cannot enter its territory or be a member of the country. Refugees are at once vulnerable individuals in need and threats to a country's sense of self, security, perhaps even economic prosperity. Consequentialist and Kantian analyses of the situation may have led us to conclude that we have *some* moral obligations to refugees,[3] but balancing these obligations with other values such as state sovereignty and economic prosperity is far more challenging.

For most people, whether or not we should accept refugees, either by offering them asylum or through resettlement, is *the* key ethical question. Should Italy grant Hashem asylum if he is able to make it to Italian shores? Should the United States or Canada resettle Rohima, or is it enough to support her in a refugee camp in Bangladesh? When the ethical debate is framed in this way, it highlights the role of

Western states as rescuers of refugees, rather than as contributors to an unjust system that makes it virtually impossible for refugees to get refuge. Yet once we take seriously the second crisis, the inability of refugees to access refuge, we will see that Western states should consider other obligations to refugees, such as aiding them in the Global South and making seeking asylum less dangerous. Yet even if we adopt this wider framing of the crisis, resettlement and asylum will remain fundamentally important solutions for refugees. It's worth taking seriously the debate over the extent to which Western states have obligations to resettle refugees.

This chapter describes the philosophical debate on sovereign states' moral obligations both to asylum seekers who have come onto their territory and to refugees waiting in camps for resettlement. Why should states help refugees in these ways? To answer this question, I'll give an overview of three strong moral arguments for allowing refugees and asylum seekers into our countries, in fairly high, though not unlimited, numbers. Are there good reasons that justify states excluding some or all refugees from their territory? In the view of some, yes. I'll explain three arguments for why our obligations to refugees do not necessarily include resettlement or asylum. While views that oppose refugee resettlement can sometimes be framed in xenophobic or racist terms, I think it's important to take seriously morally grounded views that oppose admitting large numbers of refugees and asylum seekers. I include both sets of arguments in this chapter because citizens should be able to understand each other's perspectives, even if they fundamentally disagree.

Though these debates over morality can seem abstract, they have important practical consequences. The debate between those who believe we have strong moral obligations to asylum seekers and those who prioritize cultural homogeneity, self-determination, or national identity makes a real difference in the lives of millions of people around the world. Though many people believe that we should be doing more to help refugees, the harder question is, why us? What is the ground or basis for our obligation to help Hashem and Rohima? These are questions that philosophy can help us to navigate.

REASON 1: CAUSALITY, OR YOU BREAK IT, YOU BOUGHT IT

The US war in Vietnam in the 1960s and 1970s may have been complex, but many believed that the United States was directly responsible for hundreds of thousands of people fleeing Vietnam. Even US officials accepted the truth of this claim. The United States ultimately accepted over 120,000 refugees in 1975 for resettlement.[4] If you were to ask average Americans why the United States was morally responsible for helping these refugees, they would probably answer that we had to take them because we were responsible for the war.

This is an example of the you-break-it-you-bought-it principle. Because the United States was involved in a conflict that "broke" Vietnam and created hundreds of thousands of refugees, the United States had to take responsibility for the outcome. The United States' moral obligations to Vietnamese refugees were grounded in the fact that it, effectively, created them.[5]

This is an intuitive way of grounding moral responsibility. If we harm someone—intentionally or not—we often feel the right thing to do is to try to repair the harm in some way. This is an appealing way to ground our responsibility to refugees because it connects to a moral intuition that many people share. Yet despite its intuitive appeal, it has not proven politically effective in recent years. There are a few reasons for this, hinging on questions of the intentionality, complexity, and uncertainty of responsibility.

First, it may be that though we are causally connected to a situation that produced refugees, the reason for being involved is itself morally justifiable and the creation of refugees was unintended. Some observers in the recent past have viewed this fact as relieving states of their obligations toward refugees.

When the United States and coalition forces invaded Afghanistan in 2001, they caused regional destabilization, leading to 2.7 million Afghan refugees fleeing the conflict. Yet many denied that the United States was responsible for the well-being of these refugees. They reasoned that the invasion was justified both as a response to the attack on the World Trade Center on 9/11 and as a way to overthrow the Taliban, an immoral, unjust regime. The result—millions of refugees displaced now for over fifteen years—was therefore, in essence, justifiable. Because the Afghanistan invasion continues to be seen as largely just, there has been little uptake in the idea that we are responsible for refugees because we "broke" Afghanistan. The exception to this is Afghans who risk their lives to work directly with the US or coalition military as translators. In this case, however, the obligation arises from a direct personal connection, rather than because the United States caused the war.

The second reason causality has proven a difficult ground on which to build support for refugees is because sometimes the causal chain is just too complex. Some people have argued that asylum seekers coming to the United States from Central America should be given asylum because US policies have made the gangs in these countries powerful. Specifically, in 1996 the Illegal Immigration Reform and Immigrant Responsibility Act led to the deportation of thousands of young men to Central America in the early 2000s. This sparked the expansion of gangs like MS-13 and Barrio 18, which originated in the United States and took what they learned back to their homes in Central America. El Salvador now has 65,000 active gang members.[6] This can plausibly be said to be the reason that Alberto, the man we read about in Chapter 1, fled El Salvador. Yet because the causal chain is long, because there were other factors in the rise of these gangs in Central America, and because many continue to defend the United States' immigration policy that led to the deportation of gang members, the you-break-it-you-bought-it principle has not been convincing.

Finally, sometimes causality is simply hard to determine. Climate change is causing people to be displaced by rising sea levels and intensifying food scarcity and resource conflict, which also results in displacement. Yet it's hard to tie these displacements to a single culprit. Some would say that because industrialized countries in the West produce more of the greenhouse gases that cause climate change, we are all in essence responsible for this wave of displacement. Others might argue that it is the result of overpopulation and the demand for energy. Establishing a causal chain for climate change is so complex that it is hard to link any one particular government or set of actions to the resulting crisis.

Ultimately, the you-break-it-you-bought-it principle may be plausible when a clear and direct causal chain can be established but is less effective in cases where causality is more complex and more difficult to establish. This is why it may not be the most persuasive ground for establishing moral obligations to refugees in the twenty-first century.

REASON 2: THE INTERNATIONAL SYSTEM

The world is broken up into sovereign states, each with legitimate authority over both its territory and people. Each state has the power to make laws and decide who can vote or participate in the government. Because each state has the obligation to look after its people, other states respect its sovereignty, its right to run the country however it wants. Ideally speaking, this should mean that every human being has citizenship in some country with a government whose job it is to protect human rights.

Sometimes this system breaks down. Individuals lose the protection of their state or suffer human rights violations. In such situations, they should be able to leave their country and go to a new one. Other states, then, have a collective responsibility to correct the situation when the usual institutional rules breakdown. Normally the international system works for us—we protect our citizens, you protect yours—and this is why when it occasionally breaks down, states have to step in to correct the failure. The political theorist Joseph Carens sums up this argument, writing that "the normative presuppositions of the modern state system" can ground our moral obligation to admit refugees.[7] Let's call this the "international system" argument for short.

To apply this argument, take the cases of Hashem, Rohima, and Sina, who all began as citizens of their respective countries. Those countries—Syria, Myanmar, and Eritrea—were each responsible for upholding their human rights, and each failed to do so. In the case of Hashem from Syria and Rohima from Myanmar, the government sought them out to rape, torture, or kill them. In Sina's case, Eritrea was authoritarian and so cruel that it was impossible to live a life with the minimum conditions of human dignity; she lived in constant fear that the state would put her in prison, torture or kill her. All three people lost the protection of their states and crossed a border, asking other countries to help. Because in such a circumstance the system of state sovereignty has broken down, the international community has a responsibility to step in.

This ground is also tied directly to human rights. As I discussed in Chapter 2, human rights are moral norms that have more or less become accepted international principles. While each state has the obligation to respect, protect, and fulfill its citizens' human rights, the international community is supposed to step in when countries fail to do this. In cases of genocide or ethnic cleansing, countries have an obligation to intervene in some way to stop these massive human rights violations. But when people leave their country because their human rights are being violated by the state (as in Hashem's, Rohima's, and Sina's cases) or the state cannot or will not protect human rights (as in Alberto's case), other states can protect their human rights by offering them a place. Refugees whose human rights are violated have a legitimate claim on other states for protection, either temporary or permanent. The international system rationale is backed up by human rights principles.

This is a strong ground to support our moral obligations to refugees.[8] Among its virtues is that it makes clear the failure of the refugee-producing country to uphold widely recognized human rights norms, and as result, this country can be rightly criticized. That it can communicate this clearly is an advantage it has over the Good Samaritan principle discussed later.[9] Though there is a lot to be said in favor of this reason for our moral obligation to accept refugees as participants in the international system, it does have some practical limitations. The international system ground takes more explanation—has perhaps more rational appeal than emotional—than the you-break-it-you-bought-it principle, for example, and may be less likely to motivate people. Further, in the view of some, we don't yet have an effective cosmopolitan structure to really fulfill this obligation, a global structure that would allow us to determine who should do what when the international system breaks down. In principle, it may be difficult to deny this ground, but in practice, it's harder to see how it might convince people to accept more refugees or significantly help refugees in other locations when they believe that it goes against their interests.

REASON 3: THE GOOD SAMARITAN OR THE PRINCIPLE OF HUMANITY

Perhaps the most widely appealed-to principle is the principle of the Good Samaritan, also called the principle of humanity. This principle says that if you come across a person in desperate need and you are able to help at a relatively low cost to yourself, you ought to help; in fact, it would be morally wrong not to do so. As we saw in Chapter 2, we would think our friend monstrous if she told us that she let a child drown in a shallow pond because she didn't want to get her shoes wet. If someone is in desperate need of your help and you are able to easily help, it should not matter who the person is. It is this last point that makes this moral ground particularly helpful in the global context of people to whom we have no direct connection who appeal to us for help.

A number of philosophers have adopted this as the primary reason that we ought to help refugees: they are in desperate need and we can provide help at relatively low cost to ourselves. When you compare the amount of suffering experienced by refugees to what it costs relatively wealthy states to take them in, it becomes clear that the principle of humanity can explain why many people believe that we have inescapable duties to refugees. This intuition is classically put in consequentialist terms—that morality demands that we act in ways that do the most good for the most people—but it can equally be grounded on respect for human dignity. Even if you don't find consequentialism compelling as a general moral framework, it might still seem plausible that in cases where there is such extreme need (refugees) and so many extremely wealthy countries that are able to help, one still ought to follow the principle of humanity. It just seems right that if a human being is in need and we can help, we ought to. This may be the strongest grounds discussed so far for supporting robust resettlement policies.

It's easy to see how this principle would apply to the refugees we've been discussing. Rohima, who watched her daughter die from the actions of her government, became responsible for her grandchildren but has nowhere to live and no ability to earn a living. If Bangladesh did not allow her to enter and live, and the international community did not provide food, water, and medicine, she would not be able to survive. Her need is about as great as it gets. Bangladesh, though a very poor country, was able to provide a temporary home. Other countries are now in a position to offer her a permanent home, given that it is highly unlikely that she will be able to return safely to the country that caused her so much suffering. Her need is extreme, and she could easily be helped by a Western state.

Yet there are a few limitations to this principle as a comprehensive ground for supporting refugees. First, it doesn't help us navigate the specifics of aiding refugees or tell us how much we have to sacrifice before we can say we've done enough. For some people in Europe, allowing in asylum seekers in 2015 was enough to fulfill their moral responsibility to refugees. They did not see themselves as having any further obligations to make the process of seeking asylum safer, to create better conditions in camps or reception centers in Italy and Greece, or to grant asylum seekers citizenship. Many Europeans believed that they had already done more than enough for refugees and had no further moral obligations. Had Europe done enough? In 2015, a little over 1 million asylum seekers arrived in Europe, with its population of 508.2 million; by contrast, Lebanon hosts 1.1 million refugees, with a local population of only 4.4 million.[10] Though Europeans felt that they were sacrificing a lot, it was not nearly as much as other states. Nevertheless, how much countries perceive they are sacrificing to help refugees can nullify the effectiveness of this as a ground for moral obligations.

The principle of humanity tells us that we must help refugees because of the urgency of their need. However, as the philosopher

Michael Walzer pointed out, this principle doesn't tell us how we should help.[11] Ultimately, it is up to democratic states to decide how many refugees they want to take and from what countries, based on their own principles, attitudes, history, or whims. A country may decide that it will only accept people who have some connection to that country—perhaps they speak the same language or share the same religion—and would then be justified in excluding others who do not fall into this category, even if this means excluding the vast majority of refugees. Once a state's self-interest enters the picture, even the moral grounding of humanity becomes negotiable. We can't let in too many people like Rohima, people might say, because doing so will cost us too much or change the culture of our country.

The principle of the Good Samaritan is an important moral ground for our obligations not to ignore the pleas of refugees. Yet it doesn't tell us much about what kind of help is required. It also doesn't help us navigate between two legitimate moral claims, namely the claims of refugees for help and the claims of states to promote their own interests and guard their sovereignty. In other words, it doesn't specify how much states should be obliged to help or how much they should sacrifice. For these reasons, it is perhaps not as strong a foundation for our moral obligations as it might initially seem.

REASONS FOR QUESTIONING OUR MORAL OBLIGATIONS TO REFUGEES

Not everyone will find these arguments persuasive. In 2016, at the height of the European refugee crisis, a wave of countries rejected moral obligations to refugees, instead demanding that borders be better controlled so that asylum seekers could not enter. People had many specific reasons to oppose refugees, but all believed that accepting refugees was not good for their country—it went against their self-interest in some way, whether for economic, political, religious, or cultural reasons.

Many who support refugees are inclined to dismiss this response as sheer prejudice or nativism. Perhaps people who reject refugees do so because they believe that Muslim refugees are more prone to criminality and sexual violence (prejudice) or that they want to protect what they see as the white, Christian character of their country (nativism), or perhaps they are afraid of how welcoming refugees will change their culture (xenophobia). There are certainly good reasons to resist the principles expressed in these ideas. But are these the only reasons why someone might oppose resettling refugees or taking in asylum seekers? A number of philosophers would argue that there are principled, moral reasons a country can give for limiting or rejecting refugees, reasons that don't rely on racial, religious, or cultural prejudice.

It's important to stress that all philosophers agree that refugees have stronger moral claims on us than immigrants do. There is a consensus that because of the position of vulnerability and danger people are in when they lose the protection of their state, we must help refugees in some way that is different from what we offer other kinds of immigrants. But for at least a few philosophers, this doesn't require us to resettle large numbers of refugees or allow entrance to too many asylum seekers. It is informative to explore why.

NATIONALISM AND POLITICAL SELF-DETERMINATION

While most philosophers would likely consider themselves cosmopolitan, believing that all human beings matter equally and that national boundaries or citizenship shouldn't make a difference in whom we are willing to help, there are some who consider themselves nationalists. Though "nationalists" is a very broad term, they generally believe that though we have some obligations to noncitizens, we have stronger moral obligations to fellow citizens. For many, nationalism is inextricably linked to Hitler, National Socialism, and the horrors of the Holocaust. While this kind of crude nationalism—the kind that says *only* members of my nation matter and others aren't worth any moral consideration—has largely been rejected, there remains a kind of nationalism that has been defended by some philosophers.

David Miller defends a position of liberal nationalism, a view of nationalism that is consistent with liberal values, such as equality, tolerance, and human rights. In his view, nationalism can be supported for a number of reasons.[12] Among them is that many people experience their national identity as important. The fact that I may be Ecuadorian or Turkish matters to who I am and shapes my sense of self; this in itself is a good reason to treat it as valuable. The importance of this aspect of my identity may mean that I place more weight on the values and interests of my fellow nationals than I do on those of other people. Nationalism is further rooted in the fact that citizens have special relationships to each other and these relationships generate obligations. Citizens are related to each other through economic cooperation, political and legal participation, and sharing of a nationality identity, "a broadly similar set of cultural values and a sense of belonging to a particular place."[13]

Nationalism on this view means that though we are still obliged to treat all people with equal moral respect, we are allowed to take more seriously and give more weight to the interests and needs of fellow citizens because of the special relationship we have to them. For Miller, nationalism can sometimes be a way of helping us reach legitimate political goals such as social justice and democracy. Nationalism can motivate us to pursue justice within our own countries and support robust social programs that fulfill the needs of fellow citizens (universal healthcare, for example).

Because nationalism can be valuable in this sense, national self-determination—the ability of nations to decide their own fates, policies, laws, and so on—is fundamentally important. Just as individual adults want to be able to live their lives on their own terms, nations also want to determine the collective life of their members. This is in part why national self-determination permits states to control their immigration policies. Miller, for example, believes that states have a morally defensible right to control immigration, a right that is grounded in the value of national self-determination.[14] A state may believe that it has a moral right to control immigration but still decide that it is in the nation's best interest economically or culturally to accept immigrants. Canada made a conscious choice to be a welcoming place and considers helping refugees to be a way of affirming its national identity. Nationalism doesn't necessarily lead to a more closed society and can, in some cases, lead to a more open one.

This connects to our moral obligations to refugees in important ways. If you are a nationalist in this sense—someone who believes it is morally legitimate to consider the interests of fellow citizens above others, even though all people must still be treated with dignity—you may hold that we should weigh national needs and interests of citizens more heavily than the needs of refugees for a new home. In Miller's view, while states do have obligations to help refugees, these obligations are not unlimited or unconditional and must be distributed fairly among all states who are able to admit refugees. He stresses that though states have a right to exclude refugees in some circumstances—namely, once they have reached the limit of their fair share of admissions—they must also consider the effects of their policies on refugees and must be able to give them morally defensible reasons for their decisions.

When Alberto made his way to the United States from El Salvador and filed a claim for asylum, the United States had a legal obligation to consider his asylum claim and take seriously the possibility that, if he were forced to return to El Salvador, he and his family might be tortured and killed. For Miller, states also have a moral obligation to consider Alberto's asylum claim because in making the claim, he's made a specific connections to the United States and is made vulnerable by the decision it makes. Yet after seriously considering Alberto's claim and weighing the impact of their decision on him, the United States may decide on the basis of a good-faith estimate of its fair share that it cannot admit Alberto without risking its own social cohesion or ability to provide goods to its citizens. If these were in fact the reasons for excluding asylum seekers like Alberto—and this language wasn't being used to disguise xenophobic or racist motives—then the state may be justified in not admitting Alberto. This would only be morally acceptable if the state had in fact done its fair share to help other refugees and could find some other way to ensure that his human rights would be protected.

What is interesting about the nationalist position is that even though it justifies the exclusion of refugees in some circumstances, it also stresses that states have obligations to do their fair share to help refugees, that they must take seriously their interests and rights, and that they have particularly strong obligations to refugees who have made some kind of connection to the country. It's only after all this that states are morally permitted to limit the help they provide to refugees. If we take the nationalist position seriously, states will be required to do a lot more for refugees and treat them much better than most states do at the current time. It is noteworthy that even the nationalist view leads us to this conclusion.

CULTURAL SELF-DETERMINATION

A second way to justify nationalism is through the principle of cultural self-determination. The best-known version of this view is put forth by Michael Walzer.[15] He argues that we have strong moral obligations to help refugees rooted in the principle of the Good Samaritan, or as he called it, the principle of mutual aid: because the urgency of the needs of refugees are so strong and we are positioned to be able to help them by admitting them to our countries, we cannot simply ignore them. Yet at the same time, this obligation to refugees does not require that we admit all people in need of our help because of the importance of what he terms "communities of character." States retain the right to decide how many refugees they will accept and, more controversially, which refugees they will accept. Like Miller, Walzer does not deny the force of the claims made by refugees on states that are able to take them in, but rather argues that this must be balanced by the importance of maintaining culturally specific communities.

Why is culture so important here? The moral defense of cultural communities holds that being a part of a culture and feeling rooted in a place is an important part of human life. Humans need roots and deep social connections in order to flourish, and this is often found in our particular cultures or "communities of character," in Walzer's phrase. Cultural communities must be allowed to exercise closure—deciding who will and will not be allowed to be a member—in order to preserve what is distinctive about their communities.

It is important for all human beings to be part of some kind of distinctive cultural community, in which they feel rooted and a sense of belonging, where people share special commitments to each other. But in order to establish such distinctive communities, some people may need to be excluded. Take aboriginal communities in Canada, for example. Nonaboriginal Canadians cannot live there without permission. For most Canadians, this doesn't seem objectionable or racist, but a common-sense strategy to protect a vulnerable cultural community. This same principle for cultural nationalists justifies restricting some immigrants and refugees who do not fit into the culture, despite their urgent and forceful moral claims. Self-determination around issues of who to include goes to the core of what it means to be a distinctive community.

A country may to say to Hashem: we understand how much danger you are in and how desperately you need a place to live and move your family, but because you are from a culture that is so different from ours, we don't want you to live here. If those countries choose not to resettle refugees from Syria because of their desire to preserve a certain kind of culture, for a cultural nationalist, this is not immoral—they are just balancing the interests of Hashem with those of their fellow citizens. Such a country may prefer someone who comes from an ostensibly Christian country.

Though countries have a moral right to control immigration and exclude those that they do not think will fit into their cultural communities, in Walzer's view, this must be subject to some constraints that take seriously the moral demands of refugees. Walzer, like Miller, thinks that we ought to take seriously the claims of asylum seekers—refugees who are already in our countries asking for help. But beyond that, taking seriously the demands of refugees means that countries must take in some refugees, but it is up to them to decide which refugees and how many. If a country decides to only accept refugees with an affinity—they have the same ethnic origins or share the same religion—this, Walzer argues, would be morally acceptable.

There is a danger, of course, with both varieties of nationalism. Promoting nationalism for the sake of political or cultural self-determination can give cover to other, more chauvinistic kinds of nationalism. What if Hungary in 2018 were to claim that it can't maintain its social democracy if forced to admit refugees? Given what leaders of the country have said in other contexts, it's not clear that we should take them at face value.

It's also important to remember that most liberal democracies are culturally pluralistic and that cultural identity is often contested. A white nationalist in the United States might be very happy to adopt the language of cultural self-determination and argue that we should reject all Muslim refugees because of America's white, Christian "cultural heritage." But this of course would be disputed by many Americans who believe that because of their cultural diversity and the fact that the United States is home to people from many different religious—and nonreligious—traditions, it would be wrong to consider America culturally Christian. The ban on Muslim refugees proposed by the Trump administration in 2017 was challenged by many as being, in fact, "un-American," highlighting the importance of cultural plurality to their understanding of American identity.

A morally legitimate kind of nationalism, where you help fellow citizens for the sake of promoting social justice, can easily become a more pernicious of kind nationalism, where the interests of fellow citizens are achieved at the expense of other's well-being or human rights. It may be hard in practice to separate out what might be understood as the use of this principle for xenophobic purposes, and what, for some, is a more morally sound version. Given the West's history of deeply entrenched racism, both structural and individual, you might even think that it is naive to suggest that countries can use self-determination, whether cultural or political, as a justifiable reason to exclude refugees, without taking seriously the ways that this would tap into feelings of racial animosity.

In sum, for those who believe in the value of either political or cultural self-determination, our moral obligations to refugees are real and must be taken seriously but be balanced by the right of self-determination and moral commitments to fellow citizens. If this means not resettling many refugees, they will acknowledge that this is unfortunate, perhaps even tragic, but nonetheless unavoidable.

FREEDOM OF ASSOCIATION

There is one last principled justification for excluding refugees that is worth considering. Christopher Wellman argues that even though refugees have strong moral claims, states have no moral obligation to allow them into their countries because of the value of freedom of association.[16] Freedom of association is the idea that in a free society, nobody should tell you whom you should associate with—whom you should marry, for example, or be friends with. We are free to join any club that will accept us and refuse to be part of any association if we so choose. This freedom is part of a larger value—*autonomy*, the freedom to direct your course of life as you think best. How does the value of freedom of association relate to excluding refugees?

The right of freedom of association entails the right not only to decide whom you will associate with in your personal life, but a right not to associate with people you choose not to. Likewise, citizens of a country should be free to include—that is, associate with—people they want to and exclude anyone they don't want. If a country decides that it does not want to associate with Syrian refugees, it should be free to do this. The conclusion is that countries have no moral obligation to admit refugees if they do not want to associate with them in their political communities.

States, however, still have to take the claims of refugees very seriously because of the Good Samaritan principle. What does this mean in terms of helping refugees? For philosophers like Wellman, it means that if we choose not to allow them into our country, we must help refugees abroad—and this may mean getting involved militarily to stop conflicts that produce refugees and sending aid—even though our obligations to refugees do not require we share our countries with them.

Under the freedom-of-association view, we can refuse to admit refugees, but we still have to help them in some way because of the urgency of their claim and our ability to help. For example, if France were to decide that it does not want any more refugees from Eritrea, because of the value of freedom of association France is morally permitted to deny Sina entrance—but France must still do something to help her. It's not clear what this would mean in practice. Perhaps it would require that France begin the hard work of changing the Eritrean government so that it is less authoritarian, a task that is far more difficult than admitting refugees. France is free to decide what it will do to discharge its duty toward refugees from Eritrea, but it is morally justified in excluding them from its political community if it so chooses.

The problem with freedom of association as a ground for rejecting asylum seekers and refugees is that it cannot be universalized or exercised by all countries.[17] Imagine a world in which each country said that though it feels sorry for Syrians like Hashem and Eritreans like Sina, it would prefer not to associate with them. Certainly, the murderous leaders of those countries would be delighted—they would only need to expand their torture chambers and mass graves. If no country in the world allowed refugees and other displaced people onto its territory, we would have to be comfortable knowing that they would be raped, tortured, and killed in their home country. The more likely reality, and what is in fact happening, is that countries with the wealth and power to exercise freedom of association—and keep refugees out—will continue to do so, while other countries that for various reasons cannot or will not do so will continue to host refugees. It is no accident that 85 percent of the world's refugees are hosted in the poorest and least powerful countries in the world.[18]

CONCLUSION

So what does this mean for our moral obligations to refugees? None of these thinkers denies that we have some moral obligations to refugees and asylum seekers. They all believe that we have *some* moral obligations to refugees rooted in the principle of the Good Samaritan—their need is strong and we are able to help them at relatively low cost. Yet all three views provide a principled reason for why we can exclude some or all refugees from countries if their citizens do not want them. It is not that refugees aren't worth considering, but that there is a conflict between values: the principle of humanity conflicts with national self-determination, cultural preservation, or freedom of association. For the thinkers I discussed and their supporters, these values may legitimately take precedence over the needs and moral demands of refugees. While one can imagine that all three views can be used to justify xenophobic policies of exclusion and isolation, it's important to take seriously the moral core of these arguments.

What seems to underly many of these views justifying limiting refugees is a tacit assumption: that refugees have their human rights protected *somewhere.*[19] If a country decides it does not want to take in refugees, the assumption seems to be that refugees can live somewhere else with minimum conditions of human dignity, either in another country or in a refugee camp. Further, if one country does not want to contribute to a durable solution by resettling refugees, another durable solution will be found. Refugees can just wait it out or return to their home in a relatively short period of time. As I've stressed throughout this book, these assumptions are untrue—most refugees will not be able to go home,[20] few will be integrated, even fewer resettled, and refugee camps and informal urban spaces are often unable to provide the minimum conditions of human dignity. Those sympathetic to the view that nationalism or freedom of association justifies excluding refugees must consider what happens to refugees who have been excluded.

When we view the debate over the extent to which Western states have a moral obligation to rescue refugees in these terms, it's easy to see how we can wind up with the status quo. Yes, we should help refugees, but once doing so becomes unpopular, democracies have a moral right to close their doors when they feel they have had enough. This is true even if you believe that relatively wealthy Western states have strong moral obligations to resettle refugees, based on the principle of the Good Samaritan: at some point, we can say that we have sacrificed enough and we have no further obligations to refugees. With this way of thinking, it's easy to see how less than 2 percent of refugees find refuge.

What I will suggest in the next few chapters is that though the debate over whether or not we have moral obligations to resettle refugees is important, it is not the only moral question regarding refugees. More problematic is that the debate itself presumes that the only role the West plays is one of rescue. As I'll argue, Western states play an active role in shaping the options available to refugees and benefit from refugees' exclusion. What will emerge is a new grounding for our moral obligation to refugees—one based on the *structural injustice* that we have created. This is one reason why we owe refugees the minimum conditions of human dignity and why we must rethink how we fulfill our obligations to them.

PART II

THE SECOND CRISIS

The Crisis for Refugees

Chapter 4

Refugee Camps and Urban Settlements

The Problem We Have Created

Life in the refugee camps in Bangladesh is extremely difficult for Rohingya refugees like Hasina.[1] Close to a million Rohingya refugees live in makeshift accommodations in the Cox's Bazar district, on sandy slopes that have been cleared of trees and other vegetation. Though they are grateful to be alive and safe from the violence of the Myanmar military, their daily life is challenging.

Living in one of the most densely populated refugee camps in the world, they must navigate inadequate access to clean water, sanitary facilities, and healthcare. Food is also scarce. Though the UN and other aid groups provide food, usually rice, beans, and vegetable oil, the quantities are often insufficient and lack the nutrients that you can only get from fresh fruit, vegetables, and fish or meat. Not allowed to work, refugees are reliant on these handouts and grow increasingly malnourished. Even though the Rohingya have been subject to extreme violence in Myanmar for years, the Bangladeshi government insists that their stay in the camp is temporary and they will return soon to Myanmar. This is why Rohingya children are forbidden to enroll in school or receive instruction in their national language.[2]

Before Hasina was able to flee the violence in Myanmar, she was brutally tortured by the military. "They beat me, tied my hands and feet and hung me from a tree. Next to me there was another woman. The soldiers cut her belly and vagina. They cut off her breasts and put them in plastic bag. I started screaming and a solder bit a piece of my cheek off. Then they pulled me down and gang-raped me." When she woke up naked, three days later, with stab wounds on the side of her face, she immediately began her journey to Bangladesh. When she arrived at the refugee camp a friend asked her if she would like a job in a garment factory and she accepted willingly. The friend turned out to be a trafficker, and she was taken to a brothel and made to work as a sex worker. She works seven days a week and gets about one dollar per client. The poor pay and degradation is not the worst part for Hasina: working as a prostitute, she has to relive the trauma of her torture by the military every day. Though prostitution is of course illegal and highly stigmatized, it is fairly common, especially at night when there is less security and fewer aid groups around. Pimping has become an easy and lucrative business, with the influx of thousands of young, vulnerable female refugees. As one pimp said, "When the Rohingya girls arrive in Bangladesh, they don't know anything. They are so innocent, scared, and unaware. I tell these little girls, look you have nobody, I'll marry you, but we need money to get married. Rohingya girls are easy to convince. I have sex with all my girls, I take their virginity. Then I share them with the clients."

Life outside of refugee camps is scarcely less difficult for refugees who find themselves living informally in urban centers. Fathiya Ahmed is grateful to be safely out of Syria, though she misses her life in Aleppo.[3] In the old days her husband drove a taxi and they were able to lead a calm, middle-class life, buying an apartment of their own. But in January 2013, her husband was killed by a piece of shrapnel from a bomb dropped by the Assad regime. Fathiya, along with her six children and two grandchildren, decided to leave Syria after that and crossed over into Turkey.

They lived with seventeen other people in a tiny compound in the Turkish city of Gaziantep, near the Syrian border. Fathiya shares a twelve-foot by twelve-foot bare room with her four daughters and two sons, where they eat, sleep, cook, and bathe. The compound is composed of four cinder-block rooms, with tin roofs that don't keep out much of the rain. There is no furniture—people sit on the ground or a rock—and there are clotheslines everywhere. Fathiya cooks on a tiny propane stove and is careful to keep food in jars or in bags hung from the ceiling to make sure the rats don't get to it. There is a pit in the ground the seventeen residents use as an outhouse.

A "nice Turkish lady" allows them to live rent free in this compound for the time being. Her sons are able to find work as day laborers, but Fathiya and her children and grandchildren are mostly dependent on donations from Turkish citizens. She dreams about returning to Syria but believes that if she does, her family will starve or be killed in the fighting. "If we go there now, we will go to our death."[4] For now, she will stay in Turkey and hope the generosity of the Turkish people continues.

In the chapters thus far we have examined the usual ways that ethical obligations to refugees are discussed. Everyone—politicians, the media, philosophers, and the general public alike—focuses on our obligations to *rescue* refugees from the terrible circumstances that their governments place them in. Ethically, the question hinges on whether we have an obligation to admit refugees, and if so, how many, or whether it's permissible to help them without admission, through sending aid abroad, for example. We parsed the principled reasons on both sides of this debate, finding that nearly everyone agrees that refugees, unlike other kinds of immigrants, are entitled to some kind of help from other states.

Yet this exploration was not complete. I am sympathetic with the idea that states have a strong obligation to resettle refugees based on the principle of humanity, but I think the whole debate is missing something important. It leaves out what I call *the problem we have created* for refugees.

Hasina and Fathiya are typical of what happens to most refugees who are "rescued"—they are put into less than adequate refugee camps, often for long periods, or left to fend for themselves in a city for as long as they can handle it. This is the outcome for over 90 percent of refugees: most refugees remain in camps or urban settlements in the Global South—less than 10 percent seek asylum in the West, and less than 1 percent are chosen for resettlement. Yet despite this, most philosophers, politicians, the media, and the general public alike focus on the relatively small proportion of refugees who come to the West. The result of this is that we have fundamentally neglected to think about our moral obligations to the 90 percent of refugees who, like Hasina and Fathiya, remain in the Global South. We have forgotten to fund them, too: globally, we spend $75 billion a year on the 10 percent of refugees who make it to the West, and $5 billion on the 90 percent of refugees who remain in the Global South.[5] We ought to continue to support asylum and resettlement of refugees in the West while at the same time taking seriously the struggles of refugees who remain outside the West.

This is the problem we have created: we have tolerated, financially supported, and even encouraged a situation in which the vast majority of refugees are effectively not able to get refuge. Globally, refugees are not able to access the *minimum conditions of human dignity*. All of the options that the international community offers to refugees who are in dire need of aid and protection may serve to keep refugees alive, but they do not provide sufficient autonomy, dignity, or security. Any assessment of the moral obligations we have to refugees or the policies we ought to support must also take seriously the fact that refugees need to be rescued from this condition as well.

In what ways have Western states supported refugee camps? In the view of many scholars, refugee camps further the interests of Western states by keeping migration flows far from their shores so that they can protect their sovereignty and control immigration. Arthur Helton, for example, argues that "the relatively capable states in Europe and North America seek to contain human displacement elsewhere, particularly in Africa."[6] This has been done in part through encouraging the UNHCR to adopt policies that made refugee camps that standard way of helping refugees and discouraged a focus on resettlement. In Mark Franke's view, "States funding the UNHCR have managed to cultivate a shift in the organization's ethic from one of facilitating resettlement to one largely concerned with containing refugee flows close to the regions of displacement."[7] It's not that Western states set out to harm refugees. But the lack of real options for refugees can be understood as a result of the particular policies states support that further their own interests and priorities. The outcome of this approach, however harmful for refugees as a whole, is not considered.

Put another way, if you have the misfortune of being persecuted by your state, undergoing extreme violence at the hands of private actors that the state cannot or will not protect you from, or simply fearing for your life because of general insecurity and instability, and are able to take your family and flee your country, the international community has put in place three more or less terrible options: squalid refugee camps, urban destitution, or dangerous migrations to seek asylum in the West.[8] None of these options genuinely allows refugees to get refuge, over and above keeping them alive; in many ways, these options themselves deny the basic and fundamental rights of refugees. Our failure to provide refugees with genuine options that protect human rights and ensure dignity is the reality that we have created and an outcome that is largely overlooked.

I think we should counter the excessive focus on refugees in the West by paying more attention to the experience of refugees in camps and urban settlements in the Global South. This is in part why we ought to move beyond focusing on whether we have obligations to admit refugees. While we in the West debate whether we should resettle 1 percent or 0.5 percent of refugees, refugees themselves are choosing whether to register with the UNHCR in a refugee camp, fend for themselves in the city, or make the grueling journey to seek asylum in the West. These are the real choices that refugees have. Below, I explain each of these options and show that none is morally acceptable because they all fail to provide the minimum conditions for human dignity.

Part of the second crisis is that fewer than 2 percent of refugees have access to the solutions that were envisioned after World War II—voluntary return to their home country, integration in the country hosting them, or permanent resettlement from a refugee camp to a new country.[9] This is largely the result of how Western states have interpreted the obligations outlined in the UN Refugee Convention of 1951. The Convention contained two sets of normative obligations: one set relates to what states are required to do when asylum seekers arrive on their territory, such as Sina arriving in Greece or Alberto arriving in the United States, while the other set has to do with state obligations toward refugees who have fled their own countries and are currently living in a refugee camp (like Rohima, Muna, and Hasina) or informal settlements (like Fathiya).

States' strongest moral obligation relates to people seeking asylum. States are required to uphold the principle of non-refoulement; that is, they cannot send back any refugees they find have a "well-founded fear of persecution." States must assess their asylum claims and, if found to be credible, they must be allowed to stay. This explains why states are so eager to keep potential asylum seekers away, using various deterrence measures—once asylum seekers arrive in a country, they become that country's responsibility. By contrast, the Refugee Convention contains few obligations to refugees who are not on a state's territory. States have no obligation to resettle refugees living in other countries. This in part explains why resettlement, which for many people is their only hope, is so tragically uncommon: fewer than 1 percent of people officially classified as refugees will be resettled. States are not even obliged to help to pay the cost of helping refugees not on their territory, through the UNHCR or other refugee aid organizations.

What this political calculus means for refugees themselves is little discussed. In this chapter, I examine the first two options for the 90 percent of refugees who remain in the Global South in refugee camps and urban settlements. In the following chapter, I look at the remaining option for those who find the first two unbearable: migration to the West to seek asylum. The final chapter of the book will assess what our moral obligations to refugees mean in light of the problem we created.

OPTION 1: REFUGEE CAMPS

When most people envision the life of refugees, they think of refugee camps, but what exactly are these camps? In their most general definition, they are temporary shelters where refugees can stay in the immediate aftermath of their flight from persecution. They are often built quickly and are intended only to be temporary. Refugees, once they cross a border, will try to make their way to a UNHCR-run camp, and after registering with the UNHCR, will be given an ID card, food rations, and a place to live. These camps are considered by many to be the best way to provide life-saving aid in the immediate aftermath of a crisis. Many refugees are extremely grateful to make it to a refugee camp, which at least affords them safety from the danger in their home country.

There are refugee camps all over the world, taking many different forms. For example, Bangladesh hosts what is, at the moment, the world's largest refugee camp. Cox's Bazar hosts over eight hundred thousand refugees from Myanmar. This is where Hasina and Rohima found themselves after they escaped from Myanmar. Camps here are considered some of the most precarious in the world, with shelters made out of bamboo and plastic tarpaulins. Dadaab in Kenya, where Muna lived, hosted close to five hundred thousand people at its peak in 2012. Though people have been living in this camp for close to thirty years, shelters are still temporary and makeshift, constructed from grass and sticks. As in Bangladesh, refugees in this camp are scarcely protected from the elements and vulnerable to heavy rains. Though most refugees in Jordan live in urban centers, about eighty thousand refugees live in a UN-run camp called Zaatari.

Refugee camps are supposed to be temporary but may exist for decades. Over time they develop the feel of a small town with shopping areas, places for religious worship, community centers, and legal clinics—though refugees are not permitted to build more permanent, durable structures. Most camps are surrounded by fences and other barriers that make it difficult to leave. Permanent temporariness or "permanent precariousness" is a defining feature of refugee camps.[10]

This precariousness is intentional. States that host large numbers of refugees—the vast majority of which are in some of the poorest countries in the Global South—have not agreed to integrate or include refugees in their societies. Accordingly, refugees are kept at a distance. This limits contact with the local population (to avoid tensions that may arise as well any positive contact, say, falling in love) and prevents refugees from competing with locals for scarce economic resources such as jobs, access to education, and healthcare. Refugee camps are effective ways of isolating refugees, keeping them separate, and managing them more efficiently. They also make it easier to count refugees, which is necessary to attract financial donations.[11] In short, camps serve an important bureaucratic function, but to work politically, they must be seen as temporary, no matter how long they actually last.

Given that camps remain the standard way of helping refugees in the aftermath of a crisis, one might conclude that they must be an efficient way of providing aid. But this is not the case. Providing aid via refugee camps has "the rare folly of being both inhumane and expensive."[12] In fact, refugee camps are considered to be the most expensive way of responding to the needs of refugees, usually costing well over the per capita gross national product of the host nation.[13] Scholars have shown that when refugees are allowed to integrate in host states, even poor ones, they benefit the local economy.[14] Economically speaking, refugee camps make little sense, but their political benefits—keeping refugees separate, more easily controllable, ready to be sent back to their countries whenever necessary—seem to outweigh the cost. This is why refugees like Muna and Hasina from Myanmar will likely spend their lives in a camp, unless stability is somehow returned to their home countries, or they simply can't bear the circumstances any longer and go home or leave for the West.

Yet despite their geographic and material variability, refugee camps around the world share a number of important features, both positive and negative. On the positive side, refugee camps are able to provide immediate security from the threats refugees are fleeing. The UNHCR and NGOs that operate them provide food, water, medicine, and shelter, goods highly coveted by refugees. Perhaps equally important, children are able to go to school and receive an education. This is why many people are comfortable thinking that when we support refugee camps, we have rescued refugees. The problems with refugee camps emerge as people begin to settle into their new life in the camp.

The average length of time a person can expect to live in one of these camps is twelve years.[15] For that long duration, one's life is put on hold. Once given a ration card and a place to live, refugees have little to do. They are not allowed to work in most countries (the exception is Uganda, and more recently, Ethiopia); they are expected to wait for the UNHCR to find a solution for them, knowing full well the small chance they have to access one of the promised durable solutions. Refugees understand that they only have a 1 percent chance of being resettled and, depending on the conflict they are fleeing from, little or no chance of returning to their home.

People who spend their whole lives in the Dadaab refugee camp in Kenya, like Muna, have children who will be raised and educated in a camp. Though they are lucky to have an education, once they finish it they are still not permitted to work or use their education and skills in a meaningful way.[16]

This is one of the reasons that refugees who can avoid camps do so. Take Azraq in Jordan, billed as a "model" camp. The Azraq refugee camp opened in April 2014, 120 kilometers northeast of Amman, Jordan's capital, and 20 kilometers from the nearest town. Though built to hold 120,000, as of 2017, it held 30,000.[17] The low number of inhabitants might seem puzzling given that over 5 million Syrian refugees have fled to different countries throughout the Middle East; Jordan itself hosted over 650,000 refugees at that time. The other big camp in Jordan, Zaatari, had, by 2014, more residents than it could hold. Unlike other camps that are put up hastily, Azraq was carefully planned by the UN to avoid the shortcomings of other refugee camps and improve on the delivery of services.[18]

So why aren't there more refugees in Azraq? According to one journalist who visited the camp in 2015, "Families said they spent their days stuck inside the stark metal containers, with different generations and genders squashed together in one-room sheds that lack power for fridges and fans. . . . Families live on four pieces of bread per day plus monthly food vouchers worth £19 that they say run out after two weeks. One woman told me children's shoes cost four times as much in the camp as at outside markets, while toilets and taps for water are communal."[19] Conditions are so unbearable at this camp, located far from any other city or town, that refugees use vacation passes to escape. "It was like being in prison," claimed one refugee who managed to escape from the camp.[20] Refugee camps tend to have a lot in common with prisons. In the words of Ben Rawlence, a journalist who spent years documenting the lives of refugees in Dadaab, the "geography of a refugee camp is about two things: visibility and control—the same principles that guide a prison. The refugee camp has the structure of punishment without the crime."[21]

A sign in the camp reads: "SRAD [the Jordanian police] Is, Together with You, Responsible for Your Security in the Camp" and immediately after, "The Consequences for Leaving the Camp Without Official Authorization from SRAD Are Severe."[22] This sign nicely encapsulates one of the problems with refugee camps: refugees understand that they are imprisoned and must cede control of their lives in order to receive food and shelter. This makes it less surprising that some refugees in Azraq say they would prefer to be anywhere else, including back in Syria, than in this camp.[23] It's not surprising that Syrian refugees like Hashem and Fathiya refuse to live there.

Of course, though refugees in camps are *supposed* to be idle, not work, and passively wait for the UNHCR to offer an exit, this is not what many refugee camps are actually like—they are vibrant, bustling places that often resemble cities more than camps. They contain thriving black markets where many things can be bought and sold, both licit and illicit, and complex social networks have developed. Even though not officially permitted, refugees continue to act as agents and build complex, interesting lives. I don't mean to suggest that this makes the structure of camps acceptable—just because people *can* survive terrible circumstances does not make those circumstances justifiable. It does make clear that refugees, even in these circumstances, do whatever they can to maintain their agency, their dignity, and their humanity.

Life in a refugee camp, then, forces refugees into a situation of enforced idleness,[24] limiting their ability to maintain their agency and sense of control over their lives, not merely for a brief period but for, on average, twelve years, sometimes much longer. Refugees often see their bargain as trading in their autonomy, their ability to guide their own lives, for the sake of security and food. The journalist Charlotte McDonald-Gibson, who followed a number of refugees on their journey to Europe, noted that many dreaded refugee camps. Writing about Hanna, a refugee from Syria, she noted that "there was no way she would allow her family to end up in a Turkish refugee camp. Hanna could imagine no worse horror than sitting in a tent, helpless and impassive, waiting for someone to come and give you and your family a meal."[25] Syrians like her were looking for an option that offered "at least a semblance of control over your own destiny."[26]

But there is another more concrete set of problems with refugee camps: they are not actually sufficient to protect the human rights of refugees. Refugee camps both fail to uphold the human rights refugees are entitled to in the Refugee Convention and place refugees in positions of such extreme vulnerability that their human rights can be routinely violated—by both state and nonstate actors—with little recourse. Sexual violence is paradigmatic of this last point. Think, for example, of the experience of Hasina, who was lured into prostitution in the refugee camp in Bangladesh.

Refugees, like everyone, have the right to life, to basic subsistence, and to security. With regard to food, camps are so poorly funded that refugees have access to a meager number of calories, enough to keep them alive, but not necessarily healthy. From time to time, food rations are cut and people must choose between starving and returning to war and violence. In the context of Dadaab, Rawlence writes, "There was a crime here on an industrial scale: confining people to a camp, forbidding them to work, and then starving them; people who had come to Dadaab fleeing famine in the first place."[27] Food rations were so meager that some refugees in Dadaab consider returning to Somalia, even though they would likely be targeted by al-Shabaab and killed. Subsistence rights, the right to basic food and material goods needed to live a life with dignity are often absent in camps, and without any other way to survive, such as through work, refugees are systematically prevented from accessing the basic goods needed to live a minimally dignified life.

Other rights are regularly denied as well. Refugees are entitled to the protection of *all* their human rights, including those listed in the Universal Declaration of Human Rights, the International Convention of Civil and Political Rights, and the Convention on the Rights of the Child. In human rights law, states are required to protect the rights of *all residents* (not just citizens) on its territory. But even beyond that, the 1951 Refugee Convention enumerates a number of rights that apply to refugees in camps. According to the Convention, refugees in camps are entitled to access to courts (Article 16), treatment at the same level as or better than other aliens (Article 7), access to elementary education (Article 22), and, perhaps most importantly, access to employment and the right to seek employment for wages (Article 17). These rights are all routinely denied in camps, and very little pressure is put on host states to respect these rights of refugees. In fact, Article 26 requires that refugees have freedom of movement, "the right to choose their place of residence and move freely within [the state's] territory." Yet this is precisely what is denied to refugees placed in camps. In other words, the very existence of refugee camps in their current form is a denial of human rights.

Refugee camps should, at minimum, be able to ensure that refugees live with a basic level of security. Yet the prevalence of sexual and gender-based violence against women and children shows that this is not the case. Though officially prohibited, sexual violence is so common as to be considered almost routine. Women and children experience sexual violence in refugee camps at the hands of other refugees, members of the local population, and NGO and other aid workers, and it is known to occur globally in all camp settings, including Australia. In Europe, there have been reports of widespread sexual violence among women and children in camps in Greece and Italy.[28] Despite this, programs that prevent and treat gender-based violence only receive 0.5 percent of all humanitarian funding.[29]

Even with the horrific effects it has on its victims, sexual violence is often considered "normal" and "routine" in camp settings. As one aid worker put it, refugee women "are used to rape."[30] The dismissal of sexual violence even by UN aid workers is symbolized in this statement: "What's so terrible about rape? You don't die from it."[31] Basic measures that would reduce the risk to women and girls are often not taken: "There are refugee camps without proper lighting, latrines without locks, food distribution that requires women to traverse unsafe ground."[32] Because of their total dependence on international institutions for their survival and inadequate access to resources, many refugee women, in order to survive, are forced to sell sex to other refugees, local residents, the police, and men who work for international humanitarian agencies and NGOs.[33]

Some have argued there is a *structural* connection between refugee camps and sexual violence. Refugee camps are full of poor, traumatized people who are not able to work and are entirely dependent on the international community for food. This is compounded by the fact that one of the most effective measures for protecting women—allowing her to move away from areas that she finds dangerous or threatening—is not permitted.[34]

Much as refugee camps can be beneficial to refugees in the short term, they are extremely problematic in the long term. They are founded on principles incompatible with granting refugees agency, autonomy, and basic human rights. If refugees had to tolerate this for a few months, perhaps even a few years, it might not be so bad; but in the twenty-first century, we have effectively imprisoned refugees and condemned millions of people to misery for decades, sometimes generations. Given the less than 1 percent chance of being resettled, it should not be surprising that many refugees are refusing camps and choosing instead to live informally in urban settings.

OPTION 2: URBAN REFUGEES

When Hashem al-Souki, the Syrian refugee discussed in the last chapter, left Syria with his family, he did what the majority of Syrian refugees do: he went to a city in one of the countries that surround Syria. He was able to escape Syria and take his family to Egypt.[35] Hashem wanted to avoid the camps in Jordan, which he had heard were awful, and so Egypt, still a safe place to go in the spring of 2013, seemed like the best option. Hashem would be among the last group of Syrians to enter Egypt before the border was closed.

Upon first arriving in Egypt, Syrians felt safe and could access schools and hospitals. The government more or less tolerated them. But this changed shortly after Hashem arrived. In July 2013, after Mohamed Morsi, the Islamist president of Egypt, was ousted by the army, attitudes about Syrians changed. The border was closed, Syrians without the proper paperwork were arrested, and the media claimed that Syrians were terrorists or supporters of Morsi, likely to be Islamic fundamentalists. With only $100 left to his name after the journey, life in Egypt was hard for Hashem. He found a job in a factory earning about $100 per month. As Islamist rebels became more active in the Syrian civil war, people in Egypt grew weary of the refugees, worrying that they would bring extremism to Egypt. Knowing the vulnerability of Syrians, police took it as an opportunity to extort money. Hashem was arrested, and when the police found he had nothing to give them, they left him at the side of the road.

Hashem's story is similar to that of more and more refugees. Like roughly half of all refugees, he did not try to find a camp and register with the UNHCR. Instead, his goal was to find work and a place he and his family could live where he could afford the rent. Similarly, Fathiya took her family across the Syrian border to Turkey, where she found someone who let her live rent free while her sons pieced together work. For both Hashem and Fathiya, this kind of existence, though insecure, is better than the camp alternative.

This option has become increasingly widespread since 2003. After the US invasion of Iraq, middle-class Iraqis displaced by that conflict couldn't imagine living in camps and so settled in urban centers in the countries surrounding Iraq (Lebanon, Jordan, Syria). In other places around the world, the reality of *protracted displacement*—people were likely to remain refugees for long periods of time, and if confined to a refugee camp, would not be allowed to work—made life in cities more attractive.[36] When the Syria conflict began to cause massive flows of refugees, the majority of Syrians—about 85 percent—chose to live informally in cities in Jordan, Lebanon, and Turkey, despite the fact that the UNHCR built refugee camps in Jordan to house them. Currently, around half of the world's refugees live outside of camps, mostly informally—that is, without the official permission of the country they are living in—in urban or peri-urban areas. Refugees are increasingly "voting with their feet" to reject refugee camps and live autonomously in cities.[37]

It's not hard to understand Hashem's and Fathiya's decision to live outside of camps. There are some clear advantages: refugees can live where they want and come and go freely. The informal economy, though uncertain, offers the possibility of earning an income and potentially even saving up money. Urban refugees can feel that they are working to make their lives and the lives of their families better. They are able to avoid the passivity that many dread so much in refugee camps.

Yet there are some major disadvantages to this choice. The biggest drawback is that refugees do not receive material assistance from the UNHCR for housing, food, healthcare, or, often, education. Fewer than one in ten of the four million Syrian refugees in Turkey, Lebanon, and Jordan receive any material support from the UN or its partners.[38] Though the informal economy in which refugees participate provides a means to access resources, this source is often insufficient. As a recent UNHCR report pointed out, as of December 2017, most Syrian refugees in Lebanon are now destitute, living with extreme debt, and nine out of ten do not have sufficient food.[39]

Urban refugees endure a kind of quasi-legal status. Countries are aware that they are there and mostly *tolerate* them, allowing them to live and work without being arrested and deported. While they tolerate Syrian refugees, Jordan does "as little as possible to welcome them, and sometimes as much as possible to deter their arrival."[40] Sometimes a country may start out being tolerant, even welcoming, and then turn hostile due to political circumstances. This was the case for Syrians in Egypt like Hashem, who were initially welcomed. But after July 2013, when President Morsi was ousted, Syrians began to be viewed with suspicion and hostility. Conditions became extremely difficult for Syrians, often forcing them to move again, either to a different country in the Middle East or, as in Hashem's case, to Europe. Their legal precariousness means that refugees can never be sure of their status or source of income.

Every aspect of day-to-day life is challenging for urban refugees. Take Syrian refugees living in Turkey, the vast majority of whom live outside of camps. According to an Amnesty International report,[41] finding sufficient work to support themselves is difficult. Those who are able to find jobs earn, on average, 56 percent of the minimum wage, a wage that Amnesty International argues is itself not sufficient to provide an adequate standard of living. Because refugees' circumstances overall are so precarious, it's not surprising that they also experience insecurities and exploitation in their jobs: wages unfairly withheld or reduced, arbitrary firing, poor working conditions. It's particularly difficult for women to find work, and this increases the likelihood of poverty in female-headed households. Because of the difficulty in securing basic material goods like food and shelter, many children are sent to work, with Amnesty International reporting that children as young as ten were sent to work by their parents. A Syrian doctor whose four children worked said, "If these children don't work, they will die from hunger."[42]

Housing is another challenge.[43] The UNHCR is not able to provide support to urban refugees to help them pay rent. As a result, large numbers of refugees live "in accommodation that ranges from inadequate to inhumane."[44] Those who are able to find housing often live in overcrowded circumstances and without a guarantee that they will not be kicked out at the whim of their landlord. Think of Fathiya, who lived in one room with her children and grandchildren, at the mercy of the person permitting her to stay. Like exploitation in the labor market, refugees are unable to address injustices around housing. Though not prevented from lodging complaints, many refugees are unaware of what can be done, unable to seek redress due to the language barrier, and afraid to do so because their legal status is so precarious.

One of the most significant outcomes of Syrian refugees choosing to live in cities is the high percentage of Syrian children who are not able to attend school. In Turkey, which hosts 3.5 million Syrian refugees, 80 percent of refugee children are not able to go to school.[45] Some observers refer to these Syrian children as a *lost generation* because of their lack of formal education. Though the UNHCR recognizes the importance of educating refugee children, both inside and outside of camps, the organization has not been able to figure out how to educate urban refugee children. For many refugees, not being able to educate their children is worse than their cramped, squalid quarters and inadequate food.

To put it in terms of human rights, it seems that refugees have to choose which set of rights they want help with. In camps, their social and economic rights are more likely to be fulfilled—they are likely to be given housing and food rations, and their children have some access to education. But they do not have the self-determination or autonomy that urban refugees have. Yet urban refugees often face dire struggles for their social and economic rights to food, housing, and education. Though they are able to work, work is exploitative and often insufficient to sustain them. Though life in urban centers and in the informal economy may be preferable to life in refugee camps, at least for some refugees, life is far from secure, and many, perhaps most, fail to secure an adequate material existence.

CONCLUSION

Refugees are told that the job of the UNHCR is to provide material assistance while it secures one of three durable solutions—resettlement in a new country, repatriation, or local integration in their host country. In reality, they know that their options are impoverished camps with a slim hope of resettlement or urban slums without international support. Neither option offers much in the way of a future—no one dreams of raising their children in either of these circumstances.

In order to understand the true nature of the second refugee crisis, it is crucial to grasp that these are, in effect, the two "durable solutions" that refugees have access to. Neither is sufficient to provide the minimum conditions of human dignity. This speaks to a failure of the international community to do what the Refugee Convention requires: provide refugees with physical protection, material resources, and human rights. Instead, refugees have been more or less abandoned by the international community. The lives of Hasina and Fathiya as I described them at the beginning of this chapter are likely to continue for years, if not decades. These refugees, and the millions like them, are by and large unable to get refuge.

This is in part why refugees are increasingly choosing a third option: seeking asylum in the West.[46] But because Western countries are eager to limit the number of asylum claims and, even more, the number of asylum seekers they have to accept, they have put in place strong, sometimes brutal, policies that prevent asylum seekers from reaching the West. As a result, would-be asylum seekers have no choice but to engage smugglers to try to get around the blocks officials have put up. In the next chapter I look at what this vicious game of cat and mouse means for our moral responsibility to refugees.

Chapter 5

The Price We Demand for Asylum

When Blanca Vasquez arrived at the US border from El Salvador to ask for asylum, her son Luis was taken from her.[1] She was placed in federal prison and no one would tell her what had happened to her twelve-year-old child. Her punishment was the result of a relatively new policy prosecuting parents who enter "illegally," even though it's never illegal to cross a border and claim asylum. Parents claiming asylum with small kids were now detained, without their children, until receiving or being denied asylum. Blanca was detained for five weeks before her trial and was not allowed to speak to Luis the entire time. Found guilty of the misdemeanor crime of improper entry to the United States, Blanca was sentenced to a year of probation. She was transferred to immigration detention, from where she would likely be deported. Children are not allowed to be detained for extended periods and Luis was allowed to go live with his older brother who was already living in the United States and waiting for an asylum hearing. Neither of them would be allowed to see their mother, let alone live with her.

Blanca insisted that she was eligible for asylum. Her story is a familiar one to many who know the violence in Central America. In El Salvador, she lived with her two children and husband in a three-bedroom house in a quiet neighborhood. Her husband worked in the armed forces and oversaw a prison. One morning as he dropped Luis off at school he was shot by two teenagers, known to be part of the Barrio 18 gang. Luis recognized the teens who shot his father but was too scared to say who they were. Members of Barrio 18, which controlled the neighborhood, began to follow him. The gangs attacked his brother and even killed a neighborhood teen they mistook for him. Blanca took her two sons and left their home; they moved fifteen times in five cities throughout El Salvador before realizing that the only way out of the gangs' reach was to leave the country. Her older son, William, age twenty-one, had already paid smugglers to take him to the United States, where he was detained, claimed asylum, and was released pending his asylum hearing. Blanca and Luis followed a few months later after a stranger told her that she had to leave if she didn't want to see her son dead.

Despite her story, she was told that she did not have a credible fear of persecution if she returned to El Salvador. Her claim for asylum was denied. Though they plan to appeal—her older son is searching desperately for legal help—the vast majority of decisions like these are not overturned. Though her two sons will likely get asylum, freeing them from their fear of gang violence, the price they have to pay is moving on with their lives without their mother.

After a harrowing journey from Syria to Europe, Nart was relieved to see the Bulgarian police.[2] He immediately declared himself to be a Syrian refugee and asked for asylum. He was summarily thrown in jail. This was a violation of international law—a person fleeing conflict cannot be punished for not having the correct paperwork to claim asylum—but the Bulgarian authorities did not appear to care. Many other countries, like Italy, Malta, Greece and Hungary, have done the same, and no country has ever been penalized or faced real criticism for doing so. Bulgaria's deterrence plan included having border guards threaten, beat, and set guard dogs on people trying to enter. This was successful to some extent—knowing this, many refugees choose to find other ways to enter Europe—but Nart managed to make it in.

Nart spent sixty-four nights in detention—five nights in a jail cell, fifteen nights in a refugee camp with a locked door and a guard at the gate, and forty-four nights in a closed camp. Nart was charged with illegal entry, given a six-month suspended sentence, and told that he would be jailed for two years if he crossed the Bulgarian border again. But even then he was not free to go—he spent another fifteen days in detention before being transferred to the capital, Sofia. Conditions in prison were horrible, and when Nart and others tried to protest, the guards threw cold water on them and prodded them with electric batons. When he was released, he slept on the street for a while before finding cheap accommodations; he had already spent most of his money on the journey and in paying fines in Bulgaria. He now had to wait for his asylum application to be processed with no idea of when, or even if, that would happen.

Conditions in Bulgaria only grew worse as more refugees arrived. The refugee camps were deluged with rain, and children faced the freezing weather in sandals. The EU eventually donated some emergency funds and beds, blankets, and cutlery, but it wasn't enough. Nart, like all the other refugees he met, simply wanted to leave. In many ways, this is exactly what the Bulgarian government was hoping for.

Since age eighteen, Benjamin has been living in the Australian-run detention center on the island of Nauru in the South Pacific.[3] He arrived in 2013 with his parents and sisters who, like all asylum seekers who try to enter Australia by boat, were transferred to an "offshore processing center." Conditions on the island are very poor, and refugees have reported terrible treatment. Because they don't know if or when they'll be released and officials have said they will never be allowed to settle in Australia, a sense of hopelessness pervades.

When Benjamin told a psychologist that he was considering suicide, she told him that she didn't care and he should do what he wanted. When he cut his wrists, they took him into custody.

His friend Omid from Iran had a similar, though more dramatic, idea. He soaked himself in gas, said, "I'm tired and we are all tired and I cannot take it anymore," and set himself on fire. Benjamin ran to him and put the fire out using blankets. Omid was airlifted to the hospital, but suffered in excruciating pain for twelve hours before he died. Though Benjamin sympathized with Omid—he was tired of living without hope, without happiness—he blames himself for not doing more to stop his friend from killing himself. "We are desperately seeking other powerful countries to help us and release us from this inhuman policy," he told the journalists who interviewed him. "This is the most painful part of my story—when you realize no one cares."

The utter hopelessness, the indifferent or cruel treatment by the staff, and the feeling that the world doesn't care contribute to many on the island committing acts of self-harm. For his part, Benjamin tries his best to stay motivated and refuses to hurt himself anymore. He wants to prove to the Australian government that he's a good person, worthy of respect. But when he hears Australian politicians say that refugees are uneducated or that they will never resettle in Australia, he is once again tempted to take his life.

Contributing to his feeling of hopelessness is the breakdown in social relations. Benjamin reports that even though his family is together, their relationship is cold. Everyone is frustrated and it's hard for them even to speak to one another given how much they have been punished. Even his friends, fellow refugees, can't tolerate each other anymore. "We see each other every day, talk about the same old things. We get tired of each other. I'm not saying this in a bad way, but this is a human being—you feel discouraged. Seriously, we don't have anything to say to each other anymore! We know everything, whatever happened from when he's born until now. It's like time has been stopped."

Yet Benjamin remains optimistic and dreams about the day he'll be allowed to start his new life. "It will be like I'm reborn. It'll be a big event. I'm sure it's going to happen and it will be soon. It will be very soon." As of 2017, the last time anyone outside the camp had contact with him, Benjamin remained on Nauru.

Every night Yaser's biggest concern is making sure that rats don't bite his children.[4] Yaser is a Syrian refugee waiting with his family in a Greek refugee camp on the island of Samos.

Life here is not what he imagined. His family lives in a tent mounted on wooden pallets, with plastic bottles filled with pee and plastic crates used for poo beside them. In this refugee camp, it's too dangerous to let your children use the toilet at night; there are many reports of women and children being raped on their way to the toilet in the dark. There are few toilets in the camp, and most of them are broken anyway. People go to the bathroom wherever they can, and this leads to the unbearable smell throughout the camp.

Showers are no better. They are shared with hundreds of people, are dirty and often don't even work. Yaser stopped letting his children take showers because he is afraid of infections; his son already had a bad skin infection, and they have had to deal with lice and scabies.

At least Yaser can take his children to school. His daughters go for two hours a day, and his son is on a waiting list. Of the 520 children in the camp, not one is able to go to a normal school on the island, but about 100 of the children are taught informally by NGOs. The majority of children have no access to formal education, so Yaser feels lucky that at least some of his children can go to school for a few hours.

Not everyone is able to stay so sanguine in the face of what seems like hopelessness in the camp. Everyone is struggling—there is just not enough food, water, clothes, electricity. Part of the hopelessness comes from uncertainty; people have no idea how long they will be forced to live in these conditions. There are two to three suicides every week, and lots of people cope through drinking and drugs. "I try to live from day to day, but the hopelessness really gnaws away at you. We have totally no idea how long we will have to live here. The conditions in which we must survive are inhumane," says Yaser.

Few refugees foresee that if they make it to Europe, Australia, or the United States, having paid all their savings to smugglers and endured dangerous travel in trucks and boats, that they will be detained, have their children taken away, or be put in squalid camps. It is certainly not how people envisioned the right to asylum when it became part of international law. But this is part of the second crisis, the inability of refugees to find refuge.

In many ways Blanca, Nart, Benjamin, and Yaser embody a routine experience. Nart was more or less treated as a criminal; Blanca was separated from her children in order to send a message of deterrence to others; Benjamin, though he remains hopeful, is likely to be detained indefinitely; and Yaser shows that squalid refugees camps are not only a feature of refugee life in the Global South but are now common in Europe as well. None of them was able to access the minimum conditions of human dignity.

Given what I've just described, it might be hard to understand why people continue to seek asylum in the West. But it becomes easier to understand when the other aspects of the second crisis, the bleak options for refugees who remain in the Global South, are kept in mind. As described in the last chapter, there are basically two real options. Refugees can choose between registering at a UNHCR refugee camp or making their way to an urban area and trying to live below the radar. Considering that they are likely to be a refugee for, on average, seventeen years, they will be living with the consequences of their choice for a good portion of their life. It will likely determine the conditions in which their children will grow up as well. As many refugees are aware, if they choose to wait patiently in a refugee camp, they only have a small chance of resettlement in a Western country.

If you were a refugee trying to figure out the best course of action for yourself and your family—with the goal of having a real life, a life where you can work towards building a future and not merely staying alive—what would you do? For many who ponder this question, both camps and urban settlements are unbearable. This is why they look towards a third option: asylum.

Asylum is the last hope. Some seek it out after enduring the hopelessness of camps or destitution in cities. For others, such as Central Americans coming to the United States, asylum is the only option for escaping the gangs hunting them down in Mexico or other countries in Central America. Eritreans also feel that they need to leave Africa and come to Europe in order to be safe from retribution of the Eritrean government, which has been known to find Eritrean refugees who escaped the country and punish them. Others may desperately want to be reunited with family members who have gone abroad. Sweden and Germany, the most generous countries during the 2015 refugee crisis, have strong family reunification policies. They made it clear, at least at times, that they will grant asylum in their countries and allow refugees to reunite with family members. For many refugees, seeking asylum in the West is the best choice; for others, it's really the only choice.

But here's the rub: there are few legal channels for refugees to come to Western countries. In order to claim asylum, an individual must be physically inside the country in which they are seeking asylum. Entering a Western country legally is often a challenge for people from certain countries in the Global South. The safest way to apply for asylum is to request a visa, buy a plane ticket, and, once in the country, turn yourself over to authorities and ask for asylum. But refugees from the biggest refugee-producing countries—Syria, Afghanistan, Eritrea, South Sudan, Myanmar, Somalia, Iraq—are usually not granted visas, precisely because European and other Western countries fear that once they land, they will claim asylum. Without a visa, no commercial airline, boat, or bus will allow them on board; commercial carriers are heavily fined if they transport asylum seekers. It is thus extremely difficult, often impossible, for asylum seekers to enter Western countries through legal channels.[5]

It is worth stressing: seeking asylum is a human right. This is stated in the Universal Declaration of Human Rights and agreed to by almost all countries that existed in 1948. It has since become the universal standard of how decent countries treat their own citizens and foreign citizens on their territory. The right to asylum has achieved the status of customary international law, which simply means that it is so widely accepted that all countries are expected to live up to it even if they have not formally agreed to it. What this means in practice is that refugees who attempt to come to Europe, the United States, or Australia without permission are not doing anything illegal; they are only exercising a basic, fundamental human right.

Despite this, many countries try to prevent asylum seekers from seeking asylum in their countries. All Western countries have put in place deterrence policies that are meant to send a clear message—do not seek asylum here! If they can deter refugees from coming and claiming asylum, they can avoid non-refoulement obligations—they don't have to worry about processing claims, housing and feeding asylum seekers, and attracting more of them next year. It is now commonplace to treat asylum seekers like illegal immigrants at best or security threats at worst, and this helps to justify extreme measures to exclude asylum seekers.

What are refugees to do if their only hope is asylum but they face huge barriers to seeking it? The answer is human smuggling. Asylum and smuggling go hand in hand in the twenty-first century. In fact, according to an EU report, *all* of the irregular migrants who entered the EU in 2015—more than a million—used a smuggler at some point on their journey.[6] Using a smuggler has become a necessary requirement for asylum. As one refugee from Eritrea put it, "It's not our choice to penetrate the sea. . . . But if the government won't help us, if UNHCR won't help us, if no one can help us, then the only option is to go to the smugglers."[7]

In order to understand asylum, the third option available to refugees, and the experiences of Benjamin, Nart, Yaser, and Blanca as they tried exercise their basic human right to seek asylum, two interconnected phenomena need to be understood: the deterrence policies of Western states that aim to make claiming asylum as difficult as possible, and the industry in human smuggling that has arisen in response. The price we ask refugees to pay to seek asylum—with their lives, their time, their bodies, their children, their money—is part of the second crisis. This aspect of the crisis deserves attention in order to develop a morally adequate response to it.

DETERRENCE POLICIES, OR KILL A REFUGEE TO SAVE A REFUGEE

Norms and laws surrounding asylum emerged from a very particular historical context. After World War II, Western countries realized that their failure to admit Jewish asylum seekers from Germany meant that many more people perished in the Holocaust than needed to. Without intervening in the war, the United States and Canada could have saved many lives if the people who were able to make it to these countries were granted asylum. The image of the *St. Louis*—the ship carrying asylum seekers from Germany to North America—still haunts our views of asylum. This was a ship from Germany that asked to be allowed to stop on the East Coast of the United States and Canada and disembark its 937 Jewish passengers. They were not granted permission—the United States' quota of German immigrants had already been reached, and because of widespread anti-Semitism and xenophobia, no politician would advocate for them. For many, this was not merely a matter of failing to help, that is, it was not merely a failure of the Good Samaritan principle; it made the countries that refused to help responsible for what happened to the passengers when they returned to Europe. Some were accepted as refugees in other parts of Europe, but others were eventually arrested by the Nazis; about a quarter died in concentration camps.[8] States have since taken asylum seriously, and the idea of non-refoulement continues to guide asylum policy.

Yet since the 1980s, Western countries have increasingly fortified what has been called a deterrence regime. Increasingly elaborate techniques now restrict access by asylum seekers to their countries.[9] Regardless of how many asylum seekers a country ultimately accepts, every Western country has redefined asylum seekers as unauthorized migrants. Detention, in some cases in terrible conditions, is now routinely used as a strategy both to control unauthorized immigrants, including asylum seekers, and to deter those who might follow their example. The harsher the policy, the stronger the message: you are not welcome; do not seek asylum here.

Are asylum seekers illegal immigrants? While it's true that many, perhaps most, asylum seekers enter without the correct paperwork or formal authorization, they are not, strictly speaking, illegal. According to Article 31 of the Refugee Convention of 1951, states are forbidden from imposing penalties on asylum seekers because of unauthorized entrance. Given that according to the Universal Declaration of Human Rights (1948), everyone has the right to seek asylum (Article 14), asylum seekers are not supposed to be treated as illegal immigrants, at least not until their asylum claims are processed. If a country determines that they do not have a credible fear of persecution, then these articles cease to apply and the person can be deported. But until that point, they are not supposed to be criminalized.

The stories in this book make it easy to understand why. Hashem returned from being tortured to learn that his brothers-in-law had been killed and bombs dropped near his son's school. Not only would it have been difficult for a Syrian to collect the right paperwork at that point, but there were no "correct papers" to get. No country in the world was offering Syrians visas to seek asylum. There was no legal way for Hashem to travel to any Western country. The same is true for Blanca. Alberto, also from El Salvador, ended up in the United States, not because he had a calculated plan to claim asylum, but because threats to his and his family's lives keep pushing them northward. It's not surprising that Blanca or Alberto had not secured a visa, and it makes little sense for asylum seekers like them to be penalized for unauthorized entrance.

Yet countries increasingly have come to see asylum seekers as unwanted immigrants. As routes to legal immigration in the West tightened, asylum came to be seen by Western states as a "back door" for people from the poor countries in the Global South to enter richer countries in the West. Countries needed to protect themselves from the fear that economic migrants—people merely seeking to escape poverty or seek better opportunities—were abusing generous asylum policies. The result is that all unauthorized immigrants were viewed with suspicion and treated with hostility.

DETERRENCE IN THE UNITED STATES

After World War II, asylum seekers were relatively few in number and well received in the United States. Granting asylum to people fleeing communist countries served to demonstrate the superiority of the US political and economic system. But starting in the 1970s, people from Haiti began seeking asylum in the United States in large numbers. Haitians were extremely poor and didn't have much strategic value (Haiti wasn't a communist country, so accepting its people had little use as propaganda). The US response was not only to deny that they were asylum seekers, but to have the Coast Guard interdict them at sea before they could claim asylum. This policy was eventually replaced by a policy of detaining Haitian asylum seekers in the infamous camp at Guantánamo Bay, Cuba, a policy supported by both Republican president George H. W. Bush and Democratic president Bill Clinton. This way of thinking about asylum seekers was ultimately codified into law in the United States in the 1996 Illegal Immigration Reform Act, which aimed to reduce incentives to asylum seekers through increasing strict border control and more expedited removal proceedings. This is the framework that has basically remained in place ever since with more or less bipartisan support.[10]

One way that the United States has recently tried to deter asylum seekers is through policies of mandatory detention and criminal prosecution.[11] This policy was intensified in the spring of 2018 in an important way. In April of that year, the US government began separating children from their parents who entered the United States to claim asylum.[12] This was an outcome of the "zero tolerance" policy that had been put in place that required all people entering "illegally," including asylum seekers, to be sent to federal jail and be prosecuted. Because children were not allowed to be with their parents in federal jail, they were taken from their parents. In some cases, parents were told that their children were being taken to have a bath only to have them not return, and in other cases, children were taken and their parents were told they would never see them again.[13] Many infants and toddlers were sent to foster homes, often hundreds of miles away from where their parents were being held. Other children were sent to government-run facilities that were already over capacity. This resulted in the infamous images of "kids in cages" that many in the United States were shocked to see.

Even more alarming was the reported treatment of children, both those who had been separated from their parents and "unaccompanied minors" who crossed the border without a parent.[14] According to testimony from a doctor who visited a facility for minors, conditions, which included cold temperatures, lights on twenty-four hours a day, no access to basic sanitation (including toothbrushes), water, or adequate food, were "tantamount to intentionally causing the spread of disease."[15] An ACLU report documented other forms of abuse of children: children being kicked, denied permission to move freely for days, and threatened with solitary confinement in freezing rooms. Pregnant minors were denied medical care, leading in some cases to stillbirths or other complications.[16] There have been thousands of allegations of sexual assault on minors in US custody.[17]

President Trump was explicit that separating parents from their children was intended to be a deterrent to stem the flow of "illegal immigration" and make it less likely that asylum seekers would come to the United States with their children.[18] This form of deterrence is a policy of "inflicting trauma on children, to influence parents," as one US senator put it.[19] Masha Gessen has argued that taking children from their parents is one of the most effective tools known to terrorize a population into doing what you want them to do.[20] It is perhaps not surprising that the UN has told the United States that this method of deterring asylum seekers, separating children from their parents, is illegal and a breach of human rights.[21] Even more strongly, in the view of some human rights scholars, intentionally inflicting harm on children as part of a plan to deter others from migrating meets the definition of a mass atrocity: a deliberate, systematic attack on civilians for the sake of a political end.[22]

DETERRENCE IN AUSTRALIA

One of the best-known examples of detention as a form of deterrence is the "offshore processing centers" in Australia. In 2001, Australia instituted policy measures called the "Pacific Solution" to deter asylum seekers. The most controversial policy involved moving detention centers for asylum seekers—all asylum seekers entering by boat were put in mandatory detention—from Australia to Christmas Island, Nauru, and other sites in the South Pacific. The idea was that by keeping asylum seekers off Australian soil, Australia could dodge obligations to them under international law. The country accomplished this by paying the government of Nauru millions of dollars in development funds while allowing detention centers themselves to be run by private companies. This is the policy that Benjamin was swept up in, keeping him in detention on Nauru for the past five years. This policy remains in effect even though most asylum seekers in these offshore processing centers are found by Australia to be genuine refugees entitled to asylum protection.[23]

The deterrent lies both in the indefiniteness of the detention and the horrible conditions asylum seekers are forced to live in. Nauru is so remote that Australia's treatment of refugees there is shielded from international scrutiny. Any aid workers coming to the island must sign a confidentiality agreement promising not to disclose what they see on the island and are liable to a two-year jail sentence for violating it. Nonetheless, reports were leaked and in 2016 *The Guardian* newspaper published more than two thousand leaked reports from Nauru, amounting to eight thousand pages, detailing the conditions there between 2013 and 2015. Without these files, we would know nothing of life there.

The Nauru files, as these became known, revealed routine humiliations, violence, and assaults at the hands of those who were supposed to protect the refugees. Many of the most disturbing incidents had to do with sexual violence against children. For example, a child requested a four-minute shower instead of a two-minute shower and was granted it in exchange for sexual favors. Women reported routine sexual violence; one scholar reported that she spoke to women who have been sexually assaulted on a nightly basis.[24] Other violations include beatings, harsh living conditions, terrible sanitation, and inadequate medical treatment. Conditions are reported to be "prison-like" because of the high wire fences, cage-like structures, CCTV surveillance, and metal grills on detainees' bedroom windows. Reports about these conditions and complaints by refugees and aid workers were routinely ignored by the Australian government and those who oversaw the functioning of the camp.

One of the most notable features of Nauru is the level of self-harm that refugees inflict upon themselves, including suicide, stemming from the utter hopelessness of their situation, untreated trauma, and mental illness. The head of mental health services in the Australian immigration detention centers, Peter Young, said that the environment was deliberately made to be harmful; a trauma counsellor described conditions as the worst "atrocity" he had seen in forty years of trauma counseling.[25] As one aid worker, Viktoria Vibhakar, put it, "I felt like my job was just convincing people to stay alive."[26] The extreme squalor, outright violence, and prolonged detention have led to a petition being submitted to the International Criminal Court (ICC) asking that the prosecutor open an investigation into crimes against humanity.[27]

DETERRENCE IN EUROPE

Like the United States and Australia, Europe has adopted strategies for deterring asylum seekers. Some of these policies are designed to make entering the EU, especially by crossing the Mediterranean, as difficult as possible. Though this strategy has taken many forms—increasing border control, putting up fences, paying sending countries like Turkey and Libya to restrict migrants from leaving—it has come to be symbolized by the canceling of Operation Mare Nostrum.

The *Mare Nostrum* was a ship operated by the Italian navy that conducted search-and-rescue missions near the coast of Libya between October 2013 and October 2014. After it rescued over one hundred thousand migrants from drowning,[28] it was replaced in October 2014 by Operation Triton. Operation Triton was much less effective at rescuing migrants who were drowning during the crossing between Libya and Europe: between November 2014 and April 2015, 1,866 people died in crossing; during the same period a year earlier, when the *Mare Nostrum* was operating, the death toll was 108.[29]

What could motivate the cancellation of a search-and-rescue operation that was so successful? The British foreign minister, Lady Joyce Anelay, explained it this way: search-and-rescue operations like the *Mare Nostrum* become a "pull factor" encouraging "more migrants to attempt the dangerous sea crossing and thereby leading to more tragic and unnecessary deaths."[30] Canceling the *Mare Nostrum*'s mission would deter potential asylum seekers from making the dangerous journey and being killed in the process.

This is the same way of thinking that has caused the EU to criminalize people giving aid to asylum seekers. Italy has banned humanitarian organizations from operating rescue ships in its waters, and Malta will not allow them to dock if they have refugees on board.[31] The nongovernmental rescue ship run by Doctors without Borders, the *Aquarius*, rescued thirty thousand people, but was forced to terminate its operations in the waters between Libya and Italy because of pressure from the EU.[32] The logic of this deterrence policy has been summed up as "save a migrant by killing a migrant."[33]

The problem, of course, is that deterrence policies assume that people have a genuine choice. If a refugee could have a minimally decent life without trying to seek asylum in Europe, perhaps this policy would seem more reasonable. But by withdrawing this rescue mission, the EU simply made it more unsafe for migrants to seek asylum. The policy of offering asylum without any safe or legal way to claim it is "so irresponsible that it is morally closer to the recklessness of manslaughter than to the virtue of rescue."[34]

Another way that the EU has sought to discourage asylum seekers is through neglecting conditions in receiving EU countries. In 2015, Greece received the largest proportion of asylum seekers in that dramatic year—of the million people who entered the EU, about 850,000 entered via Greece; according to the UNHCR, 85 percent came from the world's top refugee-producing countries, Syria, Iraq, Afghanistan, and Eritrea.[35] Detention of asylum seekers in Greece was among the deterrence measures put in place in response. "We have to make their lives miserable," the head of the Hellenic Police is quoted as saying; "otherwise they will be under the impression that coming to Greece they will be free to do what they want."[36] The hope was that if conditions in detention centers and camps were so deplorable, asylum seekers would be discouraged from making the journey. While the Greek policy did not appear to significantly deter asylum seekers from coming to Greece, it did succeed in creating conditions so appalling they shocked even seasoned human rights reporters.

The conditions in Greek camps were considered some of the worst in Europe: extremely overcrowded, badly heated, damp, unsanitary; gastrointestinal and dermatological diseases were common. Very little was provided to refugees by Greece—there was no soap, no clothing, no medicine, and little food. Indeed, things were so bad in Greece that the European Court of Human Rights ruled as early as 2011 that an Afghan refugee in Belgium could not be returned to Greece, because it breached the prohibition of ill treatment.[37] One of the most infamous refugee camps, Idomeni, was called a "modern day Dachau" by the Greek interior minister; more than half a million people passed through it in 2016.[38]

Most refugees arrive in Greece through Turkey. In March 2016, the EU signed an agreement with Turkey to take back all migrants who do not apply for asylum or whose asylum claims are denied. All asylum seekers are detained while the government makes its determination. In order to implement that deal, Greece had to open detention centers on the islands where asylum seekers were arriving, as they were no longer allowed to be transferred to the Greek mainland.[39] Like the refugee camps on the mainland, these detention centers have been reported to have appalling conditions: severe overcrowding, insufficient and poor-quality food, lack of medical care, and lack of protection from violence.

Unaccompanied children have been systematically detained as well. As in Australia and the United States, children in these centers are particularly vulnerable to violence and deprivation. The UN Special Rapporteur on the human rights of migrants noted that detained children faced conditions that were "deplorable," leaving them "at heightened risk of abuse, neglect, violence and exploitation." In some cases, they were locked in police stations for twenty-four hours a day, without access to the outdoors, recreation, or educational activity for over two weeks. Another report by Bhabha and Digidiki elaborated on these findings, showing that living conditions failed to meet minimum health and safety standards, amounting to inhumane treatment that was dangerous for child migrants.[40] Further, it's extraordinarily difficult to help the children in these camps. As a child psychologist working in a Greek refugee camp put it: "We try to support children psychologically as part of the child protection service, but often the children laugh at us. They say, 'Look at us. We wear sandals in the middle of winter. We are cold. Give us clothes first.' How can you support them psychologically when they are extremely cold?"[41]

Some of the EU's policies actually increase women's vulnerability to gender-based violence as well.[42] Though EU member states have agreed to take gender-based considerations seriously in the reception of refugees and in refugee status determination, in practice they do not offer much protection for women who are victims of violence. In some cases, "Border guards may be the source of violence and human rights abuses against migrants."[43] There has been little action taken to punish perpetrators or prevent future violence.[44]

We see that, taken together, many Western countries are doing everything in their power to deter asylum seekers from coming and, once they are in the country, are detaining asylum seekers in appalling conditions. From the perspectives of these states' political leaders, they are merely controlling their borders and exercising their right of self-determination. From the point of view of refugees, they are preventing them from seeking asylum and denying them the ability to claim their human rights. And in spite of the deterrence measures, refugees keep coming.

According to many scholars, most asylum seekers don't take deterrence measures into account when deciding how they will find security for their families; many aren't even aware of them. The separation of children from their parents, the lack of search-and-rescue operations, and the appalling conditions of refugee camps in asylum countries don't play a large role in the calculation refugees make about how to seek refuge.[45]

What deterrence policies are successful in doing is making the journeys more dangerous and costly for refugees. Despite the justification that deterrence policies indirectly save the lives of asylum seekers by persuading them to stay home, deterrence polices make their journey more deadly, but no less likely.[46] Research has shown that at both the US border with Mexico and the Mediterranean Sea, deterrence policies have increased the number of border deaths.[47] The stronger the deterrence policy, the more deadly the journey. The

UNHCR has pointed out that closing borders and making asylum-seeking harder has made women more vulnerable to sexual violence from smugglers and made it more likely that they will have to provide sexual favors in exchange for passage.[48]

States are aware of this. In May 2016, a report by the British Parliamentary Select Committee was released in regard to Operation Sophia, an EU naval operation aimed at undermining smuggling routes. It makes the point that deterrence at sea doesn't save lives but only makes the crossing more deadly: "The mission does not . . . in any meaningful way deter the flow of migrants, disrupt the smugglers' networks, or impede the business of smuggling on the central Mediterranean route. The arrests that Operation Sophia has made to date have been of low-level targets, while the destruction of vessels has simply caused the smugglers to shift from using wooden boats to rubber dinghies, which are even more unsafe."[49]

Why do they fail to deter would-be asylum seekers from making very dangerous trips? The reason is simple: people who are coming to the West to claim asylum believe that they have no other choice. If they stay where they are, they will die or live a life that is intolerable. If you cannot stay in your home country and you understand how difficult and hopeless life will be in a refugee camp or an urban slum, asylum may be your only choice. According to an Eritrean saying, "A dead goat doesn't fear the butcher's knife."[50] In other words, many refugees consider their lives over in their current country—either they realize they will likely be killed soon or hope for the future is so extinguished that they have no other choice. They, like the dead goat, feel like they're already dead. Such people will continue to do whatever they can to improve their lives and the lives of their children. Deterrence policies seem only to make this otherwise reasonable goal more deadly.

Because asylum is often the only choice for refugees and because all Western states have enacted harsh deterrence regimes, smuggling has become a requirement of seeking asylum in the twenty-first century. In order to understand the morality of our asylum policies, it's imperative to understand what it means to have oneself and one's children smuggled to the West. For many, smugglers are the real problem, and if states could just eradicate these bad apples, refugees would be safer. I want to suggest that we abandon this view of smuggling and focus instead on the harms faced by refugees as they navigate the choices presented to them.

HUMAN SMUGGLING: A REQUIREMENT OF SEEKING ASYLUM?

In August 2015, the German government suspended the Dublin Regulations for Syrian refugees. These regulations required all asylum seekers to register in the first country they landed in in Europe and be processed for asylum; if they failed to do this, they could be deported back to the country they first arrived in. In practice, since most refugees were coming by boat rather than air, Italy and Greece would be required to register and process the majority of people seeking asylum. By the summer of 2015, these countries had become overwhelmed—refugees were placed either in camps or detained and were told that their claims would take months to process. Many wanted to go to Germany, Sweden, or the United Kingdom where conditions were perceived to be better, and in August 2015 the relaxing of the Dublin Regulations by Germany allowed them to do so. For many, this was a sign of Germany's magnanimity toward refugees—an open door to safety that few other countries were willing to provide.

It was undoubtedly a generous and courageous act, rebuffing the growing xenophobia of other countries in Europe. Yet there was still no legal way for asylum seekers to get to Germany. A policy of offering asylum without also providing any safe or legal way for refugees to access this policy meant that refugees had to employ extralegal means in order to come to Europe. As I noted earlier, *every single person*—more than a million irregular migrants—who made it to Europe to claim asylum in 2015 used a smuggler at some point on their journey.[51] What are the ethical implications for an asylum policy that more or less requires smugglers?

Though smuggling represents the new normal for people seeking to flee persecution, war, and violence, it's morally problematic that people should have to endure smuggling and the hardship that comes with it to seek refuge. It's also problematic that the refugee crisis—the masses of people living in camps or urban slums whose only hope for a real future lies in claiming asylum in the West—has made human smuggling a multibillion dollar business. It's regrettable that this is perhaps the only way people have of seeking survival, let alone dignity, in many contexts. But what does it really meant to hire a smuggler and smuggle oneself into a country? Are smugglers to blame for the suffering of asylum seekers? Yes and no.

HUMAN SMUGGLING IN THE TWENTY-FIRST CENTURY: MORAL AMBIGUITY

There is a tendency when thinking about human smuggling to view smugglers as the worst of the worst. Certainly, for European politicians, destroying smuggling rings was often used synonymously with solving the refugee crisis—if we could just get rid of smugglers, we wouldn't have to worry about the hundreds of thousands of people risking their lives to claim asylum in Europe.

Yet for many people fleeing violence, war, political persecution, the threat of torture or indefinite detention, smugglers are saviors.[52] They are the only ones who are able and willing to help them in a desperate situation. Given the global situation I've been describing in this book, smugglers working through illegal channels are often the only ones able to help people escape terrible situations and navigate through a broken international system. They are providing an invaluable service for refugees. For millions of people around the world whom smugglers have delivered to safety, they are heroes.

I think the proper approach is to see human smuggling as morally ambiguous. In itself, it's not necessarily a bad thing. For hundreds of thousands of refugees, human smugglers were lifesavers. Yet because of the conditions under which they operate and the extreme vulnerability of the people being smuggled, smugglers often exploit their clients and violate their trust. In addition, they funnel billions of dollars into illegal criminal activity. Understood in this way, a few things come to light about the market for smugglers.

First, we cannot address the refugee crisis by focusing on getting rid of smugglers. They serve an important purpose in the lives of people fleeing violence. The broken refugee system is the true problem. As Jeremy Harding put it, smugglers "are only enacting an entrepreneurial version of the disdain which refugees suffer at the hands of far more powerful enemies—those who terrorize them and those who are determined to keep them at arm's length. Human traffickers are simply vectors of the contempt which exists at the two poles of the asylum seekers journey: they take their cue from the attitudes of warlords and dictators, on the one hand, and, on the other, of wealthy states whose citizens have learned to think of generosity as a vice."[53]

Second, we have to take seriously the ways in which our deterrence policies intensify the market for smugglers.[54] The harder it is to enter a country, the more smugglers are needed and the more dangerous journeys become. When conditions are relatively easy, smuggling is something that any entrepreneurial person can do. But when deterrence policies are intensified, people need more experienced and well-connected smugglers, and this is where the Mafia and other criminal organizations come into play. With the tightening of European borders after the start of the European refugee crisis in 2015, international criminal organizations simply added human smuggling to the list of things they move illegally, including weapons, drugs, and stolen merchandise.

Smuggling is not the same as trafficking. Human traffickers are people who move others against their will; think of women and children who are trafficked for sex work, that is, forced to work as prostitutes, usually under the threat of violence. Though many confuse smugglers with traffickers because they sometimes use the same tactics—they use violence to control people and, as I'll discuss in more detail later, can be extremely exploitative. Human rights are not a priority for either group. People sometimes start out with smugglers they have contracted with only to be sold to traffickers who extort money, before being returned to the smugglers who will help them continue on their journey. But not all smugglers behave this way. The important difference is that asylum seekers willingly put themselves in the hands of smugglers in order to get what they want—entrance into a Western country.

Further, the increasing use of smugglers by asylum seekers shows us at least two things about the experience of refugees in the twenty-first century. The first is their sheer and utter desperation. This is the only way to make sense of the decision to engage a smuggler; it is not something people would do if they had any other real choice. For many, they feel their lives are over, and so risking death is better than the certainty of death, torture, detention. As the poet Warsan Shire puts it,

> you have to understand,
> that no one would put their children in a boat
> unless the water is safer than the land.

The horrors of being smuggled to safety are still better

than fourteen men between
your legs
or the insults are easier
to swallow
than rubble
than bone
than your child body in pieces.[55]

The second feature that smuggling highlights about refugees is their agency. Even in the most extreme circumstances, refugees refuse to remain passive subjects waiting for their fate to be determined by a faceless international bureaucracy. The price to be paid for this agency is high, but, for many, one worth paying. Though some asylum seekers may be fooled by their smugglers, most engage them fully aware of what they are getting into; it's a voluntary transaction, with the risks and benefits well known. Some families see it as a generational investment—putting money up front to send a family member abroad who will either send money home or apply for reunification in the West. They are right. All the evidence suggests that it is a good investment in the medium to long term, even though the cost up front—in money, in blood, and in trauma—is steep.[56] Smuggling is one of the few tools asylum seekers can avail themselves of as they make the strategic decision to leave refugee camps or urban slums for the West.

Human smuggling is now one of the only ways people have of seeking refuge and a de facto requirement for claiming asylum in the West. For those asylum seekers who engage good smugglers—who care about delivering their customers to safety—they provide an invaluable service, a service that exists precisely because the international community has abandoned refugees. This, not smugglers, is the real problem that needs to be addressed.

THE PRICE TO BE PAID FOR ASYLUM: DROWNING, DYING IN THE DESSERT, TORTURE

So if smugglers are not bad in and of themselves, but provide a service for refugees, what is the problem? It's twofold. One, because smuggling is illegal and clandestine, it is, by nature, dangerous. People must willingly risk suffocation in the back of a truck or dehydration as they walk through the dessert. Second, asylum seekers are extremely vulnerable and smugglers often treat them as a profit-generating commodity. As such, they can become victims of extreme violence. Still, many smugglers depend on their reputation in order to get business and have a vested interest in taking care of their human cargo and making sure they get to their final destination.

The danger of smuggling emerged dramatically when bodies started washing ashore in Europe in large numbers in 2015. Because smuggling is so profitable, smugglers try to put as many bodies onto a boat as possible. To save space for more human cargo, smugglers often don't take sufficient food, fuel, or even navigational tools. Boats are sent out to sea, captained by one of the refugees, in the hopes that they will be rescued in time. Not surprisingly, many die: ships capsize, people on board starve to death, or die of heat stroke or hypothermia. According to the UN, about three thousand people have died crossing the Mediterranean Sea every year since 2014, except for 2016, when over five thousand people died.[57] It's important to remember that these numbers are only speculation. When a boat packed with refugees from a failed state capsizes, most countries will not pay for a search-and-rescue operation to count the bodies. There are likely many more drownings than we know about.

THE DESERT

Though risking death by drowning or heat exhaustion is an unacceptable price that we ask refugees to pay in order to claim asylum, there may be worse aspects to human smuggling. The philosopher Hannah Arendt once pointed out that one of the powerful aspects of totalitarianism was that it made people aware that there are worse things than death. Reading accounts of what refugees endure in being smuggled to Europe serves as a reminder of this notion. Torture, rape, suffocation, and starvation are no less horrifying because they have become routine for refugees.

One of the most horrifying smuggling routes is the one taken by Eritrean refugees through Sudan to Libya or Egypt's Sinai Peninsula. After escaping from Eritrea, refugees are driven by smugglers in trucks across hundreds of miles to the Libyan border. There they are handed over to other smugglers, who split them up into pickup trucks for the trip further north. Trucks often get lost, run out of fuel; people die of thirst or heat, fall off the side, or break their limbs when a truck is overturned.[58] Eritreans who make it to Libya alive are often sold to traffickers who torture the asylum seekers in order to extort money from their family. Their network is so extensive that money can be received from family members in France, Sudan, Canada, and so on. There are numerous reports of rape, burning, mutilation, electric shocks, prolonged suspension by the ankles or wrists, being left to die; sometimes people are forced to sleep in open graves containing dead bodies.[59] An extortion technique these traffickers frequently use is torturing the asylum seekers while they are on the phone so that their family can hear them scream; the torture only stops once family members have paid the kidnappers. Once that money is paid, refugees are moved closer to the sea and wait in squalid conditions. Food is distributed once a day, men are regularly beaten, and women frequently raped. "All the suffering that a human can suffer happens here," said an Eritrean doctor.[60] This is a business that can yield as much as $50,000 per smuggled person. Over a four-year period, about twenty-five thousand to thirty-five thousand people, 40 percent of whom were children, earned traffickers over $600 million.[61]

Here is how one seventeen-year-old trafficker put it:

> I buy Eritreans from other Bedouin near my village for about $10,000 each. . . . When I started a year ago, I asked for $20,000 per person. Like everyone else I have increased the price. I know this money is haram [shameful], but I do it anyway. This year I made about $200,000 profit.
>
> The longest I held someone was seven months and the shortest was one month. The last group was four Eritreans and I tortured all of them. I got them to call their relatives and to ask them to pay $33,000 each. Sometimes I tortured them while they were on the phone so the relatives could hear them scream. I did to them what I do to everyone. I beat their legs and feet, and sometimes their stomachs and chest, with a wooden stick. I hang them upside down, sometimes for an hour.
>
> Three of them died because I beat them too hard. I released the ones that paid. About two out of every 10 people I torture pay what I ask. Some pay less and I release them. Others die of the torture. Sometimes when the wounds get bad and I want to torture them more, I treat their wounds with bandages and alcohol.
>
> I beat women but not children and I have not raped anyone. My parents don't know I do this and I don't want them to know. I'm not interested in speaking to anyone who wants me to stop doing this. The government doesn't care so I don't mind talking to you. The police won't do anything to stop us because they know that if they come to our villages we will shoot. The military might try to get us, but I am young so I don't think about that.[62]

While the callousness of the young trafficker may shock us, it is important to keep in mind that he is able to do what he does because of the policies that make it hard for someone from Eritrea to claim asylum directly. We are morally entangled in this system in complex ways. Though we are not the ones doing the kidnapping, ransoming, or torturing, we are nonetheless complicit because we have made it impossible to access Western states to claim asylum except through smuggling. We have effectively set the conditions for these human rights violations to occur. Torture, rape, bankruptcy, and potentially death are now the price we ask refugees to pay for the chance to claim asylum.

CONCLUSION

The stories that this chapter began with—Blanca, Nart, Benjamin, and Yaser—illustrate the price refugees are willing to pay to seek refuge. All Western countries that receive asylum seekers employ deterrence measures, and as a consequence, all asylum seekers use smugglers. A cat-and-mouse game now plays out between Western states and those refugees who refuse to be imprisoned in camps or remain destitute in urban centers. Those who dare to seek a meaningful, genuine future for themselves and their children will have to navigate terrifying deterrence policies from the states that they hope will help them and the unknowable black market of smuggling.

This is what it means for Blanca and Yaser to seek safety for their children and for young men like Nart and Benjamin to exercise their agency and seek a better future. The obstacles to this of course emerge from their own countries that prevent them from living dignified lives in the first place. But they also come from us and our refusal to allow them on our territory. While we may respect the right to asylum in principle, Western states will do everything they can to make sure it's not claimed.

This aspect of the second crisis often remains hidden when people discuss how to handle the main refugee crisis. Yet deterrence policies that make seeking asylum difficult or deadly, combined with the conditions that refugees find themselves in if they make it to the West, constitute a morally significant feature of the second crisis, the inability of refugees to find refuge anywhere in the world. States will defend their use of deterrence policies as the morally justifiable exercise of sovereignty and part of their right to control their borders. States do not set out to harm asylum seekers. Though they may know that ending rescue missions at sea or separating children from their parents will hurt, and even lead to the deaths of, asylum seekers, many political leaders hold that the greater good of national security is being served. This makes evaluating the morality of these decisions complex. In the next chapter, I propose that we take seriously the second crisis, the inability of refugees to find refuge, and examine this injustice in light of the right of states to control their borders.

Chapter 6

Structural Injustice

When Guled was a teenager, he lived not far from the site where Black Hawk helicopters famously crashed in Mogadishu, Somalia.[1] As an orphan, he survived without adults by living with his sisters and other orphaned children. They subsisted on the money his sister made selling biscuits and cakes and grew up amid a permanent civil war.

One morning he arrived at school to find five men wearing black, with machine guns over their shoulders. They had come seeking children to fight for al-Shabaab. Ordered to leave the room, Guled was put into a pickup truck and told he was going to fight the infidels. Though he was forced for a time to become a child soldier, Guled eventually escaped his captors, finding his way to the Dadaab refugee camp in Kenya.

By the time Guled arrived in Dadaab in 2010, Oxfam had already called the camp a "public health emergency." It was a camp the size of New Orleans that held five hundred thousand people; it was originally built in 1992 to hold ninety thousand people. A researcher working in the camp described it as "a groaning, filthy, disease-ridden slum heaving with traumatized people without enough to eat. Crime was sky high and rape was routine."[2]

Guled was happy for the relative security. He appreciated the regular food rations—every two weeks he received three kilos of flour, two kilos of rice, one kilo of beans, half a liter of oil, and a cup of salt. Every refugee got exactly the same, no matter whether you were an infant or teenager. He was surprised to find a thriving black market where everything was for sale—food, clothing, radios, mobile phones, even blocks of ice. But since the camp residents had no income and were not allowed to work, Guled, like the other refugees, would sell his rations to access these other goods. The first thing he did was to sell two kilos of rice and call his sister in Somalia.

Dadaab had existed for over twenty years (and continues to exist), yet the camp was officially temporary. This was the fiction of Dadaab—its permanent temporariness meant that infrastructure didn't need to be built and improvements didn't need to be made.

Guled commenced living his life in Dadaab. He got married and had children that he raised in the camp. He passed his days by playing soccer—he was considered by other refugees to be a very talented player. But his wife grew frustrated with his inability to provide for his family. Though they got the basics in the camp—food rations, a place to live—they weren't able to buy extras, like the powdered milk his wife thought their kids needed.

As debts mounted and rations were cut, frustration grew. Food was so sparse in the camp at certain points that Guled had to give what little food he got to his pregnant wife and children, living with a permanent stomachache. A lot of Guled's time was spent discussing going to Europe with the other camp residents. Guled thought that if he had enough money—to pay for the transport, the bribes, the ransoms—he too would undertake the long journey to Europe. He knew the risks, but felt that at least he would be doing something, taking some action that could potentially improve the lives of his family members. "The life we are in today, it is better for me to die in the Sahara or in the sea."[3]

This was likely to be Guled's life for the imaginable future—near starvation, frustration at not being able to help his family, no work or any way to improve himself, yet not having the money to pay for the expensive trip to Europe. His only hope—which he knew was extremely slim—was that the UNHCR would find him another country that would resettle him.

When the nine-months-pregnant Sina Habte was rescued off the coast of Greece, people questioned what brought her to that moment.[4] Why would a mother-to-be risk her baby's life and cross the Mediterranean on a flimsy raft? For people fleeing Eritrea, Sina's was not an uncommon story. Sina was an average, middle-class Eritrean with a degree in chemical engineering who had married her former university professor, Dani. She was a relatively privileged Eritrean as she was allowed to practice her profession once she graduated. In contrast, most Eritreans spend their lives in "national service"—working for twelve hours a day, for about $30 a month, for as long as the state requires. Dani was not as fortunate as Sina. Despite being a civil engineer and a university teacher, he was conscripted to work as a soldier about three hundred miles from his wife. They were not permitted to see each other regularly, and mobile phones were banned during national service.

One day Dani escaped. He returned to Sina even though he knew full well that when he was discovered he would be thrown in jail. Then Sina discovered that she was pregnant. They had never thought about leaving Eritrea before, but now it became the only option. If they stayed, Dani would be jailed, likely tortured, and never released. If they were caught in Eritrea, Sina too would be put in jail. The torture that was likely could lead to a miscarriage and the death of her baby.

They were certainly not the first to consider this option. Life had become so unbearable in Eritrea that there are more Eritrean refugees per capita than refugees from any other country. When President Afwerki took power in 1993, he created the most severe conscription program in the world and a security force so vast that it was impossible to evade. The state decided every aspect of life—where you lived, where you worked, how much money you earned, what you could say, and what religion you could practice. If you wanted to leave Eritrea, you had to travel great lengths—the Eritrean security apparatus had a long arm that reached all the way to refugee camps in Sudan and Kenya. If they found you, you would be returned to the living hell of the Eritrean prison system. The government had a shoot-to-kill policy for those caught trying to escape.

Sina and Dani began to make plans to leave. They managed to find the $6,000 needed to pay someone for the six-hour drive to Sudan, and another $800 to go through South Sudan. The trek to Uganda was on foot over land, followed by another drive to the capital, Kampala. They paid another smuggler $14,000 to get them to Turkey and then to Greece.

Sina and Dani were separated from each other in Uganda. The smuggler told Dani that he had to fly to Istanbul separately from Sina, and ultimately abandoned him in Uganda. Sina made it to Istanbul and had a boat ready to take her to Greece when she was nine months pregnant and several days past her due date. The smugglers talked her into getting on the boat, though she feared she might have the baby at sea. They told her the journey was only an hour and though she had to initially get on a flimsy wooden boat, she would be transferred to a bigger one with life jackets. These were, of course, lies—the smugglers needed to get her out of the apartment she was occupying in Turkey so they could fill it with other clients. When the boat started to leak and she fell into the water, she regretted being persuaded to go. Fortunately for her, she was rescued by an off-duty Greek army sergeant who could see the capsizing boat from the beach. Shortly after her rescue, she gave birth to her baby boy and named him after the man who saved her.

About three months later, she received a call from her mother-in-law saying that Dani was dead. The smuggler had told her he had died of malaria in Uganda, though it was impossible for her to know the truth. Sina had been granted a scholarship to study in Germany but couldn't take her child with her without Dani's death certificate, which was impossible for her to get from Uganda. She once again had to hire a smuggler to get her and her baby out of Greece and into Northern Europe. This required being driven to the border of Macedonia, walking for two hours with her baby to the border, taking a taxi to Serbia followed by a bus ride, paying another smuggler to usher her through Hungary, and walking for eight hours to evade the police. She eventually made it to Sweden, via train from Austria, where she and her baby were granted asylum.

Sina and Guled represent two aspects of the problem that we in the West have created. Sina, having been granted asylum in Sweden, is among the 2 percent of refugees who are able to find refuge. But to do so, she had to spend her family's life savings, pay smugglers, risk death at sea, lose her husband in mysterious circumstances, and be smuggled through Europe with an infant in her arms while being treated as a criminal. Guled, on the other hand, is among the 98 percent of refugees who do not have access to one of the three durable solutions (resettlement, local integration, or repatriation). He is likely to spend his life in the refugee camp, dependent on aid from the international community; an outcome that was scarcely imaginable at the end of World War II. While he (usually) has enough food to keep him and his family alive, he lacks the things many consider essential for a dignified life: stability, hope for the future, and the ability to shape the course of his life and provide for his family.

Their stories parallel the reality of the global refugee experience: most refugees will not be able to access refuge or one of the genuine solutions envisioned for them by the UNHCR, and if they do gain asylum, it's only after Homeric journeys.[5] The vast majority endure the conditions described in the previous chapters. Many live in refugee camps where, in order to get minimal food rations and shelter, they must give up their autonomy and the belief that they can work toward making their lives better. If they find the material conditions or the lack of control over their lives to be unacceptable, they may choose to live in an urban area. Here they can live and work where they want but receive little international aid, access to healthcare, or education. Because their situation is so precarious, they are likely to be exploited in their work or be unable to find enough work to provide food and shelter. Many will spend their family's saving or go into extreme debt. Some refugees believe both options are inadequate and choose instead to make the dangerous journey to the West to seek asylum directly. To do this, they must overcome the most drastic deterrence measures Western countries have put in place and risk drowning, heatstroke, and torture on their journey. Those who make it are likely to find themselves in squalid refugee camps in Europe, detention centers in the United States, or offshore processing centers outside Australia, where many will be kept for years, often without their family.

Stories like Sina's and Guled's show the need to develop a new frame for the refugee crisis. The full scope of our moral obligations cannot simply be resettlement and asylum, a question of whether or not we should admit refugees to our country. This question—whether or not refugees should be resettled or given asylum—*frames* the problem too narrowly. Resettlement is important, but focusing on it exclusively means that we ignore the wider set of problems. As the last two chapters have shown, focusing only on resettlement cuts out of the picture the injustice of the options the international community offers to refugees; being forced to spend your life in a refugee camp dependent on aid, as in Guled's case, or having to cross the Mediterranean on a flimsy boat, nine months pregnant, as your only way of claiming asylum, as in Sina's case.

Can we rethink our moral obligations to refugees in a way that encompasses all of these dimensions of the refugee experience? Doing so requires that we adopt a new frame for the crisis, one that includes the injustices described in this book and the experiences of refugees as they try to seek refuge.

THE IMPORTANCE OF HOW WE FRAME AN ISSUE

What does it mean to frame an issue? To frame an issue is to pick out parts that are important and exclude others that are unimportant. Frames draw our attention to some things and away from others. For example, when we talk about industrial animal farms, the idea that we should come to see animal welfare as an issue of genuine moral concern is a way of framing the issue with ramifications for what stays in the picture and what we leave out. This particular frame pushes us to look at how animals are treated on farms and ask whether it's necessary for the production of food, whether it's good for the animals or human health. Only recently have people adopted this frame and begun to see some farming practices as morally problematic. If farming were framed around questions of economic efficiency—how to make the most food for the most people as efficiently as possible—then the animal welfare dimension would likely be left out. If we don't see something as a problem, we can't even begin to discuss it, let alone develop solutions or alternative ways of doing things.

Once a frame is in place, we can begin to see who is responsible and how the problem might be addressed. If we were to frame domestic poverty, for example, as the result of personal failings in a system of equal opportunity, then it makes sense to hold the poor person herself responsible and perhaps even to penalize her through cutting welfare benefits. But if domestic poverty is seen as an inevitable outcome of global capitalism, then it is harder to blame the individual.

In this frame, poverty in the United States may rise because people invest in countries with cheaper labor costs, creating fewer jobs for workers at home. If this is framed as a problem of the system, the harm could be mitigated through job training or a universal basic income.[6] The frame we adopt matters tremendously for how we treat a problem; it will determine how we see an issue both morally and politically.

This is true for the global refugee crisis as well. In the dominant frame, Western states and their members (either as individuals or NGOs) are *rescuers* who step in to help those harmed and abandoned by their own states. According to this frame, the failed states that produce refugees are the ones who can be held morally responsible for failing to uphold their citizens' human rights. They are the ones who can be criticized for creating refugees in need of rescue by other countries. The refugees themselves are the (mostly) innocent byproducts, and Western actors are the rescuers who come to the aid of those in need. Western states help refugees *not* because they have done anything wrong but because of their commitment to human rights or humanitarian principles.

I want to suggest that we expand this frame because it misrepresents the actual crisis as I've described it in this book, leading us to misunderstand our moral obligations to refugees. In this broader frame I think we should adopt, there are two distinct sets of harms. The first is the one implicit in the rescue frame: the circumstances that drive refugees to leave their homes in the first place. The risk of torture in the underground torture chambers, the barrel bombs that killed relatives, the fear of kidnapping by a militant group. These harms, caused by the refugee-producing state, are indisputable, and they clearly give rise to an obligation to help people who are forced to flee their country. This is the duty of rescue on which most philosophers focus.

But in the wider frame that we ought to adopt, a second set of harms comes into focus. These are the harms *we* have created. The second set of harms includes all the things refugees must do in order to survive, including living in squalid, insecure camps, subsisting despite neglect and vulnerability in urban centers, or pursuing asylum on dangerous routes with human smugglers. The *we* that I am referring to here are the countries that have been involved in setting up the refugee protection system, a system that Western states have played the biggest role in creating, influencing, and supporting. We have created a situation in which the vast majority of refugees are effectively unable to get refuge in any meaningful sense; that is, they are not able to access the minimum conditions of human dignity. I will refer to this outcome as a *structural injustice,* an outcome that all countries, but especially Western states, share political responsibility for.

As I'll explain later, no one country or set of countries *intentionally* created this system. It is an outcome that can be understood as the cumulative effect of many different policies around refugee resettlement, refugee camps, humanitarian and development aid, immigration, and border security enacted by countries around the world. The ways that these policies, laws, and norms *interact* create the unjust outcome for refugees, their inability to access the minimum conditions of human dignity. Importantly, this outcome has been sustained as a result of countries failing to take seriously the consequences of these policies for refugees and asylum seekers. While individual policies in isolation may not be problematic, when looked at as a whole these policies and actions have the cumulative effect of more or less ensuring that the vast majority of refugees will not be able to access the conditions that would allow them to lead a minimally decent life, one that includes autonomy, dignity, and basic material goods. We need to frame our understanding of refugees in such a way that it includes structural as well as direct harms to refugees.

A NEW FRAMEWORK: STRUCTURAL INJUSTICE

I want to suggest that we adopt a new frame for understanding the harms refugees experience in the twenty-first century, one that can help us to see and understand both sets of harms described previously and to develop different layers of responses to it. We need a two-layered frame, one that can include both direct, intentional injustices experienced by refugees and the indirect or structural injustices that constitute the status quo I've been describing in this book for refugees seeking but unable to find refuge. With this frame in place, we will be better positioned to understand how we should respond to refugees.

The first layer of the frame encompasses the direct injustices, harms, violence, and human rights violations that refugees experience. The paradigmatic case is the treatment of refugees by their own states that often forces them to flee. It places the focus on the soldiers in Myanmar who go from village to village killing and raping the Rohingya minority; the Assad regime who drops barrel bombs in civilian areas; the gangs in Honduras who extort and brutalize civilians with impunity. These are commonly recognized as atrocities, and the people who perpetuate them are frequently, though not always, condemned.

This layer also includes the direct injustices committed against refugees once they seek refuge. The guard in Nauru who sexually molests women and children; the landlord in Jordan who exploits the urban refugees desperate for housing; the police in Eastern Europe who beat, threaten, and pepper-spray asylum seekers are all examples of direct injustices committed by people whom refugees are seeking help from. These injustices tend to be less well known than the ones committed by the refugee-producing states, but when they come to light, they are often, though not always, criticized as immoral.

These *direct injustices* constitute the first layer. One feature of these kinds of injustices is that there is a clear agent—an individual or collective entity like a government—that can be held responsible for directly and intentionally causing the harm. We know who or what caused the injustice.

To this we must add a second, less obvious injustice. This is the injustice that I've been describing throughout this book. The very structure of the refugee protection system—the status quo that requires refugees to negotiate a system that resettles very few, contains millions in camps, and neglects millions more outside of camps—is unjust in that it unfairly prevents refugees from accessing the minimum conditions of human dignity.

But this injustice is not like the direct injustices described earlier in some important ways. Most notably, unlike direct injustices, it is not clear who or what is causing the injustice. Rather, the injustice is an outcome of many different policies enacted by many different actors. The injustices described in this book arise from different states making their own policies around refugees, resettlement, immigration, and border security, and ignoring the effects that these policies have had on those seeking refuge. No one country or policy caused the situation I've been describing. We need to employ a different concept in order to understand this.

The injustice refugees experience as they seek refuge is *structural*, and this is why I will refer to this second layer of injustice as a *structural injustice*. It is structural in the sense that it emerges from the social and political structures, systems, policies, and norms that make up the refugee protection system. Though not the intentional outcome of any one actor or set of actions, it is nonetheless a system that often makes it impossible for refugees to access the minimum conditions of human dignity. The concept of structural injustice allows us to focus on this *outcome* and helps us to understand how things can be so bad for refugees without there being someone who intended it or directly caused it.

Including both kinds of harms is crucial as we frame the harms experienced by refugees and try to understand what is owed to them. I am not suggesting that one is worse than the other or should be taken more seriously than the other. We certainly need to continue to think about and find ways to redress the direct harms refugees experience at the hands of their home states and the international community when they seek refuge. However, in my view, the second layer of structural harm has not been given enough attention. Only by taking it seriously and including it in how we frame the refugee crisis can we change our collective response to refugees.

WHAT IS STRUCTURAL INJUSTICE?

Let's start with the injustice. Something is unjust if it violates some standard of fairness or decency even though it may be legal or accepted by some. A clear example of an injustice is the segregation laws that existed in the United States in the twentieth century known as the Jim Crow laws. Though legal at the time, many people saw them as unjust because they treated African Americans as inferior to whites. Martin Luther King Jr. and others challenged these laws on the grounds that they were fundamentally immoral. They harmed people of color and treated them unfairly; they were unjust laws.

I've been arguing throughout this book that the current system of refugee protection is unjust in a similar sense. This system is unjust because it denies refugees access to the minimum conditions of human dignity and permits refugees to be treated in ways that deny their human rights. Underfunded refugee camps, neglect of refugees in cities, requiring smugglers in order to claim asylum, and resettling small numbers of refugees are widely seen as unfair and unjust when people understand what they mean for refugees and the depth of suffering they cause. It is unfair that they have no better, safer options. Though the policies behind these practices are legal, they should nevertheless be challenged as fundamentally unjust because they lead to such harmful and unfair outcomes.

Though the struggle to change Jim Crow laws was long and brutal, it was at least clear what needed to be changed: the laws themselves. But there is no single set of laws that need to be changed in the case of the refugee system. The problem that I've been describing is both global and *structural*; it results not from one set of laws or one cruel and unfair leader, but from the actions of many different states working to further their own interests. Though pursuing your own interests is not in itself problematic, the outcome that arises from it can in some circumstances be unjust. This is what it means to call something a structural injustice.

The most influential account of structural injustice comes from the philosopher Iris Young. In her view, structural injustice stems from social structures, structures that constrain the opportunities of some while granting privileges to others, whether or not anyone desires or intends this outcome. Structural injustice can arise from the policies and the actions of thousands of individuals acting according to morally acceptable rules and norms. Her insight is that large-scale social processes in which individuals or collective entities seek to accomplish their legitimate goals can nonetheless result in unjust but unintended consequences when looked at structurally. In contrast, an ordinary or direct injustice can be traced back to something or someone you can hold responsible; to understand structural injustice, you have to look at the situation as a whole.

Two features of Young's account of structural injustice are particularly important when connecting this concept to refugees: its motivation and its orientation to the future. First, the harm itself, the injustice, does not need to be *intentional,* that is, the motivation doesn't matter. Structural injustice arises from the actions of many people acting according to normal rules and accepted, morally justifiable practices.[7] There doesn't need to be a racist politician or selfish bureaucrat pulling the strings in order for there to be a structural injustice. Often structural injustice is supported by well-meaning people, people who would disapprove of the outcome if they became aware of it. This is not to say that the harm is insignificant; it is often as severe as any direct injustice. But its source is different: it results from people living their everyday lives and pursuing their own interests uncoordinated with each other. In the case of a global structural injustice, it results from different states and nonstate institutions each pursuing its own agenda that it thinks is most helpful for itself.

We can think of climate change as a kind of structural injustice. It is the result of different countries using fossil fuels to further their economy and provide their citizens comfortable lives. The outcome, dramatic changes in weather and the environment that are likely to lower the quality of life of people around the world, was never intended.[8] The outcome was not created intentionally, though it resulted from the actions and policies of many different actors, as individuals and collectives, but it is still unjust insofar as it will harm millions of people.

Second, structural injustice is forward-looking, not backward-looking, in its account of injustice. The focus of a judgment that something is a structural injustice is not to blame someone or some entity for something done in the past. The focus is on how to make things more just in the future. This is of course different from direct injustice, where the point of calling something unjust is often to demand punishment or compensation for the harm. In the case of climate change, calling out particular states for burning too much fossil fuel or having too high a population growth rate would be the result of treating it as a direct injustice. Calling it a structural injustice instead focuses on what can be done to limit the harm in the future.

A full analysis will of course contain both perspectives—forward- and backward-looking—but the forward-looking structural perspective is one that is less commonly taken.

REFUGEE SYSTEM AS A STRUCTURAL INJUSTICE

The global system of refugee protection has produced dire outcomes, as we have seen throughout this book. These outcomes were not intended by any individual country or global institution, and yet the system these countries and institutions have created determines the limited options refugees have and the fates they suffer. By focusing on this outcome, not the intentions behind it, we're better able to see the injustice involved in our current treatment of refugees.

The global refugee system can be understood as the cumulative outcome of many uncoordinated norms and decisions by different states and the UNHCR along with other NGOs. The structural injustice I've been describing in this book has resulted, in part, from the different ways states have responded to refugees: through setting up and funding camps and ignoring urban refugees, enforcing brutal deterrence policies, villainizing refugees and other immigrants, and refusing to take seriously the effects that these policies have on migrants. States may very well set refugee policies with the intention of achieving their legitimate ends as a country while trying to help refugees. However, the *collective* outcome is a system where few refugees are able to live lives of dignity. In this sense, it is a paradigmatic case of structural injustice.

Structural injustice often results from norms and policies that in themselves might be consider defensible. For instance, all states have an interest in maintaining their political autonomy and controlling who enters their territory. State sovereignty, including the right to control immigration, is by and large considered morally acceptable as long as the exercise of this sovereignty does not violate human rights. Many states have interpreted this to mean that it is within their right to decide how many refugees they will resettle and which asylum seekers they will deem to be genuinely in need of refuge. This norm is even part of the 1951 Refugee Convention, which does not include an obligation to resettle refugees from abroad and leaves resettlement to the discretion of states. Yet the result of states acting in what they see as their best interest—resettling small numbers of refugees—is that on average less than 1 percent of refugees are resettled annually.

Another policy that many countries support is funding refugee camps to provide aid to refugees. One reason for this is that being housed in a camp relatively close to their country of origin makes it easier to return home (voluntary repatriation) when a refugee's home country is stable enough. This policy also aligned with the interests of many Western states. If refugees are in camps close to their home country, they are less likely to seek asylum and can be resettled at the West's discretion. These norms and policies remained in place even after it became clear that refugee camps were not able to protect human rights, were more costly than the alternatives, and far from being temporary, often lasted decades. The result of this is long-term warehousing of refugees. It is a serious injustice that nonetheless emerged out of a morally acceptable exercise of sovereignty.

States that host refugees also craft policies to serve their own goals. They may believe that it's in their economic interest to prevent refugees from working. They may believe that the security of their citizens requires them to build fences around refugee camps and limit refugees' freedom of movement. Host states claim that they are doing their best to help refugees while at the same time taking care of the interests of their citizens. Though these states may be aiming for their own morally legitimate ends, the result is an injustice for refugees living in host countries in the Global South, unable to work and prevented from moving freely, or else forced to live virtually unaided and unprotected in urban centers.

Another norm that supports the status quo for refugees is that funding refugee protection is up to the discretion of individual states. States fund the UNHCR and their own refugee agencies to the extent they believe is compatible with fiscal goals. Again, this is usually considered a morally legitimate way for states to behave and consistent with state autonomy. The result of this norm, however, is that refugee support and protection is chronically underfunded. In 2018, for example, the UNHCR received only 2.3 billion dollars of the 8.2 billion they needed to fund their programs.[9] In practice it means that there is less money for food, medicine, education, and security for the millions of refugees around the world who are dependent on the international community.

Deterrence policies, such as the ones described in the last chapter, straddle both direct injustice and structural injustice. Sometimes they result in so much suffering that we have to understand this as the intentional outcome and treat it as a direct injustice. But in other cases, deterrence policies should be seen as contributing to structural injustice. Often these policies are justified as the state's way of enforcing its immigration policies and limiting the number of asylum claims it needs to process. Some even claim that deterrence benefits refugees: they won't make dangerous journeys if they know the horrors they will have to endure. If states don't have adequate deterrence policies, the thinking goes, there will be too much of a "pull factor," and an overwhelming number of migrants will be tempted to come to claim asylum, resulting in a greater harm. Though states may be able to offer justifications for why they put these policies in place, the combination of deterrence policies with profound global violence and instability leads to refugees paying smugglers extraordinary sums of money, risking torture, rape, suffocation, or drowning just to claim asylum.

Marilyn Frye used the metaphor of a birdcage to describe this phenomenon, where rules and norms that may not be problematic in themselves can lead to a situation in which some individuals are harmed while others benefit.[10] If you look at the wires of a birdcage individually, it is hard to see why the bird is constrained; after all, it could just go around the wire. It's not until we step back and see that there are in fact several wires working together that we can understand why the bird cannot fly away.

This is the birdcage of the refugee protection system. Looked at in isolation, the policies I have mentioned are usually not seen as immoral, and they are rarely judged negatively according to the usual political standards.[11] The unjust outcome is the result of the uncoordinated actions of different actors (host states, the UN, donor states, resettlement states) each acting according to its own interests. Taken all together, the outcome is that the majority of refugees are *structurally* prevented from accessing refuge and the minimum conditions of human dignity. This structure benefits some states—Europe, the United States, and Australia, for example, are able to remain mostly in control of who is allowed onto their territory—but harms refugees themselves. A structural injustice approach asks us to take this larger perspective and look at the ways that various policies, laws, and norms dealing with refugees around the world *interact* to create the injustices described in the earlier chapters of this book. The outcome, not the intention, is what is morally relevant.

If we take a two-layered approach to the injustices refugees experience, we will also need a two-layered response. On the one hand, we need a backward-looking account that holds individual actors and states accountable for violating the human rights of refugees through their actions and policies. That is, we need to address the direct injustices that harm refugees. But we also need a forward-looking account of responsibility to address the structural issues and untangle the various ways that the unjust status quo for refugees is maintained.

RESPONSIBILITY

One of the key features of the structural injustice model is that it allows us to analyze and address unjust structures and institutions so as to make them less unjust in the future. This is different from how we would respond to a direct harm where there is one individual or one policy that can be said to be at fault or be blamed. For direct harms, it might be appropriate to look backward and punish, blame, or hold accountable whoever caused the harm. Our standard way of understanding legal and moral responsibility applies to individual actions that can be connected to the harm in question.

A different conception of responsibility is in order as we discuss responsibility for structural injustice. Iris Young refers to this as *political responsibility* so as to distinguish it from the way we are at fault when we directly commit a harm, where we may be called guilty or receive blame for the unjust outcome. To be political in this sense is to be concerned about the common good, and not with one's own guilt or responsibility. Responsibility is based on a *social connection model*. According to this model, individuals bear responsibility for structural injustice because they contribute by their actions to the processes that produce unjust outcomes. I am not responsible because I am *guilty*; my actions in relation to structural injustice may be morally neutral or even positive. Responsibility instead derives from belonging together with others in a system of cooperation and economic competition through which we seek to promote our own interests and realize our own projects.[12] It's not because we belong to a particular state or because we as individuals have committed a particular harm that we have responsibility; our responsibility arises because we participate in diverse institutional processes that produce structural injustice.

Political responsibility is shared by all those who contribute through their actions to sustaining the injustice. According to this view, we should not blame each other or call each other guilty for this, but rather encourage each other to reorganize collective relationships and discuss and debate different ways that we can undermine structural injustice.[13] Individuals never hold responsibility alone; it is always shared because many people contribute to the injustice.

What this means is that we have an obligation to join with others who share that responsibility in order to transform the structural processes to make the outcome less unjust. This may require that we work with others to revise and reevaluate institutions, monitor their effects on the people they are supposed to help to ensure that they are not harmful, and create mechanisms for collective action. It requires us to help each other see how particular policies, norms, and actions are connected to a particular structural injustice, especially when they might seem harmless in isolation. Political responsibility asks us to see how our actions fit into the larger framework and contribute to an injustice and to work, collectively, toward addressing it.

The policies I have described are adopted, at least explicitly, for morally neutral or even positive purposes. Yet it is clear that many of these policies have consequences that may be unintended but are nevertheless extremely harmful. Our political responsibility may then be to challenge other people and states to acknowledge this. We have a responsibility to anticipate and mitigate the unintended consequences of our refugee policies, and if states continue to be willfully ignorant, it is fair to no longer call these consequences unintended. In other words, if a policy designed to help refugees is in fact harming them, such as our deterrence policies, it follows that once we become aware of this, we need to change our policies. Ignoring the consequences is no longer an option. Making each other, as individuals and as states, aware of the consequences, however unintentional, is the first step required by the political responsibility model.

While philosophers have been more inclined to use the language of "duties" or "obligations" to talk about what we owe refugees,

I think "responsibility" offers a better way of thinking about structural injustice. A duty is a specific moral requirement that makes clear what we are obliged to do. Responsibilities are no less obligatory but allow for more discretion in determining how to rectify structural injustice. This is not to say that it's up to the individual alone—the collective nature of this responsibility requires that we challenge each other and engage in debate, discussion, and dialogue about how to address structural injustice. While Young insists that we should not *blame* each other for causing structural injustice, we can criticize each other for not taking action, for not taking enough action, or for taking action that is ineffective or counterproductive.

Nobody wants to be held responsible. Certainly, few countries are going to admit that they share responsibility for the fact that the only options for the vast majority of refugees do not allow them to access the minimum conditions of human dignity. No country in the world wants to take responsibility for the outcome of our refugee policies. This is a problem that will always remain a challenge, and there is certainly no easy way to make unwilling countries take responsibility for refugees.

But political responsibility helps us to approach this question in a different way. It stresses that we are responsible not because we have done something wrong, something that we should feel guilty about, but simply because we participate in unjust structures that are unfair to refugees. It is also a view of responsibility that allows discretion on what we can and should do to address this responsibility. There are different ways that an individual or collective entities like a state may be connected to an injustice, and so we must be able to think about responsibility in these different ways, keeping in mind that it is always forward looking—aiming to make structures less unjust—not to find fault, blame or punish.

Political responsibility is not something that can be determined through a causal connection to the harm. If I want to know who is responsible for breaking my vase, I need to find the person who dropped it. Because it cannot be determined by past behavior, political responsibility must be *assigned*[14] depending on how we are situated in relation to the injustice. It's more like a group of roommates trying to figure out who should do the dishes—it might be the person who cooks, the person who has friends over, or perhaps there's just a chore chart that assigns different roommates different jobs each week. However it's worked out, the problem—dirty dishes—is addressed by whoever is assigned responsibility for it.

One way to assign political responsibility would be to look at how we are connected or related to the injustice. We might be connected because we directly caused the situation; we might directly benefit from the injustice even if it was not something we aimed at in our actions; we may be connected because we have some privilege, influence, or power that could help us address the injustice; or we may simply have the capacity to deal with the problem in a way that others do not.[15]

I want to suggest that Western states share political responsibility for fixing the status quo for refugees and are particularly suited to tackling the structural injustice of the global refugee protection system. This is not to say that Western states alone have this responsibility. Indeed, because it is global, many states must play a role in remedying it. However, I want to counter the idea that it is sufficient for Western states to help refugees by resettling them or donating money, without also addressing the structural harms that prevent refugees from accessing the minimum conditions of human dignity. There is good reason to believe that Western states share political responsibility for addressing the structural injustice experienced by refugees.

To be clear, I'm not suggesting that Western states are responsible because they *caused* the situations that produced refugees. I'm not, for example, suggesting that the West caused the Syrian civil war and is therefore responsible for the refugees that have resulted. If we could trace refugees causally to some action on the part of Western states, I agree that this would be a strong ground for obligations to help. Yet most conflicts cannot be traced back so clearly, and there is much disagreement about whether or not conflicts around the world are the result of Western action. Some think that attributing global conflicts and the refugees they produce to Western actions is "a lingering vestige of colonialism."[16] Yet others think that it's transparently clear that the policies of Western countries in the Middle East, such as the invasion of Iraq and Afghanistan, laid the groundwork for the current civil war in Syria.[17] My view is agnostic on whether or not the actions of Western countries caused the war, conflict, climate change, or failed states that produce refugees. Most events that produce refugees in the twenty-first century are so complex that it is hard to track direct causal lines. Regardless, this vision of responsibility works in a different way. Political responsibility rests on the idea that we have created a situation in which the vast majority of refugees, regardless of why they were made refugees, are effectively unable to get refuge in any meaningful sense.

Western states must share political responsibility for refugees for a few reasons. First, they have a privileged position in relation to this unjust structure because they played an influential role in how the system is set up. As David Miliband, former UK secretary of state, explains, for the past eighty years, Western states have "set global rules, upheld global norms, and funded global humanitarian efforts."[18] Just as importantly, they have shaped the *norms*, tacitly understood ways of behaving toward refugees. One global norm that wealthy countries have perpetuated, for example, is that states are free to treat refugees and asylum seekers however they think best, even if this fails to adequately respect generally accepted human rights. Western states have certainly behaved in this way and rarely criticize each other for their treatment of refugees or asylum seekers. NGOs, the media, and ordinary citizens may criticize states, but states themselves rarely do. This sets the norm that it's acceptable to treat refugees, asylum seekers, and migrants in general in ways that would be impermissible with one's citizens.

Another norm that Western states have shaped is the idea that refugees and asylum seekers can and should be treated like security threats, despite evidence to the contrary. Though we have seen virulent manifestations of this idea in recent years, this discourse goes back at least to the 1980s. Even the UNHCR has taken up the idea that it's acceptable for Western states to consider refugees and asylum seekers as security threats and has tacitly agreed to help Western states "protect" themselves from this threat.[19]

Not only have Western states set the rules and norms for how refugees are understood and treated around the world, they have also *benefited* from these norms and rules.[20] For example, Western states have insisted since the end of the Cold War that the best solution for refugees is to return them to their home country, rather than resettling them in the West (which was the preference during the Cold War). What this implies is that refugee camps should be the method by which refugees are given aid. By living in camps, close to their country of origin, they can more easily return once conditions allow them to. But by insisting on encampment—which quickly became *warehousing,* putting refugees in camps for years or decades without finding any meaningful solution for them—we were able to avoid the burdens of hosting large numbers of refugees or processing their asylum claims.[21] Perhaps more abstractly, but no less importantly, by keeping the majority of refugees safely contained in camps in the Global South, Western states have been allowed to excise discretion over which refugees we allow in. We were free to resettle refugees if we felt generous and ignore them if we had other issues to deal with. If we want to put our humanitarian budget toward resettling refugees, we can, and if not, we are able to walk away in a way that other countries that host refugees—Pakistan, Jordan, Thailand, Uganda, Turkey, Ethiopia—cannot. This is a huge benefit that is largely invisible except in this context.

There is one more crucial reason for rethinking our relationship to this structural injustice. We have the capacity to change it. Though it's true that Western states have their own financial problems and domestic issues to deal with, the extraordinary inequality between countries puts a moral burden on those countries at the top end of the spectrum. In many ways, Western states are like the person watching a child die in a shallow pond—we are able to do a lot without compromising anything of comparable moral worth. Further, we've done it before. Western countries have led efforts to resettle large numbers of refugees at other times in history when we thought it was important. The war in Vietnam in the 1960s and 1970s produced millions of refugees. But rather than prolonged encampment or urban neglect, a global responsibility-sharing program emerged. Western countries such as the United States, Australia, France, and Canada accepted over half a million refugees in three years between 1979 and 1982.[22] As Alex Aleinikoff put it, in a world of more than seven billion people, it's well within our capacity to absorb twenty-five million refugees if we saw this as our responsibility.[23]

One might respond to the way I have framed the problem refugees experience by objecting that if states were just more generous and resettled enough refugees, we wouldn't need to think about the structural injustice of the international refugee system. Our focus, morally, should be on encouraging states to take in more refugees.

Though resettlement is one extremely important way to fulfill our responsibilities to refugees, we ought to still consider the conditions that refugees live in as they seek refuge, whether it is while seeking asylum or while they are in the Global South. This is because respecting the agency of refugees entails taking seriously what they say they want. Contrary to the assumption of many in the West, at least some refugees, perhaps many, would prefer to stay near their home, in countries where they may be familiar with the culture and language, and from where they may more easily be able to return home should conditions allow. In other words, even if resettlement is greatly expanded, we must still consider our moral obligations to help refugees where they are; we have to think about ways that we can support their ability to integrate and access the minimum conditions of human dignity in urban spaces and camps.

CONCLUSION

Now that we have a better sense of the nature of the injustice and why Western states share responsibility, we can begin to think of the kinds of actions and policies that might begin to address it. How should we go about dismantling the structural injustice that prevents refugees from getting refuge? This may seem like an overwhelming question—the problem may seem so big and complex that you and I as individuals may seem powerless. But making structural change requires that people in all kinds of different capacities—as individuals, citizens, policymakers, public leaders—take up the responsibility to dismantle structural injustice. There are many things that could be done to make the system less unjust for refugees. In the conclusion I examine what steps we might take if we are going to make change on a structural level.

Conclusion

What Should We Do? What Should I Do?

Why are Guled and Muna spending their lives in a refugee camp? Why did Sina have to risk her life and that of her baby, crossing an ocean on a rickety raft, just to get help? Why did Benjamin have to watch his friend kill himself in order to draw attention to the terrible conditions of his life on Nauru? Why did Hashem, after being tortured in Syria, have to be separated from his family and smuggled into Europe before being given a place to live?

These refugees are emblematic of what I have been calling the second crisis, the crisis for refugees around the world who are unable to access refuge without risking their life. Though they may have become refugees because of the actions of governments or nonstate actors, such as gangs, in their home country, the larger crisis they face is one that Western countries have created. Regardless of whether this was intentional or coordinated, the outcome of our current refugee protection system is that most refugees and asylum seekers cannot get refuge or avail themselves of a more permanent solution. This structural injustice is the moral issue we need to grapple with.

Guled is in a refugee camp because camps are the accepted way of providing aid and because no state is willing to resettle him or the millions of others like him around the world. Kenya, where Dadaab is located, is unwilling to let Guled or Muna be part of regular life in Kenya, and no other country is willing to criticize Kenya or challenge this policy. The European Union would not consider Sina a refugee until she risked her life and came directly to Greece and then Sweden. Paying smugglers and crossing the sea while pregnant was her only option, aside from staying in Eritrea and likely being imprisoned or killed. She could have gone to a refugee camp in a neighboring country, but underfunded and insecure as they are, she would run the risk of the Eritrean police forcibly bringing her back to Eritrea. While the EU would consider Hashem, a Syrian citizen, a refugee once he was in Europe, it would not grant him a visa to enter the EU, and if he went to a refugee camp to wait for resettlement, he would likely be waiting years, possibly decades, before he was allowed to come to Europe or another resettlement state. Australia justifies its use of offshore processing centers like the one in Nauru as a measure to discourage would-be asylum seekers and to allow Australia to remain in control of its borders. Though in the view of some critics atrocities at these offshore processing centers have reached the level of crimes against humanity, the policy continues.

Throughout this book I have suggested that we must take seriously the harms experienced by refugees as they seek refuge and include these harms in the way we frame the refugee problem. In thinking about our moral obligations to refugees, we need to acknowledge that many of the situations that are so detrimental to refugees are ones that Western states have created. The international community, led by Western states, has put in place the only options refugees have—squalid refugee camps, urban destitution, or dangerous migrations[1]—all of which, as we have seen throughout this book, fail to provide the minimum conditions for human dignity. In order to get food and shelter, refugees in camps must give up their autonomy and live there for years with little hope of rebuilding their lives. Resettlement from refugee camps by Western states is less than

1 percent. Because the conditions are so dire and refugees find it so painful to lack control of their lives, many avoid refugee camps and live informally in cities; the majority of refugees now make this choice. Here they scrape by largely without any international aid, subject to exploitation and the denial of such basic rights as education and healthcare. Children, who constitute half of all refugees globally, are particularly vulnerable.[2] They are often unable to go to school, and dire poverty makes it more likely that they will need to work to help the family. If refugees believe they cannot go home and are not willing to remain impoverished and marginalized, their only remaining choice is to put their life in the hands of smugglers and try to make it to a country that will grant them asylum. Once in a Western country that they hope will grant them asylum, they may face new challenges as they wait for their day in court—more squalid camps, the need for more smugglers, detention centers, being separated from their children, or going into the shadows and living precariously and without protection of any kind.

I have suggested that the situation I have just described should be understood as a kind of *structural injustice.* It is unjust that merely 2 percent of refugees have access to refuge in any meaningful sense, while the rest are stranded long term in circumstances that don't reach the threshold of a minimum standard of dignity. It is unjust that refugees don't have any better options.

Yet this is an injustice that was not deliberately caused by any individual state and, for the most part, did not originate in deliberate malice. Most often, states are acting according to morally acceptable rules and norms. Though some may think of certain policies as immoral—the child separation policy in the United States is widely seen this way—these policies are often justified by principles that are morally neutral or positive: national sovereignty, border protection, the rule of law. Focusing on this as a structural injustice helps us to see that what is morally relevant is the *outcome,* rather than the motivation or intention of states. It is this outcome that requires that we reconsider what our obligations to refugees are.

The structural injustice I have been describing is complicated in another way: it is not the result of one single policy or set of laws. It is the result of each state passing laws and acting according to its own interests in matters of border security, immigration, and refugee policy. Most states in the West have understood their best interests to lie in keeping refugees far from their borders, to prevent an onslaught of asylum seekers. This is not surprising. Once individuals make an asylum claim, the state has to assess whether they have a well-founded fear of persecution and must allow them to stay until the assessment is completed. When this happens in large numbers—as it did in Europe in 2015—it places a great burden on states. Though it is not surprising that states are eager to minimize their obligations, the outcome is injustice: refugees cannot get refuge.

This is not to say that all responses to refugees follow this pattern. Deterrence policies straddle both direct and structural injustice. In one sense, deterrence policies function like other policies around refugees that contribute indirectly to structural injustice. They are intended to protect national sovereignty and allow countries to remain in control of immigration. Most states consider this a morally legitimate aim. For example, it is standard for countries to insist that anyone entering by plane have a valid visa to enter before boarding. This in itself is not objectionable. Looked at in isolation, it's hard to see how policies like these make it more difficult for asylum seekers to come to wealthy countries, and they seem to be morally acceptable. Though they contribute to the structural injustice that refugees must navigate, they are not in themselves morally problematic.

However, not all deterrence policies are morally neutral. Some policies harm asylum seekers for the sake of sending a message to other potential asylum seekers that they are not welcome. Such policies cross a line into direct injustice. Taking away the children of asylum seekers upon arrival on US soil, putting asylum seekers on a remote island without access to the outside world, or shutting down search-and-rescue operations that have saved asylum seekers from drowning in the sea are examples of direct injustices. In some cases, the intention is to terrorize refugees; in others, the harm to refugees is a predictable outcome. Because we accept that sovereign states have a right to control immigration, many have seen these policies as part and parcel of this right and have failed to appreciate the harm they cause or how they contribute to the overall crisis for refugees.

States justify their actions as being in the interests of their citizens, their economy, or their security, ends that are in themselves not morally problematic. We might be tempted to say that the situation that refugees find themselves in is unfortunate but not unjust. Yet I want to suggest that this is not right and that seeing the global refugee regime as a structural injustice helps bring this to light.

Even though the situation I describe was not an intentional outcome, Western states have a moral responsibility to address the political structures that unjustly prevent refugees from accessing the minimum conditions of human dignity while they are refugees. These countries should be seen as *politically responsible.* They are responsible because states contribute to the processes that produce unjust outcomes and even benefit. Thinking of responsibility like this takes seriously the ways in which Western states, though seemingly distant from refugees and the problems they face in the Global South, are actually interconnected. In many ways, Western liberal democracies are dependent upon and benefit from the diverse institutional processes that produce structural injustice. Political responsibility is shared by all those who contribute through their actions to sustaining the injustice.

Responsibility for structural injustice can be seen as part of a two-layered approach to responsibility. When our actions and policies directly and intentionally harm refugees, we should take direct responsibility. Refugee children who are sexually molested while in the custody of US immigration authorities, for example, have experienced a direct harm, and the people who can be causally traced to the harm ought to be held accountable.[3]

Yet there is also another layer of responsibility. That is the responsibility Western states share for setting up an international system of protection that denies refugees access to adequate material conditions, autonomy, and security. Western states are responsible for this outcome because they largely created the rules and norms that structure it. As I suggested in the Introduction, this does not mean that other states that have contributed to the structural injustice of the refugee system have no responsibility. Rather, I have focused on the responsibility of Western states because of the special connection these states have to refugees.

This book was written in the firm conviction that we cannot make things more just for refugees until we fully understand the situation that refugees find themselves in. Having developed an understanding of the real problem for refugees and the crucial role Western liberal democracies play in it, we can begin to think concretely about what actions we can take and what policies we should support.

We can now ask: What steps should we take to ensure that refugees have access to the minimum conditions of human dignity? How should we go about dismantling the structural injustice that prevents refugees from getting refuge? There is no one answer to these questions. In fact, many suggestions have been put forth for how to tackle the global refugee crisis.[4] I don't have an exhaustive explanation of how to solve the refugee crises. In what follows, I merely suggest some ways that we can begin a conversation about dismantling the structural injustice that has thus far been largely ignored, and offer some preliminary suggestions about what Western states and their citizens should do.

WHAT CAN WE DO?

It is up to states to ensure that the minimum conditions of human dignity are accessible to refugees and asylum seekers wherever they are. One of the most promising ways to give refugees access to what they need to live dignified lives is *integration*. Western states should support policies that encourage the integration of refugees, politically, socially, and economically, in the countries where they find themselves, both in the West and in the Global South.

Our current go-to policy for helping refugees is refugee camps, even though they are expensive and inefficient and most refugees avoid them. Temporary local integration is a promising alternative. It would allow refugees to live with the local populations and attend school, use hospitals, and work just like anyone else who lives there. It does not grant refugees citizenship or permanent residency—refugees would still need a *durable* solution, such as voluntary return or resettlement—but it allows refugees to live as members of the community and contribute to the economy and culture of their place of residence while they remain refugees. It restores some of the agency that is sorely lacking for refugees in camps and would make the exploitation that comes from living illegally in cities less likely. There is a growing consensus that integrating refugees into their host countries is not only beneficial for refugees, but also for the countries that host them. It may be the single biggest way to allow refugees to access refuge, that is, the minimum conditions of dignity while they are waiting for a more durable solution.

ECONOMIC INTEGRATION

How can Western states encourage and support the economic integration of refugees in poorer countries in the Global South? There are a number of ways. First, we could rethink the way we fund refugee protection. Because of the focus on asylum, we spend the vast majority of our funding on refugees who make it to the West, even though it benefits only a fraction of refugees. Globally, we spent $75 billion dollars a year on the 10 percent of refugees who make it to the West, and $5 billion on the 90 percent of refugees who remain in the Global South. Put in other terms, we spent $135 on every refugee who comes to the West, and $1 on every refugee who remains in the Global South.[5] Our funding model now focuses on and prioritizes refugees who want to come to the West and neglects refugees who remain in the Global South.

To be clear, I am not proposing shifting money from asylum and resettlement to integration. Such a shift would put even more responsibility on the countries that already host large refugee populations. As I'll discuss later, resettlement and asylum still remain essential programs. Though we should work toward reforming structural injustice so that all refugees can access refuge, asylum and resettlement remain essential options for many refugees who cannot stay where they are. It's well within our capacity to fund both sets of programs. We should not see funding humanitarian aid to refugees in their home regions in ways that facilitate integration as opposed to funding for asylum and resettlement. They are both part of our shared responsibility to address structural injustice.

Rather than funding refugee camps, Western states should use a system of cash transfers as a way of disseminating aid to refugees. Evidence suggests that this is in fact the best way to get resources to refugees in the Global South, even though only about 10 percent of aid is distributed this way.[6] According to the development economist Owen Barder, refugees with cash could buy what they needed from the local community or development organizations, and refugee camps would cease to be necessary as a way of distributing goods and services to refugees.[7] Perhaps most importantly, cash gives refugees decision-making power and agency to determine what goods to buy and hence some control over their circumstances. A mother can decide what her child needs, for example, rather than being at the mercy of what the aid agency or host state determines is best. The lack of agency is one of the features of life that refugees report as intolerable.[8] There is evidence to suggest that cash transfers are beneficial to the local economy as well.[9]

Further, we can encourage economic policies that support economic integration of refugees through tax and trade packages. Refugees want to work—refugees themselves have said so over and over again. Many scholars believe that it would be economically useful to bring them into the labor market, rather than forcing them to remain passive recipients of aid. Betts and Collier have suggested that Western states could facilitate this by creating special economic zones in countries that host large numbers of refugees. These zones would give tax and trade incentives to companies that hire refugees, allowing domestic businesses to develop, host countries to experience economic growth, and refugees to earn wages and exert more control over their life. Using our economic policies and trade leverage to encourage refugees' ability to work and gain autonomy may be a powerful way of undermining the structural injustice of life in camps and urban centers. Further, it would chip away at the assumption that refugees are burdens to states rather than agents eager to rebuild their life and contribute to their community.[10]

The Jordan compact was an example of such an approach. In 2016, the government of Jordan agreed to allow Syrian refugees to work in exchange for grants, loans, and preferential trade agreements with the European Union. This experiment had mixed results. It gave more Syrians access to the labor market than they would have without it, though it did not help as many refugees integrate economically as policymakers had hoped. One reason is that refugees were not consulted in its implementation.[11] Another was that the program focused too much on increasing the number of work permits and not enough on helping refugees access these opportunities. Still, it remains a promising model for helping refugees gain autonomy. It points out the importance of taking seriously the ways that other macroeconomic policies can support refugees.

Economic integration is more realistic than many imagine. Uganda has successfully integrated refugees in its economy, even without Western support.[12] Under the "self-reliance strategy," it has rejected encampment and allowed refugees the right to work and freedom of movement. Rather than giving refugees food rations, as they would receive in camps, the government assigned refugees plots of land to cultivate both for subsistence and for commercial agriculture. In cities, refugees are allowed to start businesses and work for wages. In the capital, Kampala, 21 percent of refugees run businesses that create jobs for local Ugandans—40 percent of employees of refugee businesses are Ugandan citizens. In other words, allowing refugees to work and be entrepreneurial has been beneficial to the local economy and local population.[13] To be sure, there are problems and informal barriers to market participation. But insofar as refugees are able to be autonomous, take care of themselves, and even contribute to their host community, it is far better than either camps or informal and exploitative work in cities in other countries. It may not be a complete solution for refugees—most are still waiting to go home—but it at the very least allows them to access the minimum conditions of human dignity while they wait.

POLITICAL INTEGRATION

Refugees who remain noncitizens of the countries they are living in are not only economically but politically powerless. To exercise agency politically means to act in ways that express your views and to be represented when decisions that affect you are made. We usually think of political agency through activities associated with citizenship: voting in elections, running for office, or taking part in a town hall or other public forum. Ordinarily, because refugees are not citizens in the countries they live in, we would expect that it would be difficult to afford them political rights in these ways.

Yet there are policies that Western states can support that would encourage political agency among refugees. *Disaggregated citizenship* is one way for refugees who are not yet citizens to exercise political agency.[14] The idea behind this is fairly simple. Right now citizenship is all or nothing: either you get the freedom, autonomy, and rights that come with citizenship or you're denied them; either you're resettled in Canada and on a path to full citizenship or you're totally excluded in a refugee camp in Kenya; either you're given asylum and a path to citizenship in Europe or you're denied asylum and must live illegally in the shadows. Disaggregated citizenship would mean that we disaggregate or separate out the social right and political privileges that come with citizenship so that refugees in host countries or asylum seekers who are waiting for their claims to be decided could be allowed to participate politically in some, though not all, ways. States could give out certain political or social rights, without necessarily granting nationality or permanent status. This would be a way of allowing refugees to have some political agency and participate in the political life of their host community, but without insisting that states immediately and fully grant citizenship.

The EU has a model of disaggregated citizenship. A non-European citizen might receive different rights at the local, national, and supranational levels. One may have certain political rights in the EU, for instance, but not the same rights as a national. For example, the Netherlands grants "city citizenship" to nonnationals after five years of living in the Netherlands, and this allows them to vote in citywide elections.[15] This has the effect of including noncitizens in political discussions, taking seriously their need to participate as political agents. We could imagine a similar disaggregated citizenship for refugees in the Global South. Refugees there could be given a kind of "city citizenship," so they could engage in local political processes that affect their interests and make sure their opinions are taken seriously in policymaking.

Though this would only be a partial and temporary way of granting political and social rights, it would be meaningful to the many refugees who spend years or decades living as refugees in the Global South. Disaggregating social and political rights from full citizenship for refugees who are in temporary situations—either in refugee camps or without authorization in cities, both in the Global South and in Europe—could increase the agency and autonomy that are essential for a life with dignity.

One might object that this is not the kind of political integration refugees want—they want to become permanent citizens of the country they are living in so that they can live without fear that they will be forced to move again. Perhaps this is true for some, but there is good reason to believe that it is not true for all. One scholar, Alex Aleinikoff, has argued that we exhibit a "membership bias" when we assume that refugees want to become citizens. Based on his work with refugees, he believes that some refugees would prefer a flexible political membership that would allow them to keep their options open, either returning home or resettling elsewhere.[16] The problem is that refugees get stuck: when they leave their home country, they usually end up in the country next door and often have no choice but to stay there. They can't go home, aren't allowed to integrate, and can't travel elsewhere to find work. Working out regional mobility schemes, where refugees could travel to find work, would benefit host states and provide refugees a good they have been fundamentally deprived of.[17] Disaggregated citizenship could support this kind of flexibility.

Political integration may also mean that refugees play a larger role in shaping international policies. Aleinikoff has proposed the creation of a Refugee Executive Committee to ensure that refugees are represented in conversations about global responses to refugee crises. The UN has for a long time drawn upon token refugee involvement—refugees who talk about a business they've started or their success at university. While it's important to appreciate the achievements of refugees, this is very different from including them in a way that requires us to listen to them and take seriously their perspectives.

It may turn out that what refugees actually need and want is different from what we imagine, and they may have suggestions that state actors and policymakers have not considered. Much as the international community has focused on providing refugees food and housing, Aleinikoff speculates that refugees would argue that what they really need is the ability to take care of themselves. To do this, they need cash and access to the internet and electricity. These are not generally goods that the international community thinks of as needed for refugees, but they may end up being crucial for refugees in the twenty-first century.[18] The best way to know what refugees need is to include them in the political processes that determine their lives. Integrating refugees into international political processes is essential in undermining structural injustice.

Policies like these that support the integration of refugees in the Global South, rather than in camps or without support in cities, would go a long way to helping refugees gain refuge and access the minimum conditions of human dignity. Citizens of powerful states and members of the international community who share responsibility for the protection of refugees could take political responsibility for changing the nature of the international refugee system by supporting such policies.

SUPPORTING, EXPANDING, AND NORMALIZING RESETTLEMENT AND ASYLUM

Given that economic and political integration will take time to achieve, it is also incumbent on us to reform the durable solutions so that refugees who don't have access to refuge in the Global South have other morally acceptable options. Asylum and resettlement still stand as the only real options for some. The resettlement program exists to help refugees who *cannot be helped* in refugee camps in the Global South. The UN estimates that about 8 percent of refugees are in need of resettlement, including people with urgent medical needs who cannot be cared for in refugee camps, women and girls at risk, survivors of torture and violence, and children who have been orphaned or are otherwise vulnerable.[19] While most refugees would benefit from resettlement, the refugees who are referred for resettlement in the West are those who simply cannot be protected elsewhere. Failing to support resettlement of such refugees is tantamount to denying the most vulnerable protection or help.

Reforming resettlement policies will require two elements. First, more states have to be more willing to resettle refugees. Though this is a challenge, it's not insurmountable. In a world with a global population of seven billion, absorbing twenty-five million refugees is not impossible. If Western countries agreed to take larger numbers, encouraging middle-income countries to resettle and work regionally to absorb refugees, then finding permanent homes for refugees would be within reach.[20] Regardless of how it's done in practice, more states need to have resettlement programs, and those that already have them need to be willing to increase their caps.

Second, resettlement requires more global cooperation. If our policies are to dismantle structural injustice, our decisions around resettlement and asylum should be made in coordination with those of other countries and with consideration for the effects on refugees themselves. Decisions around asylum and resettlement are usually made unilaterally, without consideration of how such policies connect to the policies of other countries or of their cumulative effect. Attentiveness to structural injustice demands that we think about our shared responsibility to work with other countries. The need for greater global coordination was acknowledged in the Global Compact on Refugees recently developed by the UN. The compact reflects an increasingly global recognition that states need to work together and take the collective effects of their actions seriously.

Though global cooperation around refugees might seem aspirational today, we've done it in the past. After the Hungarian Revolution in 1956, two hundred thousand Hungarians fled to Austria, increasing the Austrian population by 3 percent. But rather than let Hungarians flounder in the refugee camp that opened to host them, a coalition of thirty-seven countries worked together to find new homes for these refugees. In less than ten weeks, half of the refugees were resettled in other countries.[21] Had any one country acted alone, rather than as a coalition, it is unlikely that this crisis would have ended the way it did. The responsibility for the refugees was broadly shared, the solution was worked out in collaboration, and, consequently, the economic and political burden was manageable.

That's the way we ought to envision resettlement—a system where responsibility is shared. Rather than simply encouraging a particular Western country to resettle more refugees—though this is a good step—we ought to be encouraging countries to work collectively to resettle larger numbers of refugees more efficiently. The Hungarian example proves that such coordinated action is possible, and that it is perhaps the only way to envision an asylum and resettlement system robust enough to address the extreme injustice refugees experience today.

There is another reason why supporting asylum and resettlement in the West is crucial. These policies signal to other countries our willingness to play a meaningful role in refugee protection. If we were to abandon resettlement, we are essentially asking the poorest countries in the Global South to bear the whole burden of helping refugees. It would be difficult to convince other countries to host large numbers of refugees—not to mention provide work authorization and political rights—if Western states ceased to take in at least some refugees. Anne Richard, the former US assistant secretary of state for population, refugees and migration, has argued that resettlement is necessary for what she calls "humanitarian diplomacy." This alludes to the difficulty in convincing countries like Jordan or Lebanon to continue letting in refugees and to improve treatment if the United States itself is not actively helping refugees.[22] It communicates a message to other countries that refugees are important and that we care enough about their well-being to allow them into our communities.

In addition to countries working together, individuals should be able to play a larger role in resettling refugees. The Canadian Private Sponsorship program provides a model for thinking about how both states and citizens can become involved in resettlement. Private Canadian citizens, either as groups of five individuals or as part of an organization (such as a faith-based community or ethnocultural group), can sponsor a refugee for resettlement in Canada. Sponsors agree to provide financial support and settlement assistance for one year after the refugee arrives. The refugees that are sponsored through this program are not included in the overall quota the Canadian government has agreed to take in. Over three hundred thousand refugees have been resettled through this program since it came into existence. One of the most noticeable effects is that the individually sponsored refugees have an easier time integrating than government-sponsored refugees. This is not surprising since a community is standing by to help them. But another effect can be seen in the general outlook surrounding refugees. Because so many people get to know refugees in such a personal way, Canadians tend to be supportive of refugees in general. Civil society is able to engage meaningfully with refugees, and these individuals and communities have begun to overturn the assumption that refugees don't matter. Though only a few countries at the moment have a similar model, there is hope that it can be exported to other contexts.[23]

WHAT SHOULD INDIVIDUALS DO?

There is no shortage of alternative policies that would dismantle some of the structural injustice that prevents refugees from accessing the minimum conditions of human dignity. Political will is always the issue. Here is where individuals come in: most democratic states are responsive to the demands of their citizens. When citizens become aware that there are other, more just ways we could be funding and supporting refugee protection, they can demand their governments take up these policies. While there are many things that individuals can do to directly help refugees—donating money, volunteering time to work with them, supporting petitions—individuals can also play a role in dismantling structural injustice.

Individuals can challenge the implicit norms that permit refugees to be treated in the ways that I've described in this book. Structural injustice of all kinds is supported by tacit acceptance of certain norms. Norms are the underlying, often unspoken, principles that guide our actions and justify them. For example, in many cultures consumerism, buying things for the sake of buying them, is a dominant norm. This norm makes it totally acceptable to own more than you need, even if it means going into debt. Norms can be powerful drivers of behavior, even though they often function without our being aware of them.

One of the strongest norms implicit in our treatment of refugees is this: refugees don't matter, or matter less than fellow citizens.

Refugees are often thought of as different from fellow citizens, as outsiders. Because they are not like us, we can help them if we feel like it, to the extent that we think we can, but if we are otherwise occupied, it's okay to ignore them. It's easy to see how this norm gives rise to the status quo. But this norm remains dominant only if individuals allow it to go unchallenged. One of the most important ways that individuals can share responsibility for the structural injustice of the refugee system is by challenging the norm that refugees don't matter.

This norm is at the core of the state behaviors and policies detailed in this book. If states rescue refugees by putting them in camps and forbidding them from working; by tolerating them in cities but not offering them education, healthcare, or basic protections; or by detaining them in squalid camps, offshore processing centers, or detention centers, we are meant to assume that this is the best they can do and refugees should be grateful for whatever help they get. The unstated norm that supports this is that because refugees are not citizens, once they are *rescued* from their oppressive governments, countries are free to impose whatever policies they want.

This norm makes it acceptable to see human rights violations as a matter of course. Documented examples of human rights violations against refugees and asylum seekers in Western countries are rarely prosecuted or even criticized. Hungarian police pepper-spray refugees who are standing still,[24] women and children are sexually assaulted in refugee camps,[25] and children are separated from their parents and detained, to name a few examples from Western countries.[26] In the Global South, human rights are routinely violated in camps and urban spaces.[27]

When brought to light, of course, this norm does not hold up to moral scrutiny. First, it goes against both the spirit and the letter of human rights. States must take seriously the human rights of all residents and cannot violate the rights of refugees in the name of security or stability. Second, *any* moral framework that asks us to take human dignity seriously—whether Kantian, consequentalist, or religious—would find the global treatment of refugees unacceptable. Even the nationalist framework argues that though we can give more weight to the interest of fellow citizens, we must treat all people with dignity and respect their human rights.

Among the most important things individuals can do to undermine structural injustice is to make this norm explicit and to challenge it. Individuals can make clear that refugees matter and that the treatment of refugees, regardless of motives, will be subject to moral scrutiny.

Individuals can begin to do so simply by learning more. There has never been a time when so much information about refugees has been available as today. It is possible to read independent human rights reports (published by Amnesty International, Human Rights Watch, Oxfam, and others), accounts from journalists on the ground, and the stories of refugees themselves. Developing a counternarrative to the all too common antirefugee rhetoric first requires an understanding of the realities of refugee life.

Individuals can then challenge the norms that support structural injustice in different ways. Sometimes it can be as intimate as talking to family and friends about refugees. Other times it may require collective political action. Groups of individuals can and have pushed back against their country's deterrence policies, challenging them through protests, online activism, and holding elected officials accountable for their lack of support for refugees. Individuals can push for safe and legal passage for asylum seekers to come to the countries that will grant asylum or the right of asylum seekers to claim asylum in embassies close to conflict. Citizens can insist that as long as asylum requires clandestine movement, we need search-and-rescue operations at sea and in the desert, and not criminalize people trying to help refugees. Individuals, acting collectively, can demand that people have the chance to seek asylum and are treated humanely when they do so.

In short, the pernicious norms that uphold structural injustice will only change if individuals insist that refugees deserve refuge. There is no shortage of creative ways for individuals to do this.

CONCLUSION: NEITHER RECKLESS OPTIMISM NOR RECKLESS DESPAIR

This book has painted a bleak picture of what it means to be a refugee in the twenty-first century. This might lead some to what the philosopher Hannah Arendt called "reckless despair"—believing that a problem is so bad that we can't do anything about it.[28] Such despair is reckless because it usually leaves the injustice in place and allows the status quo to continue unchallenged. Yet she also cautioned us to avoid "reckless optimism"—a kind of optimism that believes that making a difference will be easy and we can be certain that we can make things better. This optimism is reckless because it doesn't appreciate the depth of the problem and all that would need to change in order to address it. Reckless optimism often changes into reckless despair once we feel that we've done everything we can and things still aren't better. Both attitudes are problematic because they ultimately lead to inaction; they prevent us from engaging deeply with the problem and doing what is in our power to change it.

I think we need a different attitude to deal with complex global problems like the global refugee crisis, issues that involve profound human suffering and that do not have simple solutions. I hope that readers take a nuanced stance and acknowledge that though the problem for refugees is complex and will not be easy to change, it is an injustice so profound that we cannot ignore it. As the philosopher Kate Norlock put it, we need an attitude of "sustained moral motivation, resilience and even cheer" that would allow us a "willingness to return to the same task repeatedly, to maintain efforts and to continually renew commitments."[29] In my view, this is the best way to respond to deeply entrenched injustices like the global refugee regime, an attitude that would allow us to linger between reckless despair and reckless optimism.

Though it sometimes seems improbable, the status quo can change. One of the problems with social structures, such as the ones that I've described in this book as structural injustices, is that they come to seem natural and inevitable. Of course we put refugees in camps—where else would we put them? Of course refugees aren't allowed to work; otherwise there would be too much competition with citizens for jobs. Of course we only resettle a handful of refugees; we can't be expected to do more than that if it's unpopular with our citizens. Yet these structures are not inevitable, and they can be challenged in many different ways. Many individuals have, in fact, challenged them.

Eric and Philippa Kempson moved to Greece from England to enjoy the beautiful climate and water.[30] When refugees started showing up on the beach in front of their house, they reacted not with resentment at the people spoiling their peaceful life, but by becoming first-line responders. They kept an eye out for boats arriving and provided the voyagers food, water, and clothing. This assistance was not offered by everyone—some Greeks even threatened the Kempsons for helping refugees. The mayor of the island of Kos said that they should do nothing to help the asylum seekers, not even offer a cup of water. The Greek government located the asylum registration center forty miles from the shore where refugees were landing, and not only was there no transportation to the centers, it was illegal until late 2015 to give asylum seekers a ride. Anyone caught helping in this way could be accused of human smuggling. The Kempsons were undeterred. "When you see two-week-old children, people with cut feet and people who haven't eaten for days—you can't do nothing," Eric explained.[31]

In November 2015, Dirk Volz and his partner Mario invited a group of twenty-four refugees to live with them in their home in Berlin. At the height of the crisis, many Germans were worried about the cultural changes refugees from predominantly Muslim countries would bring to Germany. Many friends and neighbors in Berlin responded to Dirk and Mario's act of generosity by posting insulting letters on their front door or by yelling death threats on the street. Friends worried that because they were gay, these Muslim refugees might even kill them in their sleep. But no one wanted to kill them, and no one insulted their sexual orientation. The most difficult thing for them was that the refugees used a lot of sugar and salt: "So we bought it at the market and that was that." The real disappointment for them was the reaction of their fellow Germans who acted, "as if we all don't have a responsibility in the world's happenings," Dirk wrote in a blog post.[32]

In France Jean-René Etchegaray, the mayor of a town near the Spanish border called Bayonne, ignored the demands of officials in Paris and offered shelter to African asylum seekers.[33] The mayor didn't necessarily want African migrants camping out in his town's center, but if they were going to be in his town, he believed they should live in a "condition of dignity." So he found a place for them to live and figured out a way to get them hot meals. He personally accompanied them to their new place of living and showed them where the toilets were. He did this despite criticism and condemnation from officials in Paris.

Hans Breuer was a father of two in Austria, where he worked as a shepherd, herding his sheep across the countryside.[34] When he learned what was happening to refugees in Eastern Europe in the summer of 2015, he knew that he had to help them. He learned that Hungary put refugees in cages in camps and fed them like animals. So he went to Hungary with the aim of helping refugee families get to Austria, where they could continue on their journey. Hans would meet refugees at the train station in Hungary and drive them to Austria. If police came by, he would hide the refugees under a blanket in his back seat. He risked years in jail for doing this. Hans is Jewish and spent his life hearing stories about Jews escaping in creative ways from the Nazis. Hans's father was a dissident who fled Austria for Britain before the war. "It makes me cry again and again if I think of my father, of his situation, and of other immigrants—and I put it together with these people. . . . There is too much similarity between these two situations—one seventy years ago, and one now."[35]

In 2018, the Italian government passed a bill that punished rescue boats that brought migrants to Italy without permission with prison sentences of up to twenty years. This new law was at the front of the mind of Carlo Giarratano, a Sicilian fishing boat captain, when he heard the cries of about fifty migrants aboard a rubber dingy off the coast of Libya. When he realized they had capsized and were in danger of drowning, he gave them food and water and coordinated their transfer to the Italian shore. "I'd be lying if I told you I didn't think I might end up in prison when I saw that dinghy in distress," he said.[36] Others in similar positions have made the same decision. Pia Klemp and Carola Rackete are two German sea captains who also chose to defy what they saw as an unjust law and risk imprisonment by rescuing migrants at sea and bringing them to Italy.

Erica, Philippa, Dirk, Mario, Jean-René, Hans, Carlo, Pia, and Carola responded to refugees with an attitude of defiance and approached the situation with neither reckless optimism nor reckless despair. They did not do what many people around them were doing and simply turn a blind eye to the treatment of refugees; in fact, they went out of their way to help them at great personal risk. For them, the treatment of refugees that we have grown used to was not inevitable. It wasn't even acceptable. The structures that encourage us to think of refugees as less than human, as not deserving the same dignified treatment that we would insist on for ourselves, did not work on them. Carlo Giarratano, the Italian fishing boat captain, wondered "if even one of our politicians has ever heard desperate cries for help at high sea in the black of night. I wonder what they would have done. No human being—sailor or not—would have turned away."[37]

I've written this book with the belief that we cannot change unjust situations until we fully understand them. Understanding the crisis for refugees as they seek refuge and the role our states have played in creating their dire need puts us in a better position to make circumstances more just for refugees. Seeing the crisis for refugees as a structural injustice makes it harder to dismiss their demands and to dehumanize them in the ways that have become so common. My hope for this book is that understanding will lead to action and more people will respond like the courageous individuals just described. Our response must be nothing less than to insist on the rights and dignity of refugees wherever they are.

ACKNOWLEDGMENTS

I gratefully acknowledge all the help and encouragement I received from colleagues, students, friends and family over the years that I worked on this book. This book benefited tremendously from the vibrant intellectual community that I have the good fortune to be a part of. Many of the chapters were presented to academic audiences at different universities across the United States, Canada, and Europe. I am enormously thankful to those who invited me to speak and for the discussions that took place at these events. I also presented some of the ideas in this book in nonacademic settings such as churches, synagogues, and libraries. I would like to thank the audience members who came to these talks for their questions and for sharing their (sometimes strong) opinions with me.

I am fortunate to work at a supportive institution that values public scholarship. I gratefully acknowledge the support of the College of Social Sciences and Humanities at Northeastern University. I thank my chair, Ron Sandler, for encouraging me to take on this project and supporting me throughout the process of writing. I am grateful to my colleagues in the Department of Philosophy and Religion at

Northeastern for creating a friendly, collegial, and intellectually rich environment. In particular, I would like to thank those who provided feedback on the manuscript and advice on doing public scholarship: Nicole Aljoe, John Basl, Liz Bucar, Adam Hosein, Carla Kaplan, and Rory Smead. I am incredibly grateful to the group of colleagues, friends, and students who participated in a workshop on this book in January 2019: Kathy Libal, Eleni Coundouriotis, Rebecca Riccio, Patti Lenard, Marina McCoy, Karine Blandel, Francesca Batault, and Jackie Reimer. Thank you for your encouragement of the project and invaluable feedback. I would also like to thank all my students who read parts of the book and shared their thoughts about it with me.

During my sabbatical I was a fellow at the Carr Center for Human Rights Policy at the Harvard Kennedy School and benefited enormously from my time there. I would like to thank Sushma Raman, Mathias Risse, Isabela Gerbelli Garbin Ramanzini, Eric Blumenson, and Jacqueline Bhabha in particular for discussing my project with me and giving feedback on some of the chapters.

I would like to express my gratitude to the Norwegian Research Council for supporting a research group that I've been involved with throughout this project, the Globalizing Minority Rights Project. I would like to thank all the members of this research group for many stimulating conversations. I thank Annamari Vitikainen and Kasper Lippert-Rasmussen for leading this group and bringing us together at the Arctic University of Norway, sometimes in almost twenty-four hours of daylight, sometimes in almost twenty-four hours of darkness.

Lucy Randall at Oxford University Press has been a wonderful editor to work with, and I am grateful to her for her encouragement of this project even at its earliest stages. I would like to thank Brandon Proia for his guidance with the project and his keen editorial sense. I thank Henry Schull and Sam Haas for their help preparing the manuscript. I am grateful to the anonymous reviewers at Oxford for their generous comments and constructive criticism. I would like to express my deep gratitude to David Owen for his feedback and support of this project as a work of public scholarship.

I owe a large debt of gratitude to the journalists, scholars, and human rights activists who have written the stories of refugees I use in this book. Without their courageous and often dangerous work with refugees, we would not know their stories or hear their voices. I am indebted to the refugees themselves who shared their experiences so openly. My understanding of the situation that I present in this book is indebted to them.

Family comes in many shapes, and I could not have written this book without the support of friends who have become like family. Hege, Mary, Susanne, Liza, Aziza, Alice—your friendship has been so important to me. I thank Ed for his support and for being a great coparent. I am so grateful to Mark for his friendship, for the endless hours of conversation and for cheering me on every step of the way. This book is dedicated with gratitude to my father, who devoted his life to his family, and in loving memory of my mother. Finally, a special note of thanks, appreciation and love to Auggie and Kersi.

Serena Parekh

Boston, December 2019

NOTES

Preface: Turbulence and Fear

1. Brodesser-Akner, "Christie."
2. CNN, "2015 Paris Terror Attacks."
3. Friedman, "Where America's Terrorists."
4. Crisp, "Refugees"; Nowrasteh, "Syrian Refugees."
5. Nichols, "Odds of Fatal Terror."
6. Nowrasteh, "Syrian Refugees."
7. Cunningham, "Brutal, Thorough Process."
8. Pinto Arena, "Islamic Terrorism."
9. Crisp, "Refugees."
10. Arbour et al., *Global Refugee Crisis*.
11. Carroll, "European Refugee Crisis."
12. Palma, "Crime in Sweden, Part I."
13. Sikkink, *Evidence*, p. 157.
14. Eck and Fariss, "No, Sweden Isn't Hiding."
15. Stone, "Donald Trump Is Wrong"; Deutsche Welle, "Germany's Crime Rate."
16. *Economist*, "Confusion over Immigration."
17. Palma, "Crime in Sweden, Part II."
18. Ingraham, "Two Charts Demolish." The title of a scholarly article on this subject is telling: "Immigration Reduces Crime: An Emerging Scholarly Consensus." Lee and Martinez, "Immigration Reduces Crime."
19. Walker, "Russia Spreading Fake News."
20. Higgins, "Norway Offers Migrants."

21. Davis and Sengupta, "Trump Administration Rejects Study."
22. Evans and Fitzgerald, "Economic and Social Outcomes."
23. Bier 2019 notes other economic benefits of refugees to the US economy. For example: while refugees' and asylees' high school graduation rates are lower than those of US adults as a whole, refugees' and asylees' college graduation rates are slightly higher. Further, adult refugee and asylee full-time employment grows over time, to be slightly higher than all US adults. Over time, refugee and asylee median family income almost doubles, from $32,539 to $59,433, virtually identical to the US average.
24. Dearden, "Germany 'Spent More.' "
25. Clemens, "Real Economic Cost."
26. Stone, "Refugee Crisis."
27. To put it in perspective, the top ten refugee-hosting countries, which host about 85 percent of the world's refugees, have only 2.5 percent of global income. By contrast, Europe, which has 20 percent of global income, has 11 percent of the world's refugees, and the United States, which has 25 percent of global income, has only 1 percent of the world's refugees (Miliband, *Rescue*, pp. 29–30).
28. This is according to an OECD report and reports by the IMF. Cassidy, "Economics of Syrian Refugees." In Cassidy's view, "These figures make the point that, even in countries facing huge influxes of refugees, the impact on the economy as a whole is usually not very large. The biggest challenges in accommodating refugees are social and political, rather than economic."
29. Cassidy, "Economics of Syrian Refugees."
30. Airbel, "Madeline Albright."
31. Alrababa'h and Williamson, "Jordan Shut Out 60,000."
32. Boston Globe, "Australia Subjects Refugees." I discuss Australia's policies in more detail in Chapter 5.
33. Sharot, *Influential Mind*.

Introduction

1. Sina's story comes from McDonald-Gibson, *Cast Away*.
2. In 2013, that number had been a little over four hundred thousand. Pew, "Numbers of Refugees."
3. Agerholm, "Refugees Are 'Muslim Invaders.' "
4. Taub, "Brits Want to Deploy."
5. As Betts and Collier put it, "Refugees are effectively offered a false choice between three dismal options: encampment, urban destitution, or perilous journeys. For refugees, these inadequate options—camps, urban destitution, and boats—*are* the modern global refugee regime" (*Refuge*, p. 55).

6. Betts and Collier, *Refuge,* p. 8. That is, only about 2 percent have access to one of the official "durable solutions": resettlement, voluntary return, or local integration.
7. UNHCR, "Figures at a Glance." This is the site where the UN High Commissioner for Refugees updates statistics about refugees and forced displacement. Readers should refer to this website to see updated statistics on the refugee situation (https://www.unhcr.org/en-us/figures-at-a-glance.html).
8. Airbel, "Alex Alienikof."
9. "At least since 1994, annual refugee resettlement flows as a percentage of the global refugee populations [have] never exceeded 1 percent." FitzGerald, *Refuge beyond Reach,* p. 3. For example, in 2018, 92,400 refugees were resettled out of a total of 25.9 million (UNHCR, "Figures at a Glance"). That is, 0.357 percent of refugees, or fewer than four out of every one thousand, were resettled.
10. The UN prioritizes for resettlement those who face "specific or urgent protection risks." In 2018, 1.4 million refugees were included in this category. UNHCR, *Projected Resettlement Needs,* p. 9.
11. Betts and Collier, *Refuge,* p. 3.
12. Betts and Collier, *Refuge,* p. 3.
13. Since 2015, more than 1.4 million people have sought asylum in Europe. UNHCR, "Figures at a Glance."
14. "It is estimated that the average duration of major refugee situations, protracted or not, has increased: from 9 years in 1993 to 17 years in 2003" (UNHCR, "Protracted Refugee Situations," p. 2). To be clear, this is not the time refugees spend in refugee camps but the average period that people spend as refugees, whether in camps or elsewhere. The average length of time people spend in refugee camps is twelve years (McClelland, "How to Build," quoted in Oliver, "Abolish Refugee Detention," p. 118). The figure of seventeen years, however, only includes refugees under the UNHCR's mandate and does not include Palestinian refugees from 1948 or 1967, the inclusion of whom would increase the average significantly (BBC, "Refugee Camp Statistics").
15. Bhabha, *Can We Solve,* p. 94.
16. Betts and Collier, *Refuge,* p. 54. A protracted situation is defined as one lasting more than five years.
17. Oliver, "Abolish Refugee Detention," p. 118.
18. Though Turkey hosts more than two million refugees, the conditions for refugees are minimal at best, and often grossly insufficient (Akdemir, "Syrian Refugees in Turkey"). For example, only 9.12 percent of refugees live in camps. The rest "are trying to survive on their own—many by begging, collecting garbage, or being exploited in the informal economy," with only 3 percent getting any form of social benefits from the Turkish government. Further, only

24 percent of Syrian children outside of camps have access to education in Turkey.

19. Kingsley, "Migration to Europe."
20. Neuman, "Amnesty International."
21. Sherlock, "Migrants Captured in Libya."
22. This is an observation based on my own experience giving talks about refugees to students, academics, and the general public between 2016 and 2019.
23. Roxström and Gibney, "Legal and Ethical Obligations."
24. Betts and Collier, *Refuge*, pp. 40–41.
25. Gibney, *Ethics and Politics*; Aleinikoff, "State-Centered Refugee Law."
26. Betts and Collier, *Refuge*.
27. This is, in part, what justifies their claims of national sovereignty. As John Locke explained as long ago as the seventeenth century, political sovereignty is justified precisely because states are able to protect the human rights of their residents. Locke, *Second Treatise of Government*. In contemporary terms, this is considered the *normative basis of states*: states can exercise legitimate sovereign power because the protection of human rights that results ultimately makes everyone better off. Betts and Loescher, "Refugees in International Relations," p. 6.
28. This treaty, formally known as the Convention Relating to the Status of Refugees, at first applied only to refugees fleeing Europe before January 1951. In 1967 a protocol was added that removed these limitations so that it applied to refugees fleeing anytime from any country.
29. Abadi, "The Damn Will Hold."
30. I discuss these grounds in more detail in Chapter 6.
31. Miller, *Strangers in Our Midst*, p. 83.
32. Shue, *Basic Rights*.
33. Rawls, *The Law of Peoples*, p. 432.
34. Aleinikoff, "State-Centered Refugee Law," p. 133.
35. David Miller, for example, writes that the obligations to help refugees are parallel to "the duty of rescue borne by individuals in emergencies" (*Strangers in Our Midst*, p. 78). For Betts and Collier, providing "refuge is about fulfilling our duty of rescue" (*Refuge*, p. 6). This way of seeing the position of Western states vis-à-vis refugees is so widely accepted that David Milliband, a former UK member of Parliament and current head of the International Rescue Committee, titled his recent book on the obligations of Western states to refugees *Rescue*.
36. As David Miller goes on to explain, duties of rescue do not entail "an unlimited and unconditional obligation to carry out rescues: the duty that it imposes aims to safeguard the urgent interests of the victim without placing an unacceptable burden on the rescuers" (*Strangers in Our Midst*, p. 78).
37. Betts and Collier, *Refuge*.

38. UNHCR, "Global Trends 2018." Despite this, less than 2 percent of all humanitarian spending goes to education (Miliband, *Rescue*, p. 78).
39. Tinti and Reitano, *Migrant, Refugee, Smuggler, Saviour*, p. 32.

Chapter 1

1. Semple, "Fleeing Gangs."
2. I discuss these examples later in the chapter.
3. Convention Relating to the Status of Refugees, Article 1. This Convention is also known as the 1951 Refugee Convention.
4. Wagner, "B Is for Bisexual."
5. US Citizenship and Immigration Services, "Refugees." See also US Department of State, "Access."
6. Benner and Dickerson, "Sessions Says."
7. Betts and Collier, *Refuge*, p. 5.
8. Betts and Collier, *Refuge*, p. 47.
9. Fertig and Blue, "A Mother and Daughter."
10. Agier, *Managing the Undesirables*.
11. UNHCR, "UNHCR Global Trends 2014," p. 44.
12. This example is taken from Agier, *Managing the Undesirables*, p. 33.
13. Kingsley, *New Odyssey*, p. 42.
14. UNHCR, "Return of People."
15. Oberman, "Refugees and Economic Migrants."
16. McDonald-Gibson, "For Europe, Arab Lives." See also the International Organization for Migration, "Migration Agency Issues Report."
17. Bhabha, *Can We Solve*, p. 99.
18. McAdam, *Climate Change*, p. 16.
19. See Chapter 5, "The Price We Demand for Asylum" for a more detailed examination of the kinds of journeys many take to seek asylum.
20. Walzer, *Spheres of Justice*, p. 49.
21. Carens, *Ethics of Immigration*, p. 201.
22. Ferracioli, "Appeal and Danger," p. 125.
23. Miller, *Strangers in Our Midst*, p. 83.
24. Smith, "Warehousing Refugees," p. 42.
25. In 2018, Canada, for the first time since the United States' refugee resettlement program began in 1980, resettled more refugees than any other country in the world (Radford and Connor, "Canada Now Leads").
26. UNHCR, "Global Trends 2015," p. 3.
27. Radford and Connor, "Canada Now Leads," 2019.
28. FitzGerland, *Refuge beyond Reach*, p. 3; UNHCR, "Figures at a Glance"; and Mwangi, "Only 1% of Refugees." In 2018, 92,400 refugees were resettled out of 25.9 million (0.357 percent).

29. For example, in the US context, the 1980 Refugee Act states that "the underlying principle is that refugee admission is an exceptional *ex gratia* act provided by the United States in furthering foreign and humanitarian policies" (quoted in Singer and Singer, "Ethics of Refugee Policy," p. 116).
30. In the view of some, this was deliberate. The UNHCR was designed to help refugees in a way that did not threaten countries' sovereignty. According to Barnett and Finnemore, the UNHCR was designed "to do very little and do only what states told it to do. They made UNHCR completely dependent on voluntary contributions from states and other sources for its funds" (*Rules for the World*, p. 73). "At U.S. insistence, the organization had limited resources and little opportunity to develop any financial independence" (*Rules for the World*, p. 84).
31. UNHCR, "Underfunded Situations."
32. Betts and Collier, *Refuge*, p. 1. They note that ten countries host around 60 percent of the world's refugees.
33. UNHCR, "Seven Facts."
34. Zong and Batalova, "Syrian Refugees."
35. UNHCR, "Figures at a Glance."
36. Betts and Collier, *Refuge*, p. 8.

Chapter 2

1. Rawlence, *City of Thorns*.
2. Schuck, "Modest Proposal," p. 253. The UNHCR's "never-ending funding crisis" (Roxtrom and Gibney, "Legal and Ethical," p. 58) is the result of its structure. It does not get funding based on a UN assessment but is dependent on voluntary contributions of a handful of states: 94 percent of the UNHCR's budget comes from the United States, Japan, and the EU (Loescher, "UNHCR at Fifty," p. 6; Hammerstad, "UNHCR," p. 252).
3. Consequentalists could apply their view in other ways as well. For example, they may think that the greater good can be achieved if each country only considers what's best for its own citizens. This, some might argue, would allow each country to produce the most good consequences for its people and ultimately produce the greatest good for the greatest number.
4. Rawls, *Theory of Justice*.
5. Over ten years, refugees in the United States brought in $63 billion more in revenue than they cost. Davis and Sengupta, "Trump Administration Rejects Study."
6. For Kant, there are different types of contradictions. A "contradiction in concept" is the kind discussed previously, where the maxim cannot be universalized without contradiction. A "contradiction in will" is a case where the maxim

can be thought without contradiction but cannot be put into practice without going against something that you would rationally want.

7. In Kant's words, "Although it is possible that that maxim should be a universal law of nature, it is impossible to will that it do so. For a will that brought that about would conflict with itself, since instances can often arise in which the person in question would need the love and sympathy of others, and he would have no hope of getting the help he desires, being robbed of it by this law of nature springing from his own will." Kant, *Groundwork*, Chapter 2.
8. Singer, "Famine."
9. Kingsley, "96 Days Later." The vigil was successful—the family they were trying to protect is no longer in danger of deportation.
10. Lind, "Trump Administration's Separation." This quotation comes from the president of HIAS, Mark Hetfield.
11. Wooden, "Christians Who Reject."
12. Rahaei, "The Rights of Refugee Women."
13. UNHCR, "Islam."
14. See Donnelly, *Universal Human Rights*; and Forsythe, *Human Rights*.
15. See Beitz, *Idea of Human Rights*; Buchanan, *Heart of Human Rights*; Cohen, *Arch*; Cranston, "Human Rights"; Dworkin, "Rights as Trumps"; Elshtain, "Dignity of the Human"; Feinberg, "Nature and Value"; Gewirth, "Human Dignity"; Gewirth, *Human Rights*; Gould, *Globalizing Democracy*; Hart, "Are There Any Natural Rights?"; Ignatieff, *Human Rights*; Nickel, *Making Sense*; Parekh, *Hannah Arendt*; Pogge, "How Should Human Rights"; Rawls, *Theory of Justice*; Rawls, *Law of Peoples*; Shue, *Basic Rights*; Wellman, *Moral Dimensions*.
16. Glendon, *World Made New*, 2002.
17. United Nations High Commissioner for Human Rights, "International Human Rights Law."
18. Power, *Problem from Hell*.
19. Alrababa'h and Williamson, "Jordan Shut Out."

Chapter 3

1. Kingsley, *New Odyssey*.
2. Arnold, "Rohingya Refugees."
3. See Chapter 2.
4. Rothman, "US Can Handle." Between 1979 and 1982, five hundred thousand refugees were resettled in the United States, Australia, France, and Canada (Bhabha, *Can We Solve*, p. 24). Rothman notes that "there was a widespread feeling that the country owed something to the people whose lives had been endangered by the American military's actions in their country" and, though the number was large, they were easily absorbed.

5. Souter, "Towards a Theory."
6. Martínez, "Today's Migrant Flow."
7. Carens, *Ethics of Immigration*, p. 196.
8. David Owen gives a strong defense of this view in *What Do We Owe Refugees?* See also Owen, "In Loco Civitatas" and Hosein, *Ethics of Migration*.
9. Owen, *What Do We Owe Refugees?*, p. 65.
10. Connor, "Most Displaced."
11. Walzer, *Spheres of Justice*.
12. Miller, *On Nationality*.
13. Miller, *Strangers*, p. 26.
14. For Miller, this right is constrained by other important values such as fairness and the duty to treat all human beings as having equal moral worth. Miller, *Strangers in Our Midst*.
15. Walzer, *Spheres of Justice*.
16. Wellman, "Immigration."
17. For a longer discussion of this, see Parekh, *Refugees*.
18. UNHCR, "Global Trends 2017."
19. David Miller is the exception to this. He acknowledges that "not everyone can be rescued" (*Strangers in Our Midst*, p. 93).
20. In 2018, less than 3% of refugees were able to return to their country of origin (UNHCR, "Global Trends 2018").

Chapter 4

1. Rashid, "Inside the Bangladesh Brothels."
2. Bhabha, "Toleration Deficits."
3. Sullivan, "Sadness in the Slums."
4. Sullivan, "Sadness in the Slums."
5. Betts and Collier, *Refuge*, p. 3.
6. Helton, "What Is Refugee Protection?," p. 31. Verdirame and Harrell-Bond also argue for this position. In their view, Western states used the power they had over the UNHCR, power that came from the dependency of the UNHCR on these states for funding, to encourage UNHCR to support refugee camps in order to "protect the boundaries of 'Fortress Europe' (or 'Fortress Australia')" (Verdirame and Harrell-Bond, *Rights in Exile*, pp. 278–79).
7. Franke, "Political Exclusion of Refugees," p. 317.
8. Betts and Collier, *Refuge*.
9. Betts and Collier, *Refuge*, p. 8.
10. Agier, *Managing the Undesirables*, p. 13.
11. Stevens, "Prisons of the Stateless," p. 66.
12. Betts and Collier, *Refuge*, p. 1.

13. Smith, "Warehousing Refugees"; Verdirame and Harrell-Bond, *Rights in Exile*.
14. Betts et al., "Refugee Economies."
15. McClelland, "How to Build," quoted in Oliver, "Abolish Refugee Detention," p. 118.
16. Rawlence, *City of Thorns*.
17. Hoffmann, "Humanitarian Security," p. 103.
18. Birrell, "Ghost Camp for Refugees."
19. Birrell, "Ghost Camp for Refugees."
20. Birrell, "Ghost Camp for Refugees."
21. Rawlence, *City of Thorns*, p. 113. See also, McConnachie, "Camps of Containment."
22. Hoffmann, "Humanitarian Security," p. 106.
23. Reznick, "Jordan's Azraq Syrian Refugee Camp."
24. This is not universally true. Sometimes refugees in camps are asked to work in order to "earn" their benefits. This is true in Zaatari, where most able adults are strongly encouraged to do some work in the camp.
25. McDonald-Gibson, *Cast Away*, p. 97.
26. McDonald-Gibson, *Cast Away*, p. 80.
27. Rawlence, *City of Thorns*, p. 345.
28. Black, "Sexual Violence Rampant."
29. Miliband, *Rescue*, p. 81. Miliband goes on to note that this is problematic because funding can make a significant difference. Rapes decreased by 45 percent in Dadaab when houses were provided with firewood so that women did not need to go out and collect it, thus increasing their vulnerability to violence (p. 81).
30. Pittaway and Pittaway, "Refugee Woman."
31. Cohen, "What's So Terrible," p. 74.
32. Miliband, *Rescue*, p. 83.
33. Pittaway and Pittaway, "Refugee Woman."
34. Verdirame and Harrell-Bond, *Rights in Exile*.
35. Kingsley, *New Odyssey*.
36. Crisp, "Finding Space."
37. Crisp, "Finding Space," p. 92.
38. Betts and Collier, *Refuge*, p. 3.
39. Cherri and Hariri, "Most Syrian Refugees."
40. Betts and Collier, *Refuge*, p. 143.
41. Amnesty International, "Struggling to Survive."
42. Amnesty International, "Struggling to Survive," p. 26.
43. Amnesty International, "Struggling to Survive," p. 26.
44. Amnesty International, "Struggling to Survive," p. 28.
45. Broomfield, "Pictures of Life."
46. Betts and Collier, *Refuge*, p. 55. The surge of asylum seekers into Europe began in 2015, when 1.3 million asylum seekers made claims. This was double the

previous high mark of 700,000 asylum seekers in 1992 after the collapse of the Soviet Union. In 2014 there were 600,000, and in 2013 there were 400,000 (Pew, "Numbers of Refugees")

Chapter 5

1. Kriel, "Legal Limbo."
2. McDonald-Gibson, *Cast Away*.
3. Benjamin, "Detained on Nauru." Conditions in offshore processing centers used by Australia are highly secretive—aid workers have to sign agreements saying that they won't discuss publicly what they see and risk a two-year jail sentence if they do. Nonetheless, two journalists with *The Guardian*, Karl Mathiesen and Michael Green, posed as snorkeling enthusiasts and covertly spoke to refugees in 2014 and 2016. They reported Benjamin's story.
4. Verhaert, "Day in the Life."
5. This is a fact acknowledged even by government officials. UK minister of state for asylum and immigration Lord Rooker admitted that there were no legal avenues through which a genuine asylum seeker could enter the United Kingdom (Bhabha, *Can We Solve*, p. 83).
6. Tinti and Reitano, *Migrant*, p. 32. Migrants used smugglers to escape from their home countries, to transit through countries on their way to their desired end point, and to cross the sea to reach the EU. Some used smugglers more than once and, in some cases, at every stage in their journey.
7. Kingsley, *New Odyssey*, p. 82.
8. Lanchin, "The Ship of Jewish Refugees."
9. Fiske, *Human Rights*; FitzGerald, *Refuge beyond Reach*; Gibney, *Ethics and Politics*; Hamlin, *Let Me Be*.
10. Hamlin, *Let Me Be*.
11. Fiske, *Human Rights*, p. 196.
12. According to an ACLU report, as of October 2019, the total number of children separated from their parents tops fifty-four hundred, a number much higher than the previous estimate of twenty-seven hundred (Spagat, "Tally of Children"). One of the reasons for the uncertainty is the "lack of a coordinated formal tracking system between the Office of Refugee Resettlement, the arm of Health and Human Services that takes in the children, and the Department of Homeland Security, which separated them from their parents" (Jordan, "Family Separation").
13. Lind, "Trump Administration's Separation." See also, Miroff, "Father 'Took His Own Life'"
14. Bova, "Treated Worse than Dogs."
15. Lind, "The Horrifying Conditions."

16. Darby, "Trump on Abused Immigrant Children"; American Civil Liberties Union, "ACLU Obtains Documents."
17. Gonzales, "Sexual Assault."
18. Jordan and Nixon, "Trump Administration Threatens Jail."
19. Walsh, "Senator Jeff Merkley."
20. Gessen, "Taking Children." This was a tool long used in Soviet Russia to break people being interrogated and increasingly used in contemporary Russia to send a message to people who may speak out against Putin's rule. Gessen thinks the United States is doing something similar; as the title of her article suggests: "Taking Children from Their Parents Is a Form of State Terror."
21. Cumming-Bruce, "Taking Migrant Children."
22. Cronin-Furman, "Treatment of Migrants."
23. Hamlin, *Let Me Be.*
24. Farrell, Evershed, and Davidson, "Nauru Files."
25. Doherty, "International Criminal Court."
26. NPR, "Ex-Aid Worker."
27. Doherty, "International Criminal Court."
28. Di Giorgio and Scherer, "Italy to End."
29. McDonald-Gibson, *Cast Away*, p. 236.
30. Jones, *Violent Borders*, p. 24.
31. Hockenos, "Europe Has Criminalized."
32. "Mediterranean: MSF Rescue," Doctors without Borders.
33. Anderson, "Rescued and Caught," p. 68.
34. Collier, "Beyond the Boat People."
35. UNHCR, "Mediterranean Situation."
36. Fili, "Continuum of Detention."
37. McDonald-Gibson, *Cast Away*, p. 158.
38. Fili, "Continuum of Detention."
39. Fili, "Continuum of Detention."
40. Digidiki and Bhabha, "Emergency within an Emergency," pp. 12–13.
41. Digidiki and Bhabha, "Emergency within an Emergency," p. 14.
42. Freedman, "Sexual and Gender-Based Violence," p. 19.
43. Freedman, "Sexual and Gender-Based Violence," p. 20.
44. Freedman, "Sexual and Gender-Based Violence," p. 22.
45. Pickering, "There's No Evidence"; Doherty, "Asylum Seeker Boat.""
46. Doherty, "Asylum Seeker Boat"
47. Nevins, *Operation Gatekeeper*, 2010; Tinti and Reitano, *Migrant, Refugee, Smuggler, Saviour*, p. 123.
48. Freedman, "Sexual and Gender-Based Violence," p. 22.
49. Tinti and Reitano, *Migrant, Refugee, Smuggler, Saviour*, p. 269.
50. Kingsley, *New Odyssey*, p. 126.
51. Tinti and Reitano, *Migrant, Refugee, Smuggler, Saviour*, p. 32.

52. Tinti and Reitano, *Migrant, Refugee, Smuggler, Saviour*.
53. Jeremy Harding quoted in Kingsley, *New Odyssey*, p. 72.
54. Tinti and Reitano, *Migrant, Refugee, Smuggler, Saviour*.
55. Shire, "Home."
56. Tinti and Reitano, *Migrant, Refugee, Smuggler, Saviour*.
57. UNHCR, "Mediterranean Situation"; 3,538 died in 2014, 3,771 in 2015, 5,096 in 2016, and 3,139 in 2017.
58. Kingsley, *New Odyssey*.
59. Simpson, "I Wanted to Lie Down."
60. Kingsley, *New Odyssey*, p. 40.
61. Tinti and Reitano, *Migrant, Refugee, Smuggler, Saviour*, p. 260.
62. Simpson, "I Wanted to Lie Down."

Chapter 6

1. Rawlence, *City of Thorns*.
2. Rawlence, *City of Thorns*, p. 37.
3. Rawlence, *City of Thorns*, p. 358.
4. McDonald-Gibson, *Cast Away*.
5. In 2015, only three hundred thousand of the more than twenty-five million refugees in the world were resettled, received asylum, or returned to their home country (Betts and Collier, *Refuge*, p. 8).
6. Livingston and Asmolov, "Digital Affordances."
7. Young, *Responsibility*, p. 48.
8. Eckersley, "Responsibility for Climate Change."
9. Crisp, "As the World Abandons Refugees."
10. Frye, "Politics of Reality."
11. This may be because the policies were just to begin with but changed over time. As Rawls put it: "Fair background conditions may exist at one time and be gradually undermined even though no one acts unfairly when their conduct is judged by the rules that apply to transactions within the appropriately circumscribed local situation. . . . We might say: in this case the invisible hand guides things in the wrong direction" (Rawls, *Political Liberalism*, p. 267, cited in Ronzoni, "The Global Order," p. 241).
12. Young, *Responsibility for Justice*.
13. Young, *Responsibility for Justice*, p. 153.
14. See also Miller, *National Responsibility*.
15. These are Young's suggestions in *Responsibility for Justice*.
16. Betts and Collier, *Refuge*, p. 99.
17. Kingsley, *New Odyssey*.
18. Miliband, *Rescue*, p. 7.

19. Hammerstad, "UNHCR and Securitization."
20. See Miller, *National Responsibility*, on the way that benefitting can ground responsibility.
21. Parekh, *Refugees*.
22. Bhabha, *Can We Solve*, p. 24.
23. Aribel, "Alex Aleinikoff."

Conclusion

1. Betts and Collier, *Refuge*.
2. UNHCR, "Global Trends 2018."
3. Gonzales, "Sexual Assault."
4. Betts and Collier, *Refuge*; Bhabha, *Can We Solve*; McDonald-Gibson, *Cast Away*; Amnesty International, "8 Ways"; Taub, "We Know How."
5. Betts and Collier, *Refuge*, p. 3.
6. Bailey and Harvey, "State of Evidence."
7. Barder, "Here's a Simple Way."
8. See Parekh, "Refugees," especially chapter 3.
9. "In a trial in Lebanon, Syrian refugees were given US$100 on ATM cards: every $1 spent generated more than $2 in economic activity." Barder, "Here's a Simple Way."
10. Betts and Collier, *Refuge*.
11. Barbelet et al., "Jordan Compact."
12. This is not to say that Uganda is a model for refugee protection in all ways. In fact, Uganda's policies on the treatment of its LGBT community have forced many to become refugees in recent years. Uganda is one of seventy countries where homosexuality is illegal, and LGBT people face discrimination, arrest, eviction, and violence from police and individuals. Onyulo, "Uganda's Other."
13. Betts and Collier, *Refuge*, p. 160.
14. See Baubock, *Transnational Citizenship*; Benhabib, *Rights of Others*; Glover, "Radically Rethinking"; Hammar, "Dual Citizens."
15. Benhabib, *Rights of Others*, p. 146.
16. Aleinikoff, "State-Centered Refugee Law," p. 134.
17. Aribel. "Alex Aleinikoff"; Long, "From Refugee to Migrant?"
18. Aribel. "Alex Aleinikoff."
19. UNHCR, "Resettlement in the USA."
20. Aribel. "Alex Aleinikoff."
21. Clemens, "Real Economic Cost."
22. Airbel, "Anne Richard."
23. Hyndman, Payne, and Jimenez, "Private Refugee Sponsorship."

24. "After a while, the refugees were handcuffed and led to a little hole the police had opened in the fence. Suddenly, a [Hungarian] policeman approached Abdullah and sprayed his face with pepper spray. He could not see. The policeman forced him to crawl through the little hole in the razor wire fence. As he was crawling, the policeman kicked his butt and laughed. By the time he made it to the Serbian side of the border, he had suffered severe cuts." Bender, "Why the EU Condones."
25. UNHCR, "Refugee Women and Children." See also Freedman, "Engendering Security," and Freedman, "Sexual and Gender-Based Violence."
26. Why are human rights violations against refugees tolerated? In the view of Felix Bender, "The fact is that Hungary's cruel policy toward refugees plays into the hands of other E.U. member states. They turn their eyes from the violation of human rights and the violation of the right to seek asylum, as long as Hungary's policies keep away the refugees from their doorstep. While the dirty job is being done by countries at Europe's periphery, core E.U. member states can prove to their electorates that the refugee crisis is over, that they need not be afraid of more people entering their country." Bender, "Why the EU Condones."
27. See Chapter 4 for specific examples.
28. Arendt, *Origins*.
29. Norlock, "Perpetual Struggle," pp. 6, 7.
30. Kingsley, *New Odyssey*.
31. Kingsley, *New Odyssey*, p. 179.
32. Richards, "Refugee Crisis."
33. Nossiter, "French Mayor."
34. Kingsley, *New Odyssey*.
35. Kingsley, *New Odyssey*, p. 271.
36. Tondo, "Sicilian Fisherman."
37. Tondo, "Sicilian Fisherman."

BIBLIOGRAPHY

Abadi, Cameron. "The Damn Will Hold, Until It Doesn't." *Foreign Policy*, October 6, 2017.

Adar Avsar, Servan. "Responsive Ethics and the War against Terrorism: A Levinasian Perspective." *Journal of Global Ethics* 3, no. 3, December 2007, pp. 317–34, https://doi.org/10.1080/17449620701728030.

Agerholm, Harriet. "Refugees Are 'Muslim Invaders' Not Running for Their Lives, Says Hungarian PM Viktor Orban." *Washington Post*, January 9, 2018, http://www.independent.co.uk/news/world/europe/refugees-muslim-invaders-hungary-viktor-orban-racism-islamophobia-eu-a8149251.html.

Agier, Michel. *Managing the Undesirables: Refugee Camps and Humanitarian Government*. Translated by David Fernbach. Cambridge: Polity Press, 2011.

Airbel. "Alex Aleinikoff on Displaced: Creating a New Refugee Regime." *Medium*, podcast audio, May 1, 2018, https://medium.com/airbel/alex-aleinikoff-on-displaced-creating-a-new-refugee-regime-d541e06cf57e.

Airbel. "Anne Richards on 'Humanitarian Diplomacy' and Dealing with Anti-refugee Sentiment." *Medium*, podcast audio, October 9, 2018, https://medium.com/airbel/anne-richards-on-humanitarian-diplomacy-and-dealing-with-anti-refugee-sentiment-fc0b8d7c4cdf.

Airbel. "Madeline Albright on the Global Refugee Crisis." *Medium*, podcast audio, April 10, 2018, https://www.rescue.org/displaced-podcast/madeleine-albright-global-refugee-crisis.

Airbel. "Owen Barder: We Need an Alternative to Refugee Camps." *Medium*, podcast audio, August 28, 2018, https://medium.com/airbel/owen-barder-d4ce8d83d77.

Akdemir, Ayşegül. "Syrian Refugees in Turkey: Time to Dispel Some Myths." *The Conversation*, September 26, 2017, https://theconversation.com/syrian-refugees-in-turkey-time-to-dispel-some-myths-80996.

Aleinikoff, Alexander T. "State-Centered Refugee Law: From Resettlement to Containment." *Michigan Journal of International Law* 14, no. 1, Fall 1992, pp. 120–38.

Alrababa'h, Ala', and Scott Williamson. "Jordan Shut Out Out [*sic*] 60,000 Syrian Refugees—and Then Saw a Backlash. This Is Why." *Washington Post*, July 20, 2018, http://www.washingtonpost.com/news/monkey-cage/wp/2018/07/20/when-jordan-closed-its-border-to-refugees-the-public-protested-heres-why.

American Civil Liberties Union. "ACLU Obtains Documents Showing Widespread Abuse of Child Immigrants in U.S. Custody." May 23, 2018, http://www.aclu-sandiego.org/aclu-obtains-documents-showing-widespread-abuse-of-child-immigrants-in-u-s-custody.

Amnesty International. "8 Ways to Solve the World Refugee Crisis." October 2015, http://www.amnesty.org/en/latest/campaigns/2015/10/eight-solutions-world-refugee-crisis.

Amnesty International. "Struggling to Survive: Refugees from Syria in Turkey." 2014, http://www.refworld.org/pdfid/546f49fb4.pdf.

Anderson, Elizabeth. "Outlaws." *Good Society* 23, no. 1, 2014, pp. 103–13.

Anderson, Kenneth. "Global Philanthropy and Global Governance: The Problematic Moral Legitimacy of the Relationship between Global Civil Society and the United States." *Giving Well: The Ethics of Philanthropy*, edited by Patricia Illingworth, Thomas Pogge, and Leif Wenar. New York: Oxford University Press, 2011, pp. 149–76.

Anderson, Ruben. "Rescued and Caught: The Humanitarian-Security Nexus at Europe's Frontiers." *The Borders of "Europe": Autonomy of Migration, Tactics of Bordering*, edited by Nicholas De Genova. Durham, NC: Duke University Press, 2017, pp. 64–94.

Arbour, Louise, et al. *The Global Refugee Crisis: How Should We Respond?* N.p.: House of Anansi Press, 2017.

Arendt, Hannah. *The Origins of Totalitarianism*. New York: Harcourt, 1968.

Arnold, Katie. "Rohingya Refugees: Why I Fled; Twelve Stories of Lost Homes, Lost Lives and a Perilous Search for Safety." *CNN*, September 2017, http://www.cnn.com/interactive/2017/09/world/myanmar-rohingya-refugee-stories.

Ashford, Elizabeth. "Obligations of Justice and Beneficence to Aid the Severely Poor." *Giving Well: The Ethics of Philanthropy*, edited by Patricia Illingworth, Thomas Pogge, and Leif Wenar. New York: Oxford University Press, 2011, pp. 26–45.

Bailey, Sarah, and Paul Harvey. *State of Evidence on Humanitarian Cash Transfers: Background Note for the High Level Panel on Humanitarian Cash Transfers*. https://www.odi.org/sites/odi.org.uk/files/odi-assets/publications-opinion-files/9591.pdf.

Barbelet, Veronique, et al. "The Jordan Compact: Lessons Learnt and Implications for Future Refugee Compacts." *Overseas Development Institute*, February 2018, https://www.odi.org/publications/11045-jordan-compact-lessons-learnt-and-implications-future-refugee-compacts.

Barder, Owen. "Here's a Simple Way to Help Refugees: Give Them Cash." *The Telegraph*, September 7, 2015, https://www.telegraph.co.uk/news/worldnews/europe/11848330/Heres-a-simple-way-to-help-refugees-give-them-cash.html.

Barnett, Michael, and Martha Finnemore. *Rules for the World: International Organizations in Global Politics*. Ithaca, NY: Cornell University Press, 2004.

Baubock, Rainer. *Transnational Citizenship: Membership and Rights in International Migration*. Brookfield, VT: Edward Elgar, 1995.

Bauman, Zygmunt. *Strangers at Our Door*. Cambridge: Polity Press, 2016.

BBC. "Refugee Camp Statistics." *More or Less: Behind the Stats*. BBC, May 27, 2016, http://www.bbc.co.uk/programmes/p03wgr2n.

Beitz, Charles R. *The Idea of Human Rights*. New York: Oxford University Press, 2009.

Bender, Felix. "Why the EU Condones Human Rights Violations of Refugees in Hungary." *Open Democracy*, April 15, 2018, http://www.opendemocracy.net/can-europe-make-it/felix-bender/why-eu-condones-human-rights-violations-of-refugees-in-hungary.

Benhabib, Seyla. *The Rights of Others: Aliens, Residents, and Citizens*. New York: Cambridge University Press, 2004.

Benjamin, an Asylum Seeker. "Detained on Nauru: 'This Is the Most Painful Part of My Story—When You Realise No One Cares.'" Reported by Karl Mathiesen and Michael Green. *The Guardian*, March 23, 2017, http://www.theguardian.com/world/australia-books-blog/2017/mar/24/detained-on-nauru-this-is-the-most-painful-part-of-my-story-when-you-realise-no-one-cares.

Benner, Katie, and Caitlin Dickerson. "Sessions Says Domestic and Gang Violence Are Not Grounds for Asylum." *New York Times*, June 11, 2018, https://www.nytimes.com/2018/06/11/us/politics/sessions-domestic-violence-asylum.html.

Betts, Alexander, Louise Bloom, Josiah Kaplan, and Naohiko Omata. "Refugee Economies: Rethinking Popular Assumptions." Humanitarian Innovation Project, Refugee Studies Centre, Oxford University, 2014, http://www.rsc.ox.ac.uk/refugeeeconomies.

Betts, Alexander, and Paul Collier. *Refuge: Rethinking Refugee Policy in a Changing World*. New York: Oxford University Press, 2017.

Betts, Alexander, and Gil Loescher. "Refugees in International Relations." *Refugees in International Relations*, edited by Alexander Betts and Gil Loescher. New York: Oxford University Press, 2011, pp. 1–28.

Bhabha, Jacqueline. *Can We Solve the Migration Crisis?* Cambridge: Polity Press, 2018.

Bhabha, Jacqueline. "Toleration Deficits: The Perilous State of Refugee Protection Today." *Philosophy & Social Criticism*, February 2019, p. 0191453719831336, https://doi.org/10.1177/0191453719831336.

Bier, David. "Encouraging Findings of the Trump Administration's Report on Refugees and Asylees." *Cato Institute*, February 12, 2019, https://www.cato.org/blog/encouraging-findings-trump-admins-report-refugees-asylees.

Birrell, Ian. "The £100m Ghost Camp for Refugees That You Pay For: It Was Built with UK Foreign Aid for 130,000 Fleeing War in Syria—but Is So Grim That Only 15,000 Live There." *Daily Mail*, December 19, 2015, http://www.dailymail.co.uk/news/article-3367110/The-100m-ghost-camp-refugees-pay-Built-UK-foreign-aid-billions-130-000-fleeing-war-Syria-grim-15-000-stay.html.

Black, Chris. "Sexual Violence Rampant in Greek Refugee Camps Warns UN." *The Issue*, February 9, 2018, http://www.theissue.com/politics/sexual-violence-rampant-in-greek-refugee-camps-warns-un.

Boston Globe. "Australia Subjects Refugees to a Cruel Fate. US Shouldn't Follow." *Boston Globe*, August 12, 2018, http://www.bostonglobe.com/opinion/editorials/2018/08/11/australia-subjects-refugees-cruel-fate-shouldn-follow/RJTKCBzCRuGoCIsUbOxsUL/story.html.

Boswell, Christina. "Burden-Sharing in the New Age of Immigration." *Migrationpolicy.org*, November 1, 2003, https://www.migrationpolicy.org/article/burden-sharing-new-age-immigration.

Bova, Gus. "'Treated Worse Than Dogs': Immigrant Kids in Detention Give Firsthand Accounts of Squalid Conditions." *Texas Observer*, July 18, 2018, http://www.texasobserver.org/treated-worse-than-dogs-immigrant-kids-in-detention-give-firsthand-accounts-of-squalid-conditions.

Bradley, Megan. "Unresolved and Unresolvable? Tensions in the Refugee Regime." *Ethics & International Affairs* 33, no. 1, 2019, pp. 45–56, https://doi.org/10.1017/S0892679418000874.

Brodesser-Akner, Claude. "Christie: No Syrian Refugees, Not Even 'Orphans under Age 5.'" *NJ.com*, November 16, 2015, http://www.nj.com/politics/index.ssf/2015/11/christie_reverses_earlier_call_to_accept_syrian_re_1.html.

Broomfield, Matt. "Pictures of Life for Turkey's 2.5 Million Syrian Refugees." *The Independent*, April 5, 2016, http://www.independent.co.uk/news/world/europe/pictures-of-life-for-turkeys-25-million-syrian-refugees-crisis-migrant-a6969551.html.

Buchanan, Allen. *The Heart of Human Rights*. New York: Oxford University Press, 2013.

Burnett, John. "Amid Wave of Child Immigrants, Reports of Abuse by Border Patrol." *NPR*, July 24, 2014, http://www.npr.org/2014/07/24/334041633/amid-wave-of-child-immigrants-reports-of-abuse-by-border-patrol.

Carens, Joseph. *The Ethics of Immigration*. Oxford: Oxford University Press, 2013.

Carroll, Caitlin. "The European Refugee Crisis and the Myth of the Immigrant Rapist." *EuropeNow*, July 6, 2017, http://www.europenowjournal.org/2017/07/05/untitled.

Cassidy, John. "The Economics of Syrian Refugees." *New Yorker*, November 2015, https://www.newyorker.com/news/john-cassidy/the-economics-of-syrian-refugees.

Cherri, Rima, and Houssam Hariri. "Most Syrian Refugees in Lebanon Now Destitute, Study Finds." United Nations High Commissioner for Refugees (UNHCR), December 27, 2017, http://www.unhcr.org/en-us/news/stories/2017/12/5a3cf2a04/syrian-refugees-lebanon-destitute-study-finds.html.

Clemens, Michael. "The Real Economic Cost of Accepting Refugees." *Refugees Deeply*, August 8, 2017, http://www.newsdeeply.com/refugees/community/2017/08/08/the-real-economic-cost-of-accepting-refugees.

CNN. "2015 Paris Terror Attacks Fast Facts." May 2, 2018, http://www.cnn.com/2015/12/08/europe/2015-paris-terror-attacks-fast-facts/index.html.

Coates, A. J. "Counterterrorism." *The Ethics of War*. Manchester: Manchester University Press, 2016, pp. 347–74.

Cohen, Josh. *Arch of the Moral Universe and Other Essays*. Cambridge, MA: Harvard University Press, 2011.

Cohen, Roberta. "'What's So Terrible about Rape?' and Other Attitudes at the United Nations." *SAIS Review* 20, no. 2, Summer–Fall 2000, pp. 73–77.

Collier, Paul. "Beyond the Boat People: Europe's Moral Duties to Refugees." *Social Europe*, July 15, 2015, http://www.socialeurope.eu/beyond-the-boat-people-europes-moral-duties-to-refugees.

Connor, Phillip. "Most Displaced Syrians Are in the Middle East, and about a Million Are in Europe." *Pew Research Center*, January 29, 2018, https://www.pewresearch.org/fact-tank/2018/01/29/where-displaced-syrians-have-resettled/.

Cranston, Maurice. "Human Rights, Real and Supposed." 1967. *The Philosophy of Human Rights*, edited by Patrick Hayden. St. Paul, MN: Paragon House, 2001, pp. 163–73.

Crisp, Jeff. "As the World Abandons Refugees, UNHCR's Constraints Are Exposed." *NewsDeeply*, September 13, 2018, https://www.newsdeeply.com/refugees/community/2018/09/13/as-the-world-abandons-refugees-unhcrs-constraints-are-exposed.

Crisp, Jeff. "Finding Space for Protection: An Inside Account of the Evolution of UNHCR's Urban Refugee Policy." *Refuge* 33, no. 1, 2017, pp. 87–96.

Crisp, Jeff. "Refugees: The Trojan Horse of Terrorism?" *Open Democracy*, June 5, 2017, http://www.opendemocracy.net/can-europe-make-it/jeff-crisp/refugees-trojan-horse-of-terrorism.

Cronin-Furman, Kate. "The Treatment of Migrants Likely 'Meets the Definition of a Mass Atrocity.'" *New York Times*, June 29, 2019, https://nyti.ms/2KPupRl.

Cumming-Bruce, Nick. "Taking Migrant Children from Parents Is Illegal, U.N. Tells U.S." *New York Times*, June 5, 2018, http://www.nytimes.com/2018/06/05/world/americas/us-un-migrant-children-families.html.

Cunningham, Susannah. "Inside the Brutal, Thorough Process of Vetting Refugees." *Vox,* February 2, 2017, https://www.vox.com/first-person/2017/2/2/14459006/trump-executive-order-refugees-vetting.

Dagan, Tsilly. "International Tax and Global Justice." SSRN Scholarly Paper, Social Science Research Network, April 11, 2016, https://papers.ssrn.com/abstract=2762110.

Darby, Luke. "Trump on Abused Immigrant Children: 'They're Not Innocent.'" *GQ,* May 24, 2018, http://www.gq.com/story/trump-on-immigrant-children.

Davis, Julie Hirschfeld, and Somini Sengupta. "Trump Administration Rejects Study Showing Positive Impact of Refugees." *New York Times,* September 18, 2017, http://www.nytimes.com/2017/09/18/us/politics/refugees-revenue-cost-report-trump.html.

Dearden, Lizzie. "Germany 'Spent More Than €20bn on Refugees in 2016' as Crisis Outstrips State Budgets." *The Independent,* March 10, 2017, http://www.independent.co.uk/news/world/europe/germany-refugees-spend-20-billion-euros-2016-angela-merkel-crisis-budgets-middle-east-north-africa-a7623466.html.

De León, Jason. "The Land of Open Graves." *Jason De Léon,* May 13, 2015, http://jasonpatrickdeleon.com/?page_id=20.

Deutsche Welle. "Germany's Crime Rate Fell to Lowest Level in Decades in 2018." April 4, 2019, https://www.dw.com/en/germanys-crime-rate-fell-to-lowest-level-in-decades-in-2018/a-48162310.

Digidiki, Vasileia, and Jacqueline Bhabha. "Emergency within an Emergency: The Growing Epidemic of Sexual Exploitation and Abuse of Migrant Children in Greece." FXB Center for Health and Human Rights, Harvard University, April 17, 2017, http://fxb.harvard.edu/2017/04/17/new-report-emergency-within-an-emergency-exploitation-of-migrant-children-in-greece.

Di Giorgio, Massimilano, and Steve Scherer. "Italy to End Sea Rescue Mission That Saved 100,000 Migrants." *Reuters,* October 31, 2014, https://www.reuters.com/article/us-italy-migrants-eu/italy-to-end-sea-rescue-mission-that-saved-100000-migrants-idUSKBN0IK22220141031.

Doherty, Ben. "Asylum Seeker Boat Turnbacks Illegal and Don't Deter People, Report Finds." *The Guardian,* May 2, 2017, http://www.theguardian.com/world/2017/may/03/asylum-seeker-boat-turnbacks-illegal-and-dont-deter-people-report-finds.

Doherty, Ben. "International Criminal Court Told Australia's Detention Regime Could Be a Crime against Humanity." *The Guardian,* February 13, 2017, http://www.theguardian.com/australia-news/2017/feb/13/international-criminal-court-told-australias-detention-regime-could-be-a-against-humanity.

Donnelly, Jack. *Universal Human Rights in Theory and Practice.* Ithaca, NY: Cornell University Press, 2013.

Dworkin, Ronald. "Rights as Trumps." *Theories of Rights*, edited by Jeremy Waldron. New York: Oxford University Press, 1984, pp. 153–68.

Eck, Kristine, and Christopher J. Fariss. "No, Sweden Isn't Hiding an Immigrant Crime Problem. This Is the Real Story." *Washington Post*, February 24, 2017, http://www.washingtonpost.com/news/monkey-cage/wp/2017/02/24/no-sweden-isnt-hiding-an-immigrant-crime-problem-this-is-the-real-story.

Eckersley, Robyn. "Responsibility for Climate Change as a Structural Injustice." *The Oxford Handbook of Environmental Political Theory*. *www.oxfordhandbooks.com*, January 2016, https://doi.org/10.1093/oxfordhb/9780199685271.013.37.

Economist. "Confusion over Immigration and Crime Is Roiling European Politics." *The Economist*, June 30, 2018, http://www.economist.com/europe/2018/06/30/confusion-over-immigration-and-crime-is-roiling-european-politics.

Elshtain, Jean Bethke. "The Dignity of the Human Person and the Idea of Human Rights: Four Inquiries." *Journal of Law and Religion* 14, no. 1, 1999–2000, pp. 53–65.

Elster, Jon. "The Valmont Effect: The Warm-Glow Theory of Philanthropy." *Giving Well: The Ethics of Philanthropy*, edited by Patricia Illingworth, Thomas Pogge, and Leif Wenar. New York: Oxford University Press, 2011, pp. 67–83.

Evans, William N., and Daneil Fitzgerald. "The Economic and Social Outcomes of Refugees in the United States: Evidence from the ACS." NBER Working Paper No. 23498, June 2017, https://www.nber.org/papers/w23498.pdf.

Farrell, Paul, Nick Evershed, and Helen Davidson. "The Nauru Files: Cache of 2,000 Leaked Reports Reveal Scale of Abuse of Children in Australian Offshore Detention." *The Guardian*, August 10, 2016, http://www.theguardian.com/australia-news/2016/aug/10/the-nauru-files-2000-leaked-reports-reveal-scale-of-abuse-of-children-in-australian-offshore-detention.

Feinberg, Joel. "The Nature and Value of Rights." 1970. *The Philosophy of Human Rights*, edited by Patrick Hayden. St. Paul, MN: Paragon House, 2001, pp. 174–86.

Ferracioli, Luara. "The Appeal and Danger of a New Refugee Convention." *Social Theory and Practice* 40, no. 1, January 2014, pp. 123–44.

Fertig, Beth, and Victor J. Blue. "A Mother and Daughter Both Have H.I.V. The U.S. Lets in Only One." *New York Times*, March 6, 2019, https://www.nytimes.com/2019/03/06/nyregion/family-separation-hiv.html.

Fili, Andriani. "The Continuum of Detention in Greece." *Border Criminologies*, Faculty of Law, University of Oxford, May 25, 2016, http://www.law.ox.ac.uk/research-subject-groups/centre-criminology/centreborder-criminologies/blog/2016/05/continuum.

Fiske, Lucy. *Human Rights, Refugee Protest, and Immigration Detention*. New York: Palgrave Macmillan, 2016.

FitzGerald, David Scott. *Refuge beyond Reach: How Rich Democracies Repel Asylum Seekers*. New York: Oxford University Press, 2019.

Forsythe, David P. *Human Rights in International Relations*. New York: Cambridge University Press, 2000.

Franke, Mark F.N. "Political Exclusion of Refugees in the Ethics of International Relations." *Ashgate Research Companion to Ethics and International Relations*, edited by Patrick Hayden. Surrey: Ashgate Publishing Limited, 2009, pp. 309–28.

Freedman, Jane. "Engendering Security at the Borders of Europe: Women Migrants and the Mediterranean 'Crisis.'" *Journal of Refugee Studies* 29, no. 4, December 2016, pp. 568–82.

Freedman, Jane. "Sexual and Gender-Based Violence against Refugee Women: A Hidden Aspect of the Refugee 'Crisis.'" *Reproductive Health Matters* 24, no. 47, May 2016, pp. 18–26.

Friedman, Uri. "Where America's Terrorists Actually Come From." *The Atlantic*, January 30, 2017, http://www.theatlantic.com/international/archive/2017/01/trump-immigration-ban-terrorism/514361.

Frye, Marilyn. *Politics of Reality: Essays in Feminist Theory*. New York: Crossing Press Feminist, 1983.

Gehrsitz, Markus, and Martin Ungerer. "Jobs, Crime, and Votes: A Short-Run Evaluation of the Refugee Crisis in Germany." *SSRN Electronic Journal*, 2016, https://doi.org/10.2139/ssrn.2887442.

Gessen, Masha. "Taking Children from Their Parents Is a Form of State Terror." *New Yorker*, May 9, 2018, http://www.newyorker.com/news/our-columnists/taking-children-from-their-parents-is-a-form-of-state-terror.

Gewirth, Alan. "Human Dignity as the Basis of Rights." *The Constitution of Rights: Human Dignity and American Values*, edited by Michael J. Meyer and William A. Parent. Ithaca, NY: Cornell University Press, 1992, pp. 10–28.

Gewirth, Alan. *Human Rights: Essays on Justification and Applications*. Chicago: University of Chicago Press, 1982.

Gibney, Matthew J. *The Ethics and Politics of Asylum: Liberal Democracy and the Response to Refugees*. New York: Cambridge University Press, 2004.

Glendon, Mary Ann. *A World Made New: Eleanor Roosevelt and the Universal Declaration of Human Rights*. New York: Random House, 2001.

Global Detention Project. "United States Immigrant Detention." May 2016, http://www.globaldetentionproject.org/countries/americas/united-states.

Glover, Robert. "Radically Rethinking Citizenship: Disaggregation, Agonistic Pluralism, and the Politics of Immigration in the United States." *Political Studies* 59, no. 2, June 2011, pp. 209–29.

Gonzales, Richard. "Sexual Assault of Detained Migrant Children Reported in the Thousands since 2015." *NPR.org*, February 26, 2019, https://www.npr.org/2019/02/26/698397631/sexual-assault-of-detained-migrant-children-reported-in-the-thousands-since-2015.

Gould, Carol C. *Globalizing Democracy and Human Rights*. New York: Cambridge University Press, 2004.

Hamlin, Rebecca. *Let Me Be a Refugee: Administrative Justice and the Politics of Asylum in the United States, Canada, and Australia*. New York: Oxford University Press, 2014.

Hammar, Tomas. "Dual Citizenship and Political Integration." *International Migration Review* 19, no. 3, Autumn 1985, pp. 438–50.

Hammerstad, Anne. "UNHCR and the Securitization of Forced Migration." *Refugees in International Relations*, edited by Alexander Betts and Gil Loescher. New York: Oxford University Press, 2011, pp. 237–60.

Hart, H. L. A. "Are There Any Natural Rights?" *The Philosophy of Human Rights*, edited by Patrick Hayden. St. Paul, MN: Paragon House, 2001, pp. 151–62.

Helton, Arthur C. "What Is Refugee Protection? A Question Revisited." *Problems of Protection: The UNHCR, Refugees, and Human Rights*, edited by Niklaus Steiner, Mark Gibney, and Gil Loescher. New York: Routledge, 2003, pp. 19–33.

Higgins, Andrew. "Norway Offers Migrants a Lesson in How to Treat Women." *New York Times*, December 19, 2015, http://www.nytimes.com/2015/12/20/world/europe/norway-offers-migrants-a-lesson-in-how-to-treat-women.html.

Hockenos, Paul. "Europe Has Criminalized Humanitarianism." *Foreign Policy*, August 1, 2018.

Hoffmann, Sophia. "Humanitarian Security in Jordan's Azraq Camp." *Security Dialogue* 48, no. 2, April 2017, pp. 97–112.

Hosein, Adam. *The Ethics of Migration: An Introduction*. New York: Routledge, 2019.

Hyndman, Jennifer, William Payne, and Shauna Jimenez. "Private Refugee Sponsorship in Canada." *Forced Migration Review*, February 2017, https://www.fmreview.org/resettlement/hyndman-payne-jimenez.

Ignatieff, Michael. *Human Rights as Politics and Idolatry*. Princeton, NJ: Princeton University Press, 2001.

Illingworth, Patricia. "Giving Back: Norms, Ethics, and Law in the Service of Philanthropy." *Giving Well: The Ethics of Philanthropy*, edited by Patricia Illingworth, Thomas Pogge, and Leif Wenar. New York: Oxford University Press, 2011, pp. 196–219.

Ingraham, Christopher. "Two Charts Demolish the Notion That Immigrants Here Illegally Commit More Crime." *Washington Post*, June 19, 2018, http://www.washingtonpost.com/news/wonk/wp/2018/06/19/two-charts-demolish-the-notion-that-immigrants-here-illegally-commit-more-crime.

International Organization for Migration. "UN Migration Agency Issues Report on Arrivals of Sexually Exploited Migrants, Chiefly from Nigeria." July 21, 2017, https://www.iom.int/news/un-migration-agency-issues-report-arrivals-sexually-exploited-migrants-chiefly-nigeria.

International Rescue Committee. "Alex Aleinikoff: Let's Start with How We Define 'Refugee.'" *The Displaced Podcast*, podcast audio, https://www.rescue.org/displaced-podcast/alex-aleinikoff-lets-start-how-we-define-refugee.

Jones, Reece. *Violent Borders: Refugees and the Right to Move*. London: Verso, 2016.

Jordan, Miriam. "Family Separation May Have Hit Thousands More Migrant Children Than Reported." *New York Times,* January 18, 2019, https://www.nytimes.com/2019/01/17/us/family-separation-trump-administration-migrants.html.

Jordan, Miriam, and Ron Nixon. "Trump Administration Threatens Jail and Separating Children from Parents for Those Who Illegally Cross Southwest Border." *New York Times,* May 7, 2018, http://www.nytimes.com/2018/05/07/us/politics/homeland-security-prosecute-undocumented-immigrants.html.

Kant, Immanuel. *Grounding for the Metaphysics of Morals ; with, On a Supposed Right to Lie Because of Philanthropic Concerns.* 3rd ed. Indianapolis: Hackett, 1993.

Keck, Margaret E., and Kathryn Sikkink. *Activists beyond Borders: Advocacy Networks in International Politics.* Ithaca, NY: Cornell University Press, 1998.

Kingsley, Patrick. "96 Days Later, Nonstop Church Service to Protect Refugees Finally Ends." *New York Times,* January 30, 2019, https://www.nytimes.com/2019/01/30/world/europe/netherlands-church-vigil-refugees.html.

Kingsley, Patrick. "Migration to Europe Is Down Sharply. So Is It Still a 'Crisis'?" *New York Times,* June 27, 2018, http://www.nytimes.com/interactive/2018/06/27/world/europe/europe-migrant-crisis-change.html.

Kingsley, Patrick. *The New Odyssey: The Story of the Twenty-First-Century Refugee Crisis.* New York: Liveright Publishing, 2017.

Kingsley, Patrick. "To Protect Migrants from Police, a Dutch Church Service Never Ends." *New York Times,* December 10, 2018, https://www.nytimes.com/2018/12/10/world/europe/migrants-dutch-church-service.html.

Kriel, Lomi. "Legal Limbo: Her Husband Murdered, Her Son Taken Away, a Mother Seeking Asylum Tells a Judge, 'I Have Lost Everything.'" *Houston Chronicle,* December 30, 2017, http://www.houstonchronicle.com/news/houston-texas/houston/article/Her-husband-murdered-her-son-taken-away-a-12462658.php.

Lanchin, Mike. "The Ship of Jewish Refugees Nobody Wanted." *bbc.com,* May 13, 2014, https://www.bbc.com/news/magazine-27373131.

Lee, Matthew T., and Ramiro Martinez. "Immigration Reduces Crime: An Emerging Scholarly Consensus." *Sociology of Crime, Law, and Deviance* 13, 2009, pp. 3–16.

Lind, Dara. "HIAS, the Jewish Refugee-Aid Group Targeted by the Pittsburgh Synagogue Shooter, Explained by Its President." *Vox,* September 25, 2015, https://www.vox.com/2015/9/25/9392151/hias-jewish-refugees-immigrants.

Lind, Dara. "The Horrifying Conditions Facing Kids in Border Detention Explained." *Vox,* June 25, 2019, https://www.vox.com/policy-and-politics/2019/6/25/18715725/children-border-detention-kids-cages-immigration.

Lind, Dara. "The Trump Administration's Separation of Families at the Border, Explained." *Vox,* August 14, 2018, https://www.vox.com/2018/6/11/17443198/children-immigrant-families-separated-parents.

Livingston, Steven, and Gregory Asmolov. "Digital Affordances and the Role of Open Source Intelligence (OSINT) Communities in Framing Contests." Draft paper presented at Harvard Kennedy School, February 2, 2018.

Locke, John. *Second Treatise of Government.* New York: Hackett, 1980.

Loescher, Gil. "UNHCR at Fifty: Refugee Protection and World Politics." *Problems of Protection: The UNHCR and Human Rights,* edited by Niklaus Steiner, Mark Gibney, and Gill Loescher. New York: Routledge, 2012, pp. 3–18.

Long, Katy. "From Refugee to Migrant? Labor Mobility's Protection Potential." *Migration Policy Institute Report,* May 2015, https://www.migrationpolicy.org/research/refugee-migrant-labor-mobilitys-protection-potential.

Mark, Michelle. "Over 10,000 Migrant Children Are Now in US Government Custody at 100 Shelters in 14 States." *Business Insider,* May 30, 2018, http://www.businessinsider.com/children-in-custody-trump-administration-immigration-zero-tolerance-policy-2018-5.

Martínez, Sofía. "Today's Migrant Flow Is Different." *The Atlantic,* June 26, 2018, http://www.theatlantic.com/international/archive/2018/06/central-america-border-immigration/563744.

McAdam, Jane. *Climate Change, Forced Migration, and International Law.* Oxford: Oxford University Press, 2012.

McClelland, Mac. "How to Build a Perfect Refugee Camp." *New York Times,* February 13, 2014, https://www.nytimes.com/2014/02/16/magazine/how-to-build-a-perfect-refugee-camp.html.

McConnachie, Kirsten. "Camps of Containment: A Genealogy of the Refugee Camp." *Humanity* 7, no. 3, 2016, pp. 397–412, https://doi.org/10.1353/hum.2016.0022.

McDonald-Gibson, Charlotte. *Cast Away: True Stories of Survival from Europe's Refugee Crisis.* New York: New Press, 2016.

McDonald-Gibson, Charlotte. "For Europe, Arab Lives Matter More Than Africans.'" *New York Times,* June 22, 2016, http://www.nytimes.com/2016/06/23/opinion/for-europe-arab-lives-matter-more-than-africans.html.

"Mediterranean: MSF Rescue Ship Aquarius Forced to Terminate Operations." *Doctors Without Borders—USA,* December 6, 2018, https://www.doctorswithoutborders.org/what-we-do/news-stories/news/mediterranean-msf-rescue-ship-aquarius-forced-terminate-operations.

Meyers, Diana T., ed. *Poverty, Agency, and Human Rights.* New York: Oxford University Press, 2014.

Miliband, David. *Rescue: Refugees and the Political Crisis of Our Time.* New York: Simon and Schuster, 2017.

Mill, John Stuart. *On Liberty, Utilitarianism, and Other Essays.* New ed. New York: Oxford University Press, 2015.

Miller, David. *National Responsibility and Global Justice.* New York: Oxford University Press, 2007.

Miller, David. *On Nationality.* Oxford: Oxford University Press, 1997.

Miller, David. *Strangers in Our Midst: The Political Philosophy of Immigration.* Cambridge, MA: Harvard University Press, 2016.

Miroff, Nick. "Father 'Took His Own Life' after He Was Separated from Family by Border Patrol Agents." *The Independent,* June 10, 2018, http://www.independent.co.uk/news/world/americas/father-us-border-patrol-separated-family-marco-antonio-munoz-honduras-a8392006.html.

Mwangi, Annabel. "Only 1% of Refugees Are Resettled—Why Are We So Threatened by Them?" *The Guardian,* February 18, 2017, https://www.theguardian.com/global-development-professionals-network/2017/feb/18/only-1-of-refugees-are-resettled-why-are-we-so-threatened-by-them.

"Myanmar's Killing Fields." *Frontline,* PBS, May 8, 2018, https://www.pbs.org/wgbh/frontline/film/myanmars-killing-fields/.

Nagel, Thomas. "Poverty and Food: Why Charity Is Not Enough." *Global Justice: Seminal Essays,* edited by Thomas Pogge and Darrel Moellendorf. St. Paul, MN: Paragon House, 2008, pp. 49–59.

Neuman, Scott. "Amnesty International: Europe Complicit in Libyan Migrant Abuses." *NPR,* December 12, 2017, http://www.npr.org/sections/thetwo-way/2017/12/12/570087994/amnesty-international-europe-complicit-in-libyan-migrant-abuses.

Nevins, Joseph. *Operation Gatekeeper and Beyond: The War on "Illegals" and the Remaking of the U.S.-Mexico Boundary.* 2nd ed. New York: Routledge, 2010.

Nichols, Chris. "Odds of Fatal Terror Attack in U.S. by a Refugee? 3.6 billion to 1." *PolitiFact,* February 1, 2017, http://www.politifact.com/california/statements/2017/feb/01/ted-lieu/odds-youll-be-killed-terror-attack-america-refugee.

Nickel, James W. *Making Sense of Human Rights.* 2nd ed. Oxford: Blackwell, 2007.

Norlock, Kathryn. "Perpetual Struggle." *Hypatia* 34, no. 1, Winter 2019, pp. 6–19.

Nossiter, Adam. "French Mayor Offers Shelter to Migrants, Despite the Government's Objections." *New York Times,* February 12, 2019, https://www.nytimes.com/2019/02/12/world/europe/bayonne-migrants-jean-rene-etchegaray.html.

Nowrasteh, Alex. "Syrian Refugees and the Precautionary Principle." *Cato Institute,* January 28, 2017, http://www.cato.org/blog/syrian-refugees-precationary-principle.

NPR. "Ex-Aid Worker: Abuse of Refugee Children on Nauru Was Mostly Ignored." *Morning Edition,* NPR, August 24, 2016, http://www.npr.org/sections/parallels/2016/08/24/491170178/ex-aid-worker-abuse-of-refugee-children-on-nauru-was-ignored.

Oberman, Kieran. "Refugees and Economic Migrants: A Morally Spurious Distinction." *The Critique,* December 1, 2015, http://www.thecritique.com/articles/refugees-economic-migrants-a-morally-spurious-distinction-2.

Oliver, Kelly. "Abolish Refugee Detention: Rethinking International Law and Carceral Humanitarianism." *Refugees Now: Rethinking Borders, Hospitality, and Citizenship*, edited by Kelly Oliver, Lisa M. Madura, and Sabeen Ahmed. New York: Rowman and Littlefield, 2019, pp. 117–36.

Onyulo, Tonny. "Uganda's Other Refugee Crisis." *GlobalPost*, July 12, 2017, https://www.pri.org/stories/2017-07-12/ugandas-other-refugee-crisis.

Owen, David. "In Loco Civitatis: On the Normative Basis of the Institution of Refugeehood." *Migration in Political Theory: The Ethics of Movement and Membership*, edited by Sarah Fine and Lea Ypi. Oxford: Oxford University Press, 2016, pp. 269–89.

Owen, David. *What Do We Owe Refugees?* Cambridge: Polity Press, 2020.

Palma, Bethania. "Crime in Sweden, Part I: Is Sweden the 'Rape Capital' of Europe?" *Snopes*, March 29, 2017, http://www.snopes.com/fact-ch /crime-sweden-rape-capital-europe.

Palma, Bethania. "Crime in Sweden, Part II: Are Refugee Men Overrepresented in Swedish Crime?" *Snopes*, March 30, 2017, http://www.snopes.com/fact-check/crime-sweden-part-ii-refugee-men-overrepresented-swedish-crime.

Parekh, Serena. *Hannah Arendt and the Challenge of Modernity: A Phenomenology of Human Rights*. New York: Routledge, 2008.

Parekh, Serena. *Refugees and the Ethics of Forced Displacement*. New York: Routledge, 2017.

Pew Research Center. "Number of Refugees to Europe Surges to Record 1.3 Million in 2015." August 2, 2016, https://www.pewresearch.org/global/2016/08/02/number-of-refugees-to-europe-surges-to-record-1-3-million-in-2015/.

Pickering, Sharon. "There's No Evidence That Asylum Seeker Deterrence Policy Works." *The Conversation*, July 24, 2012, http://theconversation.com/theres-no-evidence-that-asylum-seeker-deterrence-policy-works-8367.

Pinto Arena, Maria do Céu. "Islamic Terrorism in the West and International Migrations: The 'Far' or 'Near' Enemy Within? What Is the Evidence?" Robert Schuman Centre for Advanced Studies, European University Institute, May 2017, http://cadmus.eui.eu/bitstream/handle/1814/46604/RSCAS_2017_28.pdf.

Pittaway, Eileen, and Emma Pittaway. "'Refugee Woman': A Dangerous Label; Opening a Discussion of the Role of Identity and Intersectional Oppression in the Failure of the International Refugee Protection Regime for Refugee Women." *Australian Journal of Human Rights*: Symposium: The Rights of Strangers - Part 2, Vol. 10, no. 1 (June 1, 2004), pp. 119–35.

Pogge, Thomas. "'Assisting' the Global Poor." *The Ethics of Assistance: Morality and the Distant Needy*, edited by D. Chatterjee. Cambridge: Cambridge University Press, 2004, pp. 260–88.

Pogge, Thomas. "'Assisting' the Global Poor." *The Ethics of Assistance*, edited by Deen K. Chatterjee, Cambridge University Press, 2004, pp. 260–88, https://doi.org/10.1017/CBO9780511817663.014.

Pogge, Thomas. "How International Nongovernmental Organizations Should Act." *Giving Well: The Ethics of Philanthropy*, edited by Patricia Illingworth, Thomas Pogge, and Leif Wenar. New York: Oxford University Press, 2011, pp. 46–66.

Pogge, Thomas. "How Should Human Rights Be Conceived?" 1995. *The Philosophy of Human Rights*, edited by Patrick Hayden. St. Paul, MN: Paragon House, 2001, pp. 187–210.

Power, Samantha. *"A Problem from Hell": America and the Age of Genocide*. New York: Basic Books, 2002.

Radford, Jynnah, and Phillip Connor. "Canada Now Leads the World in Refugee Resettlement, Surpassing the U.S." *Pew Research Center*, June 19, 2019, https://www.pewresearch.org/fact-tank/2019/06/19/canada-now-leads-the-world-in-refugee-resettlement-surpassing-the-u-s/.

Rahaei, Saeid. "The Rights of Refugee Women and Children in Islam." *Forced Migration Review*, June 2012, https://www.fmreview.org/Human-Rights/rahaei.

Rashid, Tania. "Inside the Bangladesh Brothels Where Rohingya Girls Are Suffering." *PBS NewsHour*, April 26, 2018, http://www.pbs.org/newshour/world/inside-the-bangladesh-brothels-where-rohingya-girls-are-suffering.

Rawlence, Ben. *City of Thorns: Nine Lives in the World's Largest Refugee Camp*. New York: Picador, 2016.

Rawls, John. *The Law of Peoples*. Cambridge, MA: Harvard University Press, 2001.

Rawls, John. *Political Liberalism*. New York: Columbia University Press, 1993.

Rawls, John. *A Theory of Justice*. Cambridge, MA: Harvard University Press, 1971.

Reznick, Alisa. "Jordan's Azraq Syrian Refugee Camp Stands Largely Empty." *Al Jazeera*, June 1, 2015, http://www.aljazeera.com/indepth/inpictures/2015/05/jordan-azraq-syrian-refugee-camp-stands-largely-empty-150526084850543.html.

Richards, Victoria. "Refugee Crisis: German Man Takes in 24 Asylum-Seekers and Describes His 'Disappointing' Experience." *The Independent*, November 5, 2015, http://www.independent.co.uk/news/world/europe/refugee-crisis-german-man-takes-in-24-asylum-seekers-and-describes-his-disappointing-experience-a6722146.html.

"Richest 1 Percent Bagged 82 Percent of Wealth Created Last Year—Poorest Half of Humanity Got Nothing." *Oxfam International*, January 22, 2018, https://www.oxfam.org/en/pressroom/pressreleases/2018-01-22/richest-1-percent-bagged-82-percent-wealth-created-last-year.

Ronzoni, Miriam. "The Global Order: A Case of Background Injustice?" *Philosophy & Public Affairs* 37, no. 3, Summer 2009, pp. 229–56.

Rose, Joel. "Doctors Concerned about 'Irreparable Harm' to Separated Migrant Children." *NPR*, June 15, 2018, http://www.npr.org/2018/06/15/620254326/doctors-warn-about-dangers-of-child-separations.

Rothman, Lily. "The US Can Handle Much More Than 10,000 Syrian Refugees." *Time*, September 15, 2015.

Roxström, Erik, and Mark Gibney. "The Legal and Ethical Obligations of UNHCR: The Case of Temporary Protection in Western Europe." *Problems of Protection: The UNHCR and Human Rights*, edited by Niklaus Steiner, Mark Gibney, and Gill Loescher. New York: Routledge, 2012, pp. 37–60.

Schuck, Peter H. "Opinion: Creating a Market for Refugees in Europe." *New York Times*, December 21, 2017, https://www.nytimes.com/2015/06/09/opinion/creating-a-market-for-refugees-in-europe.html.

Schuck, Peter H. "Refugee Burden-Sharing: A Modest Proposal." *Yale Journal of International Law* 22, 1997, pp. 243–98.

Semple, Kirk. "Fleeing Gangs, Central American Families Surge toward U.S." *New York Times*, November 12, 2016, http://www.nytimes.com/2016/11/13/world/americas/fleeing-gangs-central-american-families-surge-toward-us.html.

Sharot, Tali. *The Influential Mind: What the Brain Reveals about Our Power to Change Others*. New York: Henry Holt, 2017.

Sherlock, Ruth. "Migrants Captured in Libya Say They End Up Sold as Slaves." *NPR*, March 21, 2018, http://www.npr.org/sections/parallels/2018/03/21/595497429/migrants-passing-through-libya-could-end-up-being-sold-as-slaves.

Shire, Warsan. "Home." *Genius*, http://genius.com/warsan-shire-home-annotated.

Shue, Henry. *Basic Rights: Subsistence, Affluence, and U.S. Foreign Policy*. 2nd ed. Princeton, NJ: Princeton University Press, 1996.

Shulman, James. "The Funder as Founder: Ethical Considerations of the Philanthropic Creation of Nonprofit Organizations." *Giving Well: The Ethics of Philanthropy*, edited by Patricia Illingworth, Thomas Pogge, and Leif Wenar. New York: Oxford University Press, 2011, pp. 220–42.

Sikkink, Kathryn. *Evidence for Hope: Making Human Rights Work in the 21st Century*. Princeton, NJ: Princeton University Press, 2017.

Silverman, Stephanie J. "The Difference That Detention Makes: Reconceptualizing the Boundaries of the Normative Debate on Immigration Control." *The Ethics and Politics of Immigration: Core Issues and Emerging Trends*, edited by Alex Sager Lanham, MD: Rowman and Littlefield, 2016, pp. 105–24.

Simpson, Gerry. "'I Wanted to Lie Down and Die': Trafficking and Torture of Eritreans in Sudan and Egypt." Human Rights Watch, February 11, 2014, http://www.hrw.org/report/2014/02/11/i-wanted-lie-down-and-die/trafficking-and-torture-eritreans-sudan-and-egypt.

Singer, Peter. "Famine, Affluence, and Morality." *Philosophy and Public Affairs* 1, no. 3, 1972, pp. 229–43.

Singer, Peter, and Renata Singer. "The Ethics of Refugee Policy." *Open Borders? Closed Societies? The Ethical and Political Issues*, edited by Mark Gibney. New York: Greenwood Press, 1988, pp. 111–30.

Smith, Merrill. "Warehousing Refugees: A Denial of Rights, a Waste of Humanity." *World Refugee Survey 2004*, US Committee for Refugees and Immigrants, 2004, pp. 38–56.

Souter, James. "Towards a Theory of Asylum as Reparations for Past Injustice." *Political Studies*, February 28, 2013.

Spagat, Elliot. "Tally of Children Split at Border Tops 5,400 in New Count." *Associate Press*, October 25, 2019, https://abcnews.go.com/US/wireStory/tally-children-split-border-tops-5400-count-66516532?fbclid=IwAR1X3OguiExeTS8eNc-Hn0SGiAsi3wrUCT3fyIF9Lg2TN8xrN1N9NsDHlt4.

Stevens, Jacob. "Prisons of the Stateless: The Derelictions of UNHCR." *New Left Review* 42, November–December 2006, pp. 53–67.

Stolberg, Sheryl Gay. "How Democrats Are Using Guests to Send Messages at the State of the Union." *New York Times*, February 4, 2019, https://www.nytimes.com/2019/02/04/us/politics/democrats-guests-sotu.html.

Stone, Jon. "The Refugee Crisis Is Actually Having 'Sizable' Economic Benefits in European Countries, EU Says." *The Independent*, November 5, 2015, http://www.independent.co.uk/news/world/europe/the-refugee-crisis-will-actually-have-a-sizable-positive-economic-impact-on-european-countries-eu-a6722396.html.

Stone, Jon. "Why Donald Trump Is Wrong about Germany's Crime Rate." *The Independent*, June 18, 2018, http://www.independent.co.uk/news/world/europe/donald-trump-germany-crime-rate-immigrants-migrants-refugees-a8404786.html.

Sullivan, Kevin. "Sadness in the Slums: Fathiya Ahmed." *Washington Post*, December 2, 2013, http://www.washingtonpost.com/sf/syrian-refugees/2013/12/02/urban-poor.

Taub, Amanda. "We Know How to Solve the Refugee Crisis—but It Will Take More Than Money." *Vox*, September 9, 2015, http://www.vox.com/2015/9/9/9293139/refugee-crisis-europe-syria-solution.

Taub, Amanda. "Why 67% of Brits Want to Deploy the Army to France to Stop Migrants." *Vox*, August 12, 2015, http://www.vox.com/2015/8/12/9144079/calais-uk-immigration-identity.

Taylor, Isaac. "State Responsibility and Counterterrorism." *Ethics & Global Politics* 9, no. 1, January 2016, p. 32542, https://doi.org/10.3402/egp.v9.32542.

Tinti, Peter, and Tuesday Reitano. *Migrant, Refugee, Smuggler, Saviour*. London: C. Hurst, 2016.

Tondo, Lorenzo. "Sicilian Fisherman Risk Prison to Rescue Migrants." *The Guardian*, August 3, 2019, https://www.theguardian.com/world/2019/aug/03/sicilian-fishermen-risk-prison-to-rescue-migrants-off-libya-italy-salvini.

United Nations High Commissioner for Human Rights. "International Human Rights Law." http://www.ohchr.org/EN/ProfessionalInterest/Pages/InternationalLaw.aspx.

United Nations High Commissioner for Refugees (UNHCR). "Figures at a Glance." http://www.unhcr.org/en-us/figures-at-a-glance.html.

United Nations High Commissioner for Refugees (UNHCR). "Global Trends: Forced Displacement in 2015." June 20, 2016, http://www.unhcr.org/576408cd7.pdf.

United Nations High Commissioner for Refugees (UNHCR). "Islam and Refugees." February 18, 2019, https://www.unhcr.org/protection/hcdialogue%20/50ab90399/islam-refugees.html.

United Nations High Commissioner for Refugees (UNHCR). "Mediterranean Situation." *Refugees Operational Data Portal*, https://data2.unhcr.org/en/situations/mediterranean.

United Nations High Commissioner for Refugees (UNHCR). "Protracted Refugee Situations: Executive Committee of the High Commissioner's Programme, Standing Committee, 30th Meeting." UN Doc. EC/54/SC/CRP.14, June 10, 2004, https://www.unhcr.org/40c982172.pdf.

United Nations High Commissioner for Refugees (UNHCR). "Refugee Women and Children Face Heightened Risk of Sexual Violence amid Tensions and Overcrowding at Reception Facilities on Greek Islands." February 9, 2018, http://www.unhcr.org/en-us/news/briefing/2018/2/5a7d67c4b/refugee-women-children-face-heightened-risk-sexual-violence-amid-tensions.html.

United Nations High Commissioner for Refugees (UNHCR). "Resettlement in the United States." March 18, 2019, https://www.unhcr.org/en-us/resettlement-in-the-united-states.html.

United Nations High Commissioner for Refugees (UNHCR). "Return of People Not in Need of International Protection." September 9, 2019, https://www.unhcr.org/en-us/return-of-people-not-in-need-of-international-protection.html.

United Nations High Commissioner for Refugees (UNHCR). "Seven Facts about the Syrian Refugee Crisis." March 7, 2018, https://www.unhcr.org/ph/13418-seven-facts-syria-crisis.html.

United Nations High Commissioner for Refugees (UNHCR). "States Reach Historic Deal for Refugees and Commit to More Effective, Fairer Response." March 8, 2019, https://www.unhcr.org/news/latest/2018/12/5c1810404/states-reach-historic-deal-refugees-commit-effective-fairer-response.html.

United Nations High Commissioner for Refugees (UNHCR). "UNCHR Brochure on Underfunded Situations in 2018." September 2018, http://reporting.unhcr.org/node/21131.

United Nations High Commissioner for Refugees (UNHCR). "UNHCR Global Trends in Forced Displacement 2014." 2015, https://www.unhcr.org/en-us/statistics/country/556725e69/unhcr-global-trends-2014.html.

United Nations High Commissioner for Refugees (UNHCR). "UNHCR Global Trends in Forced Displacement 2017." 2018, https://www.unhcr.org/global-trends2017/.

United Nations High Commissioner for Refugees (UNHCR). "UNHCR Global Trends in Forced Displacement in 2018." 2019, https://www.unhcr.org/5d08d7ee7.pdf.

United Nations High Commissioner for Refugees (UNHCR). *UNHCR Projected Global Resettlement Needs 2019*, 2018, https://www.unhcr.org/5b28a7df4.pdf.

US Citizenship and Immigration Services. "Refugees." http://www.uscis.gov/humanitarian/refugees-asylum/refugees.

US Department of State. "Access to the U.S. Refugee Admissions Program." Office of Admissions, Bureau of Population, Refugees, and Migration, US Department of State, September 2006, http://www.rcusa.org/uploads/pdfs/Access%20to%20the%20U.S.%20Refugee%20Admissions%20Program.pdf.

van Elk, Noreen Josefa. "Terrorism and the Good Life: Toward a Virtue-Ethical Framework for Morally Assessing Terrorism and Counter-terrorism." *Behavioral Sciences of Terrorism and Political Aggression* 9, no. 2, May 2017, pp. 139–52, https://doi.org/10.1080/19434472.2016.1221844.

Verdirame, Guglielmo, and Barbara Harrell-Bond. *Rights in Exile: Janus-Faced Humanitarianism*. New York: Berghahn Books, 2005.

Verhaert, Greet. "A Day in the Life of a Father That Lives in a Refugee Camp." *flandersnews.be*, January 28, 2018, http://deredactie.be/cm/vrtnieuws.english/News/1.3134014.

Vitikainen, Annamari. *The Limits of Liberal Multiculturalism: Towards an Individuated Approach to Cultural Diversity*. London: Palgrave Macmillan UK, 2015.

Wagner, Neva. "B Is for Bisexual: The Forgotten Letter in U.K. Sexual Orientation Asylum Reform." *Transnational Law and Contemporary Problems* 26, no. 1, Winter 2016, pp. 205–27.

Walker, Peter. "Russia 'Playing Up Refugee Crisis to Cause Unrest in Europe.'" *The Independent*, March 22, 2017, https://www.independent.co.uk/news/world/europe/russia-europe-threat-refugee-crisis-europe-aggravate-propaganda-kremlin-farenc-katrei-hungarian-spy-a7642711.html.

Walsh, Joan. "What Senator Jeff Merkley Saw at an Immigrant Detention Center for Children." *The Nation*, June 6, 2018, http://www.thenation.com/article/senator-jeff-merkley-saw-immigrant-detention-center-children.

Walzer, Michael. *Spheres of Justice: A Defense of Pluralism and Equality*. New York: Basic Books, 2008.

Wan, William. "The Trauma of Separation Lingers Long after Children Are Reunited with Parents." *Washington Post*, June 20, 2018, http://www.washingtonpost.com/national/health-science/the-trauma-of-separation-lingers-long-after-children-are-reunited-with-parents/2018/06/20/cf693440-74c6-11e8-b4b7-308400242c2e_story.html.

Wellman, Carl. *The Moral Dimensions of Human Rights*. New York: Oxford University Press, 2011.

Wellman, Christopher Heath. “Immigration and Freedom of Association.” *Ethics* 119, no. 1, October 2008, pp. 109–41.

Wenar, Leif. “Poverty Is No Pond: Challenges for the Affluent.” *Giving Well: The Ethics of Philanthropy*, edited by Patricia Illingworth, Thomas Pogge, and Leif Wenar. New York: Oxford University Press, 2011, pp. 104–32.

Williams, John. “Space, Scale and Just War: Meeting the Challenge of Humanitarian Intervention and Trans-national Terrorism.” *Review of International Studies* 34, no. 4, October 2008, https://doi.org/10.1017/S0260210508008188.

Wooden, Cindy. “Christians Who Reject All Refugees Are ‘Hypocrites,’ Pope Says.” *Catholic News Service*, October 13, 2016, https://www.catholicnews.com/services/englishnews/2016/christians-who-reject-all-refugees-are-hypocrites-pope-says.cfm.

Yamamoto, M. Merrick. *Terrorism against Democracy*. Center for International and Security Studies, University of Maryland, pp. 31–38, https://www.jstor.org/stable/resrep05041.10.

Young, Iris Marion. *Responsibility for Justice*. New York: Oxford University Press, 2011.

Zong, Jie, and Jeanne Batalova. “Syrian Refugees in the United States.” *Migration Policy Institute*, January 12, 2017, https://www.migrationpolicy.org/article/syrian-refugees-united-states.

INDEX

For the benefit of digital users, indexed terms that span two pages (e.g., 52–53) may, on occasion, appear on only one of those pages.

aboriginal communities in Canada, 92–93
acceptance of refugees, moral arguments for
  causality, 80–82
  Good Samaritan principle, 85–87
  international system, 82–84
Afghanistan, 81
agency, 145, 186–89
Ahmed, Fathiya, 102–3, 116
Alberto (El Salvadoran refugee), 90–91, 131
Aleinikoff, Alex, 175, 188–89
al-Shabaab, 37–38
al-Souki, Hashem, 76–77, 83–84, 115–16, 131
Amnesty International, 117–18
Anelay, Joyce, 136
Aquarius (ship), 136
Arendt, Hannah, 147, 196
association, freedom of, 95–96
asylum seekers, 121–41. *See also* human smuggling
  arbitrary nature of asylum, 34–35
  Australia, deterrence in, 134–35
  child-parent separation, 132–33, 214n.12, 215n.19
  defined, 33
  detention of, 121–25, 130, 132–33
  deterrence policies, 129–31
  Europe, deterrence in, 135–41
  failed, 33
  from failed states, 32–33
  funding for, 184
  human rights of, 34
  illegal immigrants versus, 130–31
  individual efforts to help, 197–200
  moral obligation to, 106–7
  non-refoulement principle, 33, 45–46, 106–7, 128, 129–30
  number of, 4, 213–14n.46
  obligations of states to, 45–46
  political responsibility towards, 175–76
  reasons for choosing asylum, 126–29
  reforming policies, 190–93
  rejected, 33, 35, 36, 42
  structural injustice, 165–66
  United States, deterrence in, 131–33
Australia
  deterrence policies in, 123–25, 134–35
  terrorist threats in, xiii
Austria, efforts to help refugees in, 198–99
autonomy, 95, 112, 116–17
  economic integration, 183–86
  political integration, 186–89
Azraq refugee camp, Jordan, 110–11

INDEX

Bangladesh, Cox's Bazar refugee camp in, 101–2, 108
Barder, Owen, 184–85
Barnett, Michael, 210n.30
Bender, Felix, 218n.24
Benjamin (refugee), 123–25, 214n.3
Bentham, Jeremy, 57
Betts, Alexander, 206n.5, 208n.35, 213–14n.46, 216n.5
Bhabha, Jacqueline, 138
Bible, treatment of refugees in, 67–68
Boko Haram, 37–38
border deaths, 139–40
Boston Marathon bombings, xii
Breuer, Hans, 198–99
Brexit referendum, 2–3
burden sharing, 47

Cairo Declaration on Human Rights in Islam, 1990, 68
Canada
  aboriginal communities in, 92–93
  Canadian Private Sponsorship program, 192–93
  refusal to accept Jewish asylum seekers from Germany, 129–30
  resettlement in, 90, 209n.24
Carens, Joseph, 43, 83
cash transfers for refugees, 184–85, 217n.9
Cassidy, John, 206n.28
categorical imperative, 59–60
causality, 80–82
Central American refugees, 81–82, 121–22, 127
charity, 52–53
children
  asylum seekers, 132–33
  detention of, in Greece, 138
  in refugee camps, 101, 109–10, 125–26
  separation from parents, 132–33, 214n.12, 215n.19
  sexual violence against, 114, 134–35
  urban refugees, 118–19
Christianity, 66, 67–68
Christie, Chris, xi
citizenship, disaggregated, 187–88
city citizenship, 187–88
climate refugees, 39–41, 82, 164
Collier, Paul, 206n.5, 208n.35, 213–14n.46, 216n.5
communities of character, 91–92
consequentalism, 210n.3
  general discussion, 56–58
  refugees and, 61–62
contradictions, in Kantian ethics, 59, 62, 210–11n.6
Cox's Bazar refugee camp, Bangladesh, 101–2, 108
criminal organizations, 143–44
criminals, depicting refugees as, xiv–xvi
cultural plurality, 94
cultural self-determination, 91–95

Dadaab refugee camp, Kenya, 108, 110, 112–13, 151–53
dangers of human smuggling, 146–49
deaths of refugees
  drownings, 146
  of Eritrean refugees, 146–49
  by heat exhaustion, 146
  suicide, 124, 125–26, 135
desert crossings, 146–49
detention of asylum seekers, 121–25, 130
  in Australia, 134–35
  in Greece, 138
  in United States, 132–33
deterrence policies for asylum seekers, 128, 129–31
  in Australia, 134–35
  in Bulgaria, 122–23
  effect on smuggler market, 143–44
  in Europe, 135–41
  structural injustice of, 167
  in United States, 131–33
Digidiki, Vasileia, 138
dignity, human, 69–70, 71–72
direct injustices against refugees, 160–61, 167, 180–81
disaggregated citizenship, 187–88
Doctors without Borders, 136
donations, 52–53
drownings, 2, 146
Dublin Regulations, suspension by Germany, 141–42

durable solutions, Refugee Convention of 1951, 44

economic benefits of accepting refugees, 206n.23, 210n.5
economic integration, 183–86
economic migrants versus refugees, 36–37, 38–39
economic policies, consequentialism in, 58
education
  in refugee camps, 101, 109–10, 125–26
  of urban refugees, 118–19
Egypt, urban refugees in, 115–16, 117
El Salvador, asylum seekers from, 27–28, 81–82, 90–91, 121–22, 127, 131
employment
  for refugees in Uganda, 186
  tax and trade incentives, 185–86
  of urban refugees, 117–18
Eritrean refugees
  human smuggling of, 128–29, 147–49
  reasons for seeking asylum, 127
  Sina Habte, 1–2, 23, 83–84, 153–55
Etchegaray, Jean-René, 198
Europe. *See also specific countries*
  access to asylum in, 6–7
  depicting refugees as criminals and sexual predators, xiv–xvi
  deterrence policies in, 135–41
  disaggregated citizenship model in, 187–88
  individual efforts to help refugees, 197–200
  lack of evidence linking refugees to terrorism, xiii
  moral obligations to refugees in, 86
  number of refugees in, 206n.27
  open borders policy, 2–3
  public funds spent on refugees in, 4–5
  refugee crisis in, 1–6
  secondary crisis, 3–7
exclusion of refugees, justifying
  cultural self-determination, 91–95
  freedom of association, 95–96
  nationalism and political self-determination, 88–91
extortion by human traffickers, 147–49

failed asylum seekers, 32–33
failed states, 37–38
Farage, Nigel, xiv–xv
Farook, Syed, xii
Ferracioli, Luara, 43
Finnemore, Martha, 210n.30
FitzGerald, David Scott, 207n.9
food, in refugee camps, 110–11, 112–13
forcibly displaced persons, 4, 30, 35–36
France, efforts to help refugees in, 198
freedom of association, 95–96
friendship, intrinsic value of, 59
Frye, Marilyn, 168
funding
  for refugee protection, 4–5, 167, 183–85
  for resettlement, 184
  for UNHCR, 53, 167, 210n.2

gang violence, 27–28, 81–82, 121–22, 127
gender-based violence, 114, 139. *See also* sexual violence
Germany
  family reunification policies, 127
  individual efforts to help refugees, 198
  Jewish asylum seekers from, other nations refusal of, 129–30
  suspension of Dublin Regulations for Syrian refugees, 141–42
Gessen, Masha, 133, 215n.19
Giarratano, Carlo, 199
global refugee crisis
  Cold War and, 9
  conflict of national sovereignty and human rights, 9–11
  ethics and, 7–8
  minimum conditions of human dignity, 11–13
  moral responsibility of Western states, 13–20
  political factors, 9
Global South. *See also* refugee camps
  amount of public funds spent on refugees in, 4–5
  discrepancy in burden sharing, 47
  economic integration, 183–86
  impact of refugees on economy, xviii
  moral obligations to refugees in, 104–7

Global South (*Cont.*)
  political integration, 186–89
  support for hosting refugees, xviii
  temporary local integration, 183
  urban refugees in, 115–19
Good Samaritan principle, 64–65, 85–87, 95
Greece
  European refugee crisis, 1–6
  individual efforts to help refugees, 197
  refugee camps in, 125–26, 137–38
Green, Michael, 214n.3
Guardian, The (newspaper), 134, 214n.3
Guled (Somalian refugee), 151–53

Habte, Sina, 1–2, 23, 83–84, 153–55
Haitian asylum seekers, 131–32
Harding, Jeremy, 143
Harrell-Bond, Barbara, 212n.6
Hasina (Rohingya refugee), 101–2
Hebrew Immigration Aid Society (HIAS), 66–67
Helton, Arthur, 104–5
hopelessness among asylum seekers, 124, 125–26, 135
host country, defined, 31–32
housing challenges for urban refugees, 118
human dignity, 69–70, 71–72
human rights
  asylum seeking, 34, 128
  defining, 68–70
  governmental responsibilities, 72–74
  international community, moral obligations of, 82–84
  negative rights, 74
  overlapping consensus on, 71–72
  refugee protection, 73–74
  separating children from parents, 132–33, 214n.12, 215n.19
  universality of, 70–72
  violations in Europe, 218n.26
  violations in refugee camps, 112–13, 194–95
human smuggling, 214n.6
  dangers of, 146–49
  of Eritrean refugees, 147–49
  intensified by deterrence policies, 143–44
  moral ambiguity, 142–46
  as only option for asylum seekers, 128–29, 141–42
  trafficking versus, 144
human trafficking, 144, 147–49
humanitarian diplomacy, 191–92
humanity, principle of, 64–65, 85–87
Hungary, 191, 218n.24, 218n.26

Idomeni refugee camp, Greece, 137–38
IDPs (internally displaced persons), 4, 31–32
illegal aliens, defined, 36
illegal immigrants, defined, 36
Illegal Immigration Reform and Immigrant Responsibility Act of 1996, 81–82, 131–32
IMF (International Monetary Fund), xviii
immigrants versus refugees, 41–44
individuals, role in challenging policies, 193–96, 197–200
integration, 183
  economic, 183–86
  political, 186–89
  temporary local, 183
internally displaced persons (IDPs), 4, 31–32
international community, moral obligations of, 82–84
International Monetary Fund (IMF), xviii
International Organization for Migration, 39
international policies, integrating refugees in formation of, 189
intrinsic value, 59
Iraq, 116
Islam, 66, 68
Italy, efforts to help refugees in, 199

Jewish asylum seekers from Germany, 129–30
Jim Crow laws, 162, 163
Jordan
  Azraq refugee camp, 110–11
  economic integration in, 185–86
  impact of refugees on economy, xviii
  support for hosting refugees, xix
  urban refugees in, 117
  Zaatari refugee camp, 108, 110, 213n.24
Judaism, 66–67

Kadu, Rohima, 77, 83–84, 86
Kant, I., 58–59, 210–11n.6, 211n.7
Kantian ethics, 210–11n.6, 211n.7
general discussion, 56, 58–60
refugees and, 62–63
Kempson, Eric, 197
Kempson, Philippa, 197
Kenya, Dadaab refugee camp in, 108, 110, 112–13
Klemp, Pia, 199
Koran, treatment of refugees in, 68

Lebanon
cash transfers for refugees, 217n.9
impact of refugees on economy, xviii
urban refugees in, 117
legal precariousness of urban refugees, 117, 118
legal versus human rights, 69
liberal nationalism, 89
local integration of refugees, 44
Locke, John, 208n.27
lying, 59

Mafia, 143–44
Malik, Tashfeen, xii
Mare Nostrum (ship), 136
Mathiesen, Karl, 214n.3
McAdam, Jane, 40–41
McDonald-Gibson, Charlotte, 39, 112
membership bias, 188
Miliband, David, 173–74, 213n.28
Mill, J. S., 57
Miller, David, 43, 89, 208n.35, 208n.36, 212n.14, 212n.19
Milliband, David, 208n.35
minimum conditions of human dignity. *See also* structural injustice
cumulative harmful effect of Western policies, 159
economic integration, 183–86
integration, 183
political integration, 186–89
in refugee camps, 50–52, 104–5
secondary crisis, 3, 7–8
moral ambiguity of human smuggling, 142–46
moral obligations, 50–75
causality, 80–82
consequentalism, 56–58, 61–62
defining, 54–56
Good Samaritan principle, 64–65, 85–87, 95
human rights perspective, 68–74
of individuals, 52–53
international system, 82–84
justifying, 56–60
Kantian ethics, 56, 58–60, 62–63
moral skepticism and, 55–56
questioning, 87–88
to refugees, 61–63
religious ethics, 66–68
secular global ethics, 63–66
moral skepticism, 55–56
moral universalism, 63
mutual aid, principle of, 91–92
Myanmar, 77, 83

Nart (Syrian refugee), 122–23
national identity, 89, 90
national sovereignty, 208n.27
nationalism
cultural self-determination, 91–95
political self-determination, 88–91
nativism, 88
Nauru island, detention center on, 134–35, 214n.3
negative rights, 74
Netherlands, 187–88
non-expellable irregulars, defined, 36
nongovernmental actors, 37–38
non-refoulement, principle of, 33, 45–46, 106–7, 128, 129–30
Norlock, Kate, 196–97
normative basis of states, 208n.27
normative obligations, Refugee Convention of 1951, 45
norms shaped by Western states, 173–75

Oberman, Kieran, 38
obligations, Refugee Convention of 1951, 44–45, 46, 47–48
offshore processing centers, 134–35, 214n.3

open borders policy, xix–xxi
#OpenTheBorders campaign, xix
Operation Mare Nostrum, 136
Operation Sophia, 140
Operation Triton, 136
Orbán, Viktor, xi
overlapping consensus, 71–72

Pacific Solution, 134–35
parents, separating children from, 132–33, 214n.12, 215n.19
patriotism, 62–63
persecution
  principle of non-refoulement, 33, 45–46, 106–7, 128, 129–30
  Refugee Convention refugee definitions, 31, 32
  refugee status and, 28–29, 30, 32
  state, 32–33
  violence by private actors, 32–33
political integration, 186–89
political policies, consequentialism in, 58
political responsibility, 169–76, 177–93
  assigning, 171–72
  asylum, 190–93
  economic integration, 183–86
  integration, 183
  political integration, 186–89
  refugee protection, 175–76
  resettlement, 175, 190–93
  social connection model, 169–70
  two-layered approach to, 181–82
  of Western states, 172–75
political self-determination, 88–91
Pope Francis, 67–68
prejudice, 38, 88
principle of humanity, 64–65, 85–87
principle of mutual aid, 91–92
principle of non-refoulement, 33, 45–46, 106–7, 128, 129–30
prostitution, in refugee camps, 102, 114
protracted displacement, 116, 207n.14

Rackete, Carola, 199
rape
  depictions of refugees as rapists, xiv–xv
  principle of non-refoulement, 45–46
  in refugee camps, 11–12, 114, 125, 151
  by traffickers, 147–48
rationality, 59–60
Rawlence, Ben, 110–11, 112–13
Rawls, John, 58, 71–72, 216n.11
reckless despair, 196
reckless optimism, 196
Refugee Act of 1980, 210n.28
refugee camps, 107–15. *See also specific camps*
  cost of, 109
  in Greece, 125–26, 137–38
  human rights violations in, 112–13
  idleness in, 110–11
  imprisonment in, 110–11
  isolation of refugees in, 108–9
  length of time spent in, 110, 207n.14
  negative aspects of, 110–11
  political responsibility towards refugees in, 175–76
  positive aspects of, 109–10, 111–12
  precariousness of, 108–9, 151–53, 155–56
  problems created by Western states, 104–7
  Rohingya refugees in, 101–2
  security in, 50–52, 114
  sexual violence in, 101–2, 112, 114
  structural injustice, 166–67
  temporary local integration as alternative to, 183
  warehousing, 174–75
Refugee Convention of 1951, 113, 208n.28
  definition of refugees, 30
  durable solutions, 44
  hardcore cases, 44–45
  minimum conditions of human dignity, 46
  normative obligations, 45
  obligations, 44–45, 46, 47–48, 106–7
Refugee Executive Committee, 189
refugee system as structural injustice, 165–68
refugees. *See also* asylum seekers
  burden sharing, 47
  climate, 39–41, 82, 164
  economic migrants versus, 36–37, 38–39

failed states, 37–38
illegal aliens, 36
illegal immigrants, 36
immigrants versus, 41–44
inconsistencies in defining, 27–30
length of time as, 5–6
misconceptions about, xi–xvi, xvii–xix
non-expellable irregulars, 36
nongovernmental actors and, 37–38
number resettled each year, 4–5
obligations of states to, 44–48
as political tool, xvi–xvii
Refugee Convention definition of, 30
temporary protected status, 36
UNHCR definition of, 35–36
rejected asylum seekers, 33, 35, 36, 42
religious ethics, 66–68
rescuers, Western states as, 158–59, 194, 208n.35, 208n.36
rescuing migrants at sea, 1–2, 136, 140, 146, 199
resettlement. *See also* state moral obligations
consequentialist view, 61–62
funding for, 184
Kantian view, 62–63
number of refugees accepted, 4–5, 207n.9
political responsibility of, 175
reforming policies, 190–93
Refugee Convention of 1951, 44
structural injustice, 165–66
Western focus on refugee camps versus, 104–6
resettlement states, defined, 31–32
responsibility, 177–93
assigning, 171–72
asylum, 190–93
economic integration, 183–86
integration, 183
political integration, 186–89
refugee protection, 175–76
resettlement, 175, 190–93
social connection model, 169–70
for structural injustice, 169–76
two-layered approach to, 181–82
of Western states, 172–75
Richard, Anne, 191–92
Rohingya refugees, 101–2
Rothman, Lily, 211n.4
Russia, xvi, 215n.19

sea crossings, 1–2, 136, 140, 146, 199
search-and-rescue missions, 136
secondary crisis, 3–8, 177
secular global ethics, 63–66
security in refugee camps, 50–52, 109–10, 114
security threats, refugees depicted as, 174
self-determination
cultural, 91–95
political, 88–91
self-harm among asylum seekers, 124, 125–26, 135
separating children from parents, 132–33, 214n.12, 215n.19
sexual predators, depicting refugees as, xiv–xvi
sexual violence
in Nauru detention center, 134–35
preventing, 213n.28
in refugee camps, 101–2, 112, 114
by smugglers, 139–40
in Sweden, xv
in US detention centers, 133
Shire, Warsan, 144–45
Singer, Peter, 63–65
smuggling, human. *See* human smuggling
social connection model, 169–70
solitary confinement, 69
Somalian refugees, 151–53
sponsorship program in Canada, 192–93
St. Louis (ship), 129–30
state moral obligations, 76–88
causality, 80–82
cultural self-determination, 91–95
freedom of association, 95–96
Good Samaritan principle, 85–87
international system, 82–84
nationalism and political self-determination, 88–91
questioning, 87–88
state persecution, 32–33
structural injustice, 22–23, 98, 151–76. *See also* political responsibility
defining, 162–65

structural injustice (*Cont.*)
deterrence policies, 179–80
direct injustices against refugees, 160–61
framing issues, 157–59
as new framework, 160–62
refugee system as, 165–68
role of individuals in challenging, 193–96
suicide among asylum seekers, 124, 125–26, 135
Sweden, xiv–xvi, 127
Syrian refugees, 76–77
cash transfers for, 217n.9
dread of refugee camps, 112
European deterrence policies, 122–23
Jordan compact for, 185–86
responsibility of international community towards, 83
suspension of Dublin Regulations by Germany, 141–42
urban refugees, 102–3, 115–17

tax and trade incentives, 185–86
temporary local integration, 183
temporary protected status, defined, 36
terrorism, refugees not linked to, xi–xiv
Torah, treatment of refugees in, 66–67
torture by human traffickers, 147–49
Trump, Donald, 46, 133
Turkey
agreement with EU regarding asylum seekers, 138
impact of refugees on economy, xviii
refugee conditions in, 207–8n.18
urban refugees in, 102–3, 117–18

Uganda, 186, 217n.12
United Nations High Commissioner for Refugees (UNHCR)
definition of refugees, 35–36
focus on refugee camps over resettlement, 104–5
forcibly displaced persons, 35–36
funding of, 53, 167, 210n.2
purpose of, 31, 210n.30
urban refugees, disadvantages of, 116–17
United States
depictions of refugees as terrorists, xii
deterrence policies in, 131–33
impact of refugees on economy, 206n.23, 210n.5
Jim Crow laws, 162, 163
number of refugees in, 206n.27
process of gaining refugee status, xii–xiii
Refugee Act of 1980, 210n.29
refusal to accept Jewish asylum seekers from Germany, 129–30
Universal Declaration of Human Rights, 34, 70–72
urban refugees, 115–19
advantages of, 116–17
disadvantages of, 117–19
education of, 118–19
housing challenges, 118
problems created by Western states, 104–7
Syrian, 102–3
wages of, 117–18
utilitarianism
general discussion, 56–58
refugees and, 61–62

Vasquez, Blanca, 121–22, 131
Verdirame, Guglielmo, 212n.6
Vibhakar, Viktoria, 135
Vietnam, 80, 175
voluntary return (repatriation) of refugees, 44
Volz, Dirk, 198

wages of urban refugees, 117–18
Walzer, Michael, 42–43, 86–87, 91–92, 93
warehousing, 174–75
Wellman, Christopher, 95
Western states. *See also specific countries*; structural injustice
deterrence policies, 129–31
focus on refugee camps versus resettlement, 104–6
moral responsibility of, 13–20
norms shaped by, 173–75
political responsibility of, 172–75
as rescuers, 158–59, 194, 208n.35, 208n.36

xenophobia, 88

Yaser (Syrian refugee), 125–26
you-break-it-you-bought-it principle, 80–82

Young, Iris, 22–23, 163–64, 169, 170–71
Young, Peter, 135

Zaatari refugee camp, Jordan, 108, 110, 213n.24